You are Divine!
pass it on!
Namaste!

Dan Wall

For Information on booking Gene's workshop, **Follow Your Dreams---The Bottom Line**, his **One of A Kind Evening** featuring music, storytelling and slide shows, or for motivational speaking to churches, at risk youth and mentoring programs, 12-Step functions, prisons or corporations contact:

Awakening Imaginations
PO Box 2323
Asheville, N.C. 28801

e-mail: awakeningimag1@aol.com
800-614-0995
website: www.thechameleon.net

This book is dedicated

to my friend, Endre Balogh,

and my mother, Jeanne Claire Wall,

for showing me the face of

unconditional love.

A Story That Could Be True

If you were exchanged in the cradle and
your real mother died
without ever telling the story,
then no one knows your name.
And somewhere in the world
your father is lost and needs you,
but you are far away.
He can never find
how true you are, how ready.
When the great wind comes
and the robberies of the rain,
you stand in the corner shivering.
The people who go by...
you wonder at their calm.
They miss the whisper that runs
any day in your mind,
"Who are you really, wanderer?"
and the answer you have to give,
no matter how dark and cold
the world around you is:
"Maybe, I'm a king."

William Stafford

THE
CHAMELEON

ACKNOWLEDGEMENTS

At the very top of the list I want to acknowledge my higher power, God; the creator to whom I give all credit and from whom all blessings flow. Whatever I might accomplish in this world is through grace, as I'm simply a conduit of that magnificence.

Next, I want to thank my Mom and Dad for bringing me into this world in the first place. I have no doubt that without my mother's influence I wouldn't be here to tell this story. I now understand why they say a mother's love is truly one of the most powerful forces in the universe. Thanks to my dad for being the embodiment of honor and integrity, as well as giving me the opportunity to learn qualities such as compassion, forgiveness, generosity, and the ability to express intimacy. I love you both very much.

Thanks to all my teachers, both past and present, who have inspired me along this path of self discovery, whether they knew it or not. In particular, I want to thank Jim and Diana Goure, Neville Goddard, Barbara De Angelis, John Bradshaw, Walter Russell, Pat Allen, Bob Hoffman, Michael Meade, Deepak Chopra, Dennis Praegger, Bill and Bob, and the tens of thousands of people I've heard share their experience, strength and hope at Twelve Step meetings over the years.

A special thanks to Mark Bryan, Bob Earll, Stevie Wonder, Roberta Schwartz, Waylon Jennings, Robert Welsch, Roxanna Marchosky, Prince Khalid, and Susan Flanagan...all heaven sent as God's messengers to me.

Dan Donahoe, Carol Paradise, Charlie Springer, Shadoe Stevens, Clyde and Adrienne Holliefield, Weasel and Denise, Sandra Singh, Helen Dykhuizen, Endre and Mona Balogh, Beth Nielson Chapman, Ernie Blue, Tim Collins, Kaye Brett, Parvene Michaels and my sister Susan. You are friends each and every one, who have touched me in ways for which I am eternally grateful.

Thanks to Arthur Douet for his incredible artwork, and to Joan

Oliver for being the first person I dared let see this creation, warts and all. To Ron Walker (Kofi) for his inspired graphics, as well as the energy he brings to the table, and Althea Gonzales and Susan Story for shining their lights on 'Following Your Bliss/The Bottom Line'... the workshop I've been waiting all my life to create. Special thanks to Ann Walters for going way beyond the call of duty and Leah King, Gail Bowdish, Beth Shafer, and the entire gang at Awakening Imaginations Ministries for believing in me and my dream of making a difference in the world; one talk, one workshop, one concert and ultimately one person at a time. Also to Mary Kunz for helping us get non-profit and tax exempt status so we can take the ministry to the entire world.

If I tried to name all the people who have shared adventures and precious moments with me; who have touched me profoundly in ways of the heart; who have suffered my faults and frailties with infinite patience; in other words everyone who has taught me the lessons that have gotten me to this point on my journey, this little book might more resemble a tome.

If by chance you happen to recognize yourself, a place, an event or someone you know in these pages (after all, it is a mighty small planet), you could very well be carrying some of my memories. (As most children of the sixties will attest, the loss of a certain amount of gray matter was to be expected.) We are all truly in this together, and I'd love to hear from you.

INTRODUCTION

I've always thought of life as an adventure, and I've tried to live it accordingly. Over the years, many friends have told me I'm the luckiest guy they've ever known. I'm not sure about that, though I do know I've been blessed with the attitude that God created lemons not only for lemonade, but to inspire those people who could stand to pucker up more often. I also know I've had the privilege of close contact with some of the more compelling, diverse, and thought provoking people of our times. Many of them well-known and in the public eye (some names are so heavy you can't help dropping them), but often the memories and people I treasured the most were known only to those fortunate enough to have been there at the time.

Many of the lessons and much of the wisdom I've gleaned along the way I've been able to save. In fact, if I had $15...no let's make that $19.99, for every time I'd been told to put this tale in writing, I'd be a millionaire...so, all of you who urged me to do this, cough up or as my song says, "Put Your Money Where Your Mouth Is".

In ancient times, I was often a court jester or wandering minstrel, and probably a leprechaun, given my mischievous nature. The fact is, I have always tried to live by the motto, "Don't get too serious, it'll drive you delirious." Truth be known, I'm a wordsmith, otherwise known as a story-teller.

I have found it easier to tell my life story from the third person as the older, wiser self that each of us has within; from the voice that warned you right up front that the relationship you are now trying to extricate yourself from wasn't a match in the first place; the same voice that reminds you not to eat two banana splits at one sitting. You know the one. With the advantage of time and hindsight, I can now look back at myself and see my struggles toward manhood with a bit of clarity and humor, and hopefully relate it in a way that brings understanding.

I call this older wiser self 'Merlin'. He's your basic omniscient narrator (*and will be italicized from here on.*) 'Merlin' is actually a nickname I was gifted with twenty-five years ago, but one I've had a hard time accepting. The first time I was called by that name, it came as a total surprise. It was addressed to me on the credits of an album that read, "Special thanks to 'Merlin' and his bag of tricks." The band, Soul Dog, was recognizing the services I had rendered on their record '<u>Keep On Truckin'</u>. *(He's still got the tee-shirt.)* Finally, after years of adventures, mentors, and magical life transformations, I feel I've earned the right to wear it and that it actually fits. Somehow, it does seem ironically appropriate for a Twentieth century magician.

Yes, like the mythic 'Merlin' of old, I'm also a magician; an alchemist really. An "alchemist of sound" to be exact. It was a name coined for me by an 80-year-old psychic from Black Mountain, North Carolina named Veneta Mueller. Veneta used to give readings, much like Edgar Cayce (probably the most renowned psychic of this century), where she would go into a trance, answer questions, and come out totally unaware of anything that had occurred. Veneta saw and pronounced my ability to change leaden vibrations to gold through music, and predicted, in amazing detail, some of the stories told here, a full two decades before they would transpire.

Veneta was the first person who saw my deep desire to touch the hearts and souls of my fellow beings. She told me I had a highly refined analytical faculty which allowed me to recognize where things were out of balance. She also reminded me I had signed a covenant with the universe that regardless of all else, my essential purpose was to help put the planet back into alignment. *(Doesn't ask for much does she?)* Furthermore, because of my recent past lives as a monk in contemplation, she told me it was now my sworn duty to share the fruits of my spiritual endeavors in this incarnation. She also mentioned that learning to do so with tact, diplomacy, and sensitivity would be a great opportunity for me this go around. *Just in case you're wondering how come you haven't heard from me before now, suffice it to say that lesson hasn't come easily. In fact, it has been a constant struggle.*

This isn't a new story; more like the 20th century version of the prodigal son meets Icarus (the boy who flew too close to the sun and got scorched). What is new however, is that the quest is enhanced with music and poetry. When I began to tell the tale, it was simply as a backdrop to bring you into the world where the songs and poems were created; to give you some insight as to when and where they came through; or better yet... crossed over from the other side. They are an integral part of the journey.

This format was loosely designed to have the corresponding music or poem experienced where it was inspired along my sojourn. There are footnotes in the text with an asterisk placed where the musings begin. Turn to the back and read the poem, or hit the remote on your CD player to play the music, or read now and listen later, it's up to you. *Ah, the magic of technology.*

They say nothing happens by coincidence, accident or chance, that there is nothing random or haphazard about our universe. I'll go one step further. I believe all the events and experiences which happen in our lives we create as opportunities for growth, but what we do with them and how we respond to them is our choice. If this is true, then I have brought myself to this moment and to these pages for a reason, and so have you. I think you'll easily find what drove me to put these words on paper. What remains to be seen, is what you might discover about yourself and your own dreams.

I never make promises I can't keep, but I will say this. By the time you finish reading this book, if you haven't had a hearty guffaw, or at least one big Ah-Ha moment, we will gladly refund your misery.

PROLOGUE

Hi! My name's 'Merlin'. I'm an alch...oholic, oh, excuse me, wrong book. I'm an alch...emist and your omniscient narrator for the next three hundred or so pages. I guess I'm also the older, wiser self just referred to in the introduction, but let me make one thing perfectly clear from the onset. I never said you shouldn't eat two banana splits at one sitting. In fact, I think it sounds like a great idea. I've done it a few times myself. Just be warned that your stomach might not agree with you. I must also warn you that some of the story I'm about to tell will be hard to believe. It may defy your imagination, and leave you feeling a bit incredulous. You might think some of it fiction or a vivid imagination run amuck, or you might even think it to be a bold faced lie. I can't help that. My only responsibility is to tell the story. I have used a few aliases to protect people's anonymity, where it seemed appropriate, but there are no composite characters. What's written here happened just as you see it in print. It is all true. The fact is, the truth wasn't plausible enough to be fiction. How do I know all this? Because I lived it. I was there, and the telling of the story is part of my initiation.

Most of us believe there are no dragons left; that such things as enchantments and sorcerers, white knights and princesses, are only to be found in fairy tales for children; outdated fables from a time long gone that have no relevance in this 'the computer age'. Even the word magic has been dismissed as sleight of hand; certainly no mature adult believes such nonsense!

What a joy to be wrong. Not only are such mythological characters here and now, but they're all around us.

Sure, dragons no longer come screeching out of the sky breathing fire, but come lurking in pill form or a bottle, with names like greed and lust and gluttony. White knights rarely come bounding up on prancing steeds of the four legged variety, but might be found sitting at round tables running charitable foundations instead. Sorcerers have had to become much more subtle, so as to not draw attention to themselves, lest they be forced to work for the government or worse yet, find themselves on the cover of Star Magazine. You probably have one in your neighborhood. Trust me, they're out there.

This is the story of a young knight who fights many dragons and meets many princesses, while learning enchantments from modern day sorcerers along the way. It is the classic story of the boy who doesn't fit in, so runs away to join the circus to try and find himself; his search for a mentor in a kingdom that no longer teaches the relevance or importance of such things. It's one boy's rite of passage, or initiation into manhood, in a time when the distinction between men and boys has become blurred and confusing; a time when the culture has lost reverence for its elders and everyone is paying the price.

Ultimately, this is a modern day parable about the most magical of all journeys; the quest to discover oneself and fulfill one's destiny. On that note...

Southern Upbringing

"Sweet childish days, that were as long as twenty days now."

Wordsworth

*O*nce upon a time . . . and oh what a time it was, after the invention of digital time and the widespread use of daylight-savings time; back when people still had leisure time; there was a prince. Well, a wandering minstrel really, but he thought he was a prince. *

He had been born into the typical dysfunctional family of the mid-twentieth century. You know, where everyone had a role to play, and heaven forbid you try and break out of it, lest the entire family modality collapse.

His father, The King, was one of five boys raised during the depression, which unavoidably colored all his perceptions. To call him a stern, autocratic disciplinarian would be very much an understatement. Life was a struggle and you damn well better keep your nose to the grindstone.

The King, AKA 'The Captain', joined the navy at the beginning of World War II and was commissioned as an ensign, assigned to a ship. Starting out as chief engineer, he then became navigator, combat information officer, executive officer, and finally commanding officer of a destroyer. That ship was sunk by a Japanese torpedo during World War II, and many of the Captain's friends were killed. He received a Purple Heart and The Silver Star for exceptional heroism in combat.

After the war, 'The Captain' returned to complete college and law school, and then went back to active duty in the JAG Corp (Judge Advocate General). There he kept his nose to the grindstone and became a very powerful judge within the military complex.

The most popular careers among his clan seemed to be fire and brimstone Baptist preachers, and FBI agents, so it was no wonder that honor, integrity, and especially doing one's duty, was of utmost importance to the 'Captain'.

* Merlin's Theme…Chameleon CD #1

As you can see, any child with an adventurous spirit and a penchant for individuality was probably in for a rough ride.

Thank God for his mom, The Queen. If not for her, it's doubtful the Prince would have survived to tell the story. Even if he'd made it past adolescence, it was her unconditional love and support that pulled him through more times than he can remember. Brought up in a rural Mississippi town, as the mayor's daughter, she was the oldest child of four and the only girl of a very visible and powerful Southern politician and ally to Franklin Roosevelt. Always an honor student (Phi Betta Kappa in college), she was honestly embarrassed when she received an A- on her report card. (Unfortunately for the Prince, some things aren't hereditary.) Besides being editor of the school newspaper, she was on the debate team, and even played glockenspiel in the marching band. Involved with theater, music and the arts, she still managed to be very active at her Baptist church and could certainly be described as the apple of her daddy's eye. A true Southern Belle. It was about the time she started travelling to political rallies in support of his Senatorial bid, that The Queen had her first rude awakening.

Let's hear about it from the prince himself.

Having lived a rather cloistered fairy-tale existence, mom was distraught once she learned the general opinion was that Grandpa couldn't win his Senatorial bid, because of being too honest. Keep in mind, this was during the time of the big political machines and grandpa's opponent was Theodore G. Bilbo, close friend of Huey P. Long (the "Louisiana Boss"). Mom's reaction of 'what's this country coming to, when an honest man can't get elected', seemed to be a harbinger of how most of us feel these days. To this day, she loves pulling out the old scrapbooks of grandpa and 'Bilbo' going at each other in the press. One headline, in particular, she relished, was grandpa being quoted in the local Jackson paper, "Bilbo Has No More Brains Than A Hummingbird". Even though grandpa lost the election, he definitely got the last laugh, as mom would be quick to point out. Appointed head of the PWC (Public Works Commission) by Roosevelt himself, grandpa was in charge of doling out Federal money to half a dozen southern states. I can just imagine Bilbo's reaction.

Grandpa was larger than life for me. I loved visiting him and Maw Maw (my grandmother). Sometimes they'd invite me to stay the entire summer. Paw Paw would take me around town with him and of course being introduced as the mayor's grandson had lots of built-in perks like candy, Coca-Colas, piggyback rides, etc. Probably the best thing of all, was playing at grandpa's house. It seemed to me to be the grandest house, smack right in the center of town. It had all the accessories an adventurous boy could want; big antebellum porches all the way around, a staircase to slide down, a huge dank basement to hide out in with secret passages only I and my favorite cousin Rolo knew about, and a formal dining room that was off limits to the kids, which of course made it even more appealing. There was a goldfish pond with lilies and all kinds of cool stuff you'd find when you just happened to fall in. Then there was 'Patches', the black and white quilt looking pony Paw Paw bought for us, that lived in the barn and spent his days galloping in the pasture next to the house. He'd always prance over to the fence when we kids were rollicking, as he knew, more times than not, we'd have an apple or carrot or sugarcubes stuffed away in some pocket.

The job of over-seeing us; making sure we slowed down long enough to eat lunch, and putting bandaids on the cuts and scrapes we saw as badges of honor, fell to Margaret. Big and black and proud and beautiful, she had been with grandpa all her life and was as much a part of the family as I was. We must have run her ragged. I remember her walking out on the screened-in back porch bringing us those little six ounce bottles of Coca-Cola, and treats for Patches, at least a dozen times a day, and she always seemed to have a smile. I'm convinced she could read our minds, as she always had some kind of treat waiting for us in the breakfast nook to tide us over till dinner. Best of all, she could keep a secret. She didn't feel obligated to tell the grown-ups about all our misbehaving. Things like lizards and frogs in the house were just part of the deal, and if you tracked some mud in or accidently left a dead goldfish on the table, she wouldn't get her dander in an uproar. I loved Margaret.

I really only recall two things clearly about my grandmother. One, she would light up unfiltered cigarettes, while playing solitaire, and then never take them out of her mouth. I remember it would drive me crazy waiting for the two inch ash to drop, but it almost never did. The second thing I remembered about her didn't come to me till I was in my early twenties, and making out with a new girlfriend. All of a sudden in the middle of a kiss it dawned on me and I leaped to my feet, saying, "You smell just like my grandmother!"

Her look of astonishment was priceless, and I started to laugh once I realized how odd that must have sounded. I thought I'd better explain myself, lest she think I was a bit warped. So, after her initial shock wore off, I clarified that it had triggered one of the most nurturing feelings I had ever experienced, and after awhile, I think she actually believed me. Since then I have met three or four other women that had that same fragrance, and each time I had the deja-vu feeling of comfort and safety. Go figure.

This is the world my mom grew up in. Only later did I fathom the value and savor the memory of how she would devote her days to our family, and how every night around bedtime, she had her own ritual. She would go to the living room and turn off the lights, put on classical music, light candles, kerosene lanterns and pour herself a glass of wine. This was her time to reflect. We were welcome to come join her and listen to the music, but we had to be quiet. I now see this is where the importance and appreciation of quiet time, and awareness of solitude was instilled in me for the first time. For that I'll be eternally grateful.

The Prince was the middle child of three, each born four years apart, as his parents had planned. That way, they could send them to college one at a time. (At least he never had to wonder if he were a mistake.) But alas, our Prince was destined to be the black sheep; that is, if you believe in destiny. Personally, I think he'd have volunteered for the job either way. Typical of most military families, they were transferred every two to three years, so he never really knew a home or a hometown, and learned quickly to be a social chameleon.

With that came the unspoken lesson; you can't get too close to people, cause you're just going to lose them anyway, so you'd better learn to walk away and not look back.

Public Flogging

Since it's not only accepted by society but deemed quintessential that children require love at an early age, it only begs to ask the question: at what age does a person no longer need it?

GWC

*T*he first glimpse of the Prince's adventuresome and rebellious spirit had come out at a very young age. He couldn't have been more than six at the time, and was thoroughly enjoying his first jet airliner ride. He was being escorted by one of his uncles back to California from Mississippi, where he had spent the summer being spoiled by his grandparents. His uncle needed to use the restroom and had left the Prince alone for a few minutes while he went in search of relief. On the way to the restroom, he had ordered a cocktail, and the stewardess had brought a couple of those cute little bottles of hootch and left them at his seat.

Upon returning from the lavatory, his uncle was entertained to find the prince had not only downed them both, but wanted more. It wasn't long before the alcohol began to have its not so subtle effect, and the Prince, discovering his ability to sell charm in the form of hugs and kisses, proceeded to wander the aisles doing just that, much to the delight of the other passengers.

It's curious looking back; the writing was on the wall even then. Just the act of taking the bottles, knowing full well I was about to do something illicit, as well as the ritual of pouring it over ice, mimicking my parents, was all part of the thrill. I remember hating the taste and how it burned going down, but once I'd swallowed the magic elixir and my entire upper body started to shake uncontrollably, I thought it was pretty cool. I'm not quite sure how I became cognizant of the fact, but once I realized people would pay me money to act cute and give them hugs, I was hooked. Fifty cents for a smooch; no problem, how many do you want? I'd found my calling. By the time we landed in Monterey, I had collected nearly twenty dollars, which my uncle thought was hilarious. As I grew older and continued with the same patterns of behavior, the story became a family legend (much to the chagrin of my parents.)

Though the Prince's obsessive behavior was certainly pre-ordained, I wonder if getting the unspoken endorsement from his uncle exacerbated the situation. You know, the old-fashioned 'boys will be boys', just 'sowing his wild oats' mentality.

When I turned nine, dad was transferred to Treasure Island and moved the family to Marin County, California. I couldn't have known a more enjoyable life as a nine-year-old. I loved hunting lizards and Gila Monsters in the rolling hills, and salamanders in the rock strewn creek behind our house there in Lucas Valley.

My days were spent running through imaginary jungles, without a care in the world. Fields of wheat-like grass waved high over the heads of me and my cohorts. We would flatten down the tall grain, making trails to run on, and meeting halls where we could all gather, unseen by prying eyes. Cowboys and Indians * was one of our favorite games. I had a much coveted John Wayne outfit, complete with chaps, spurs and a red bandanna that I would wear. We had secret hideouts beneath low-lying shrubs where we could observe 'them' (the adults), but they couldn't spot us, and bicycling with my buddies three miles to the peacock farm, to hunt for exotic feathers, was a much anticipated weekly excursion.

Roller skating and sliding down the straw-covered hills on flattened cardboard boxes were more of our favorite pastimes. We formed a club, built a tree fort for club meetings and put up a rickety 'No Girls Allowed' sign at the entrance. I made my first political statement when I convinced the other boys into bending that rule, once I discovered the fun of playing doctor and nurse. Not an easy task, considering the fear of getting "cooties" was pretty wide spread back then. I knew my biggest problem would be convincing Danny Riggs, who hated girls, because his sister was such a tattletale. Also, since his house had the only swimming pool in the neighborhood, I knew his vote would carry a lot of weight. I plotted my strategy

* Cowboys and Indians...Chameleon CD #11

carefully, and at the next club meeting, pulled out my secret weapon; one of my big brothers girlie magazines to show Danny what he was missing. I think since his sister was flat-chested, I was able to convince him that not all girls were alike, and it would behoove us to do a careful survey on the subject. We reached a diplomatic compromise and elected to invite them to the pool first, before luring them to the fort.

Best of all, there was baseball,* playing it, dreaming about it, and listening to it on the radio. I spent hours fantasizing about hitting the winning home run in a world series. Every San Francisco Giant game that was aired, found me glued to the same aluminum paint stool, often perilously close to the edge, listening intently to the old-fashioned RCA knob radio.

I remember the crack of the wooden bat, the roar of the crowd, the longing for a game-winning play by one of my heroes. The emotions stirred up were intense, and it was the one place I never felt the need to curb my passions. I could whoop, holler and groan as much and as loudly as I wanted. Even the disappointments were bearable, as I reappeared on my stool for another chance the next afternoon.

Willie Mays, Willie McCovey, Orlando Cepeda, Juan Marichal, Gaylord Perry; they were my heroes. Even if the game carried on past my bedtime, a ballgame was the one and only excuse for staying up late that was deemed acceptable.

It's always been the same. In earlier times it was jousting and sword fighting, now it's baseball. Since boys are naturally drawn to hierarchies, a boy has had to always prove his prowess amongst his peers. The fascination today with modern technology, such as video games and computers, has me worried. So much time in front of machines and not enough time interacting with each other out in nature, can't possible lead to anything good in the long run.

Then came the weekends; the one time dad seemed to be around and involved. He would cook all the pancakes and waffles we kids could eat, sometimes even having contests to see who could devour the most. For an added treat, we got to wash the saucer-like morsels down with cups of

---

* Life As We Know It…Chameleon CD #7

coffee or "joe", as my dad referred to it from his Navy days. It was only allowed on weekends since it was believed back then that java would stunt one's growth.

It was telling how I didn't like the taste of coffee at first, but just like booze, I reasoned if the adults were doing it, it must be cool. Before long, I mastered the right combination of cream and sugar, to disguise the bitterness, and convinced myself I was really on to something. You don't even have to wonder what became my first addiction once I left home. For the time being though, olives, maraschino cherries and spooning frozen orange juice straight from the can were my childhood 'drugs of choice'.

At first, my parents found it bewildering and a bit astounding that a child could have such pronounced proclivities at such an early age. I mean, what's a parent to do with a kid that eats entire cans of frozen orange juice at one sitting? *Dr. Spock forgot to cover that one.* They finally started giving me my own private stash at Christmas and birthdays when they saw they weren't going to break my habit.

Probably the only home in America where wrapped up bottles of cherries and olives under the Christmas tree were par for the course. Looking back, it was an idyllic life for a youngster, short-lived though it was.

Unfortunately it didn't last.

The first crack in the chasm began the day the prince stole for the first time; a purple and green bathing suit and a pocket size address book. Odd how certain memories can stay so vivid, while others turn hazy, if remembered at all.

When my mom discovered the stolen items and questioned me about them, I shrugged my shoulders, averted my eyes and without thinking murmured,

"I don't know how they got here."

I was hoping she'd drop the inquisition, but quickly realized, when she didn't go away, I'd just raised the ante. Soon my palms were sweaty and I felt like I'd been punched in the stomach. I stuck to my story, as long as I could stand the discomfort, until my mom finally ran out of patience and exasperatedly demanded, "Just tell me the truth, I promise you won't be punished. I just want to hear the truth."

I deliberated long and hard on what she said, and then made what I thought was a valiant effort. I mustered up all available courage, took a huge risk and leap of faith and whispered "Yes ma'am, I took them, I'm so sorry," before I broke down sobbing.

The guilt and remorse the prince felt at that moment for not only stealing and lying for the first time, but for letting his mom down when he knew he had been raised better, would have been punishment enough, had it been left there. His mom, though, didn't have the skills necessary to handle the situation, and upon hearing his confession, went on to do one of the most damaging things you can do to a child. She shamed him.

It was one of those experiences that has dramatic 'repercussions' years after it's been consciously forgotten. If handled differently by his parents, it might have been the one and only time the Prince ever stole or lied, but we'll never know.

She dragged me back to the store and made me hand back the items in person, as well as apologize, to the store owner in front of what seemed like a multitude of people standing there. I wasn't even sure if my vocal cords would work when the manager of the store said, "What do you have to say for yourself young man?"

I managed to stammer out, "I'm sorry...", but before I could finish my sentence, he jumped in again, "Speak up. I can't hear you."

I hadn't bargained on a mob witnessing this entire spectacle and I could feel their eyes boring into me condemningly, "What a loser."

My emotional dam could hold back the flood of tears no longer and I burst into blubbering wails. It was the first time, of many to come, when I wished the ground would open up and swallow me whole.

I felt humiliated. The message which had started out "you've done a bad thing", now became "you are a bad person." From then on, a little part of me started to wonder if maybe Mom was right.

To make matters worse, the chastening didn't end there; the knots in my stomach almost doubled me over when she told me on the way to the car, "Just wait until your father hears about this."

Dreading his arrival home was probably worse than either the beating or the restriction that was to ensue, and my young mind translated it into "all because I told the truth," and then to the obvious conclusion, "telling the truth doesn't work."

To this day, whenever anyone close to me says "I need to speak with you later", or "We need to talk", I immediately expect the worst. *(Now there's a pattern that could sure use reprogramming.)*

That was just the beginning of the Prince's trials and tribulations. Later that year, after getting off restriction for the stealing incident, he and a couple of his buddies were rollicking out in the woods and had taken a break from catching lizards to perfect their cigarette etiquette. (You know, weighty lessons like how to inhale without coughing all over the guy next to you, and how to roll a pack up in your T-shirt sleeve like James Dean... really substantial stuff to a ten-year-old page trying to emulate the older knights.)

We had a flattened grass meeting hall there, and had dragged in an old torn up mattress so we'd have something to lounge on. We were passing the smoke around in ritual fashion, taking turns coughing and choking and trying to still act cool in the process, when Danny showed up late from being kept after school. He came bounding, trampoline style, onto the mattress which caused me to drop the cigarette.

"Oh great" I yelled, "Everyone get up!"

"It fell in one of the holes," Danny shouted and now we all started to panic.

It started to smolder and, of course, the more agitated we became jumping around on the mattress trying to get it out, the more air was being fanned on the sparks.

"Someone run to the creek and get a bucket of water," I countered, but we all knew it was too late. The entire mattress was sending up smoke signals, giving away our hiding place, for all the world to see.

"Someone's gonna see this and call the police. I'm not sticking around", one of the other boys yelled.

Sure enough, just then we heard the sirens in the distance and we took off running. Since I lived the closest (my backyard fence was just seventy-five yards from the action), we spontaneously headed there to watch the arrival of the fire trucks. After all, it was a prime vantage point, and like most criminals, we wanted to return to the scene of the crime.

We were standing atop the raised strawberry patch in my back yard captivated by the action, when my dad came out to see what all the ruckus was about.

"Don't you boys want to go over closer where all the other kids are?" as there were at least a dozen other children over by the fire trucks.

"No sir, we'd rather watch from here," I responded for all of us.

Big mistake.

Being a legal man, between our snickering and our plaintive looks, it didn't take him long to deduce what was going on.

Sure enough, I was busted and publicly humiliated again. This time he took off his belt, beat me in front of my friends, then picked me up by the scruff of my neck and forced me to go and apologize to the fire chief.

Next, I was not only restricted to the house for a month, which forced me to drop out of little league baseball, but I couldn't even listen to games on the radio during that time. I later found out the other boys not only didn't get manhandled and have to publicly apologize; they weren't even put on restriction.

Once I realized I was the only one who'd really been disciplined, I started to feel a seething anger towards my dad. That was when I first started fantasizing how I was going to get even.

*For the prince, growing up was to become like a gathering storm destined to become a hurricane. First the cool breeze blowing in small cumulus clouds that blocked out the sun, with that tangible feeling of electricity in the air. Then the far off rumblings, barely audible, as the winds picked up, bringing in thick ominous clouds that darkened until they looked bruised and swollen, and he knew it was just a matter of time before the torrential pounding and violence began. ***

* Speak The Truth…Awakening Imaginations CD #7

Wild Child

"Boys will be boys," "And even that," I interposed, "wouldn't matter if we could only prevent girls from being girls."

Anthony Hope from 'The Dolly Dialogues'

The Prince loved adventure and, when you mix that with an innate curiosity, as well as a fearlessness bordering on foolhardiness, it kept him in constant trouble. There wasn't a scurrilous or malicious bone in his body, but he did have a stubborn streak and was dogged in his single-minded dislike of authority figures, and since he always felt different from the other kids, he would do just about anything to try to fit in.

By the time the Prince reached the sixth grade, his older brother had discovered he could get him to do just about anything on a dare, or especially a double dog dare. Since the Prince loved being with the older guys, he found if he'd steal cigarettes for them they'd let him hang around. Unfortunately, stealing became like a drug to him and his exploits had to become more and more daring to impress his comrades, as well as to get the adrenaline rush he was craving.

Junior High was spent in Virginia Beach, where it was relatively quiet. I stayed away from home and my dad as much as possible, usually fishing or tagging along with the older guys. It didn't hurt matters, from my perspective, that my older brother was keeping a lot of the attention off me by getting into his own share of mischief. He was skipping school, smoking cigarettes, sneaking girls into the house, that sort of thing. One day, more on a whim than anything else, I bet a couple of his buddies I could walk into the local hardware store and come out with a wheelbarrow. They laughed at me,

"Yeah right, even you aren't that good," which just made me more determined than ever.

"Just watch, you'll see," I retaliated.

So while they waited around the corner to see if I really could, I sauntered into the hardware and browsed around as if looking for some-thing for my father. My heart was pumping as it always did when I was about to steal, and as soon as the one clerk was helping someone else and had his back turned, and the other had disappeared into the backroom, I walked over to a brand new cement wheelbarrow and started pushing it in front of me. I ambled toward the front entrance. I knew if I looked like I knew what I was doing, most people would just assume I was legitimate. Anyway, I wheeled the barrow right out the front door, around the corner and straight over to my brother's friends who were standing there with their mouths agape. Their approval felt terrific, and after laughing at their incredulity, I casually tooled on down the street and left it on the sidewalk, a couple blocks away. I felt like I'd just passed an initiatory rite.

Unfortunately, it was before his peers instead of his elders. A common mistake in this day and age of gang mentality; boys trying to initiate boys. Only later, did the Prince realize that stealing (just like doing cocaine would do later), was one way of connecting the synapses in his brain, so he was able to focus for the first time in his life. All the Prince knew at the time, was that he always felt like the cartoon character who runs out over the cliff with his legs still pumping, but since he's standing on air, knows full well he's about to have a long fall.

All my life, I was described by my teachers as an over active, intelli-gent kid with a lot of imagination and potential. Hyperactive was another term often used, as well as daydreamer, underachiever, and space-cadet.

"If he could just stay focused . . . ," they'd write on my report cards at school. Each time the family would move, I would gratefully leave behind the latest nicknames I'd been given. 'Space face' was my least favorite, and 'Happy Harry' was probably the least offensive, but they all ate at me. Around the house I grew up hearing things like, "You'd lose your head, if it wasn't glued on," or "If you had a brain, you'd be dangerous." The worst had to be "What's wrong with you? Why can't you be more like so-and-so!"

It would be thirty years before the Prince discovered all the names were synonymous with Attention Deficit Disorder.

Full Moon Over Cuba

"My father taught me to work, but not to love it. I never did like to work and I don't deny it. I'd rather read, tell stories, crack jokes, talk, laugh-anything but work."

Abraham Lincoln

round this same time, the Vietnam War was just getting into full swing and his older brother went and enlisted into the Marine Corps, so there went his leading blocker. Soon after his enlistment, the family was transferred to Guantanamo Bay, Cuba, where the Prince would spend the next three years, mostly on restriction. At first, it seemed like an adventure; free outdoor movies, lots of sports and fishing with his buddies, and since they were all military brats as well, he never had to feel 'different than', or 'apart from', his school chums.

One night one of my new buddies and I got hold of a bottle of Ron Rico Purple Label 151 proof rum, and tried it out underneath the grandstands at a Marine vs. Navy baseball game. We mixed it in a paper cup with Coke, and every time I'd take a sip, I remembered my entire body would practically go into contortions, my head would shake, and I'd get a hot burning sensation through my middle. It was great, at least for the first hour or so. For the first time in my life, I felt like I fit in; like I didn't have to do anything to be OK in other peoples eyes. I was enough just like I was.

Then everything started to swim in circles and I threw up all over myself. I somehow managed to stagger home, where I hugged cold porcelain for the next three hours, but to me, that hour of contentment was worth it. *Little did the Prince know he would later pay a dear price for that philosophy.*

It was while living in Cuba, I joined the work force for the first time. *Being raised Protestant, that act took on disproportionate ramifications.* I still recall the explicit speech 'The Captain' delivered that compelled me to procure my first gainful employment.

"I will provide food, basic clothing and shelter; anything else you want in life, you need to earn it yourself."

I ruminated at the time, "None of my other friends have to work. They all receive allowances from parents that make less than you", but if there was one lesson I had gotten down pat, you didn't cross swords with 'The Captain'. There was no way you could win.

Even if I alluded to something totally erroneous in his logic, he would at first scoff at me, then upbraid me, and then become enraged and start threatening a beating or restriction if I persisted in 'talking back'. I learned to keep my mouth shut, as much as possible. *(Which by the way is almost totally impossible for someone with ADD.)*

When I heard about an opening for a stable boy to shovel manure at the base corral, I jumped into it with both feet (no pun intended). I loved horses and had been taking riding lessons anyway, so any reason to spend more time there was a blessing in my eyes, and to get paid for it besides?

The stable was neighboring our house, so I could trek over every day after school. Many of the herd corralled there on the base were Jamaican race horses that hadn't quite make the grade, or had been retired. My esteemed favorite was a big gentle roan named Bronson. He was 17 hands tall and seemed to have an insatiable appetite for apples and carrots, which I would provide by the bagfuls. We hit the trails together almost daily and soon became best of friends.

Soon the Prince had graduated from shoveling manure to training the horses for jumping and had become a member of the exclusive Jack and Jill Club (a club that welcomed only the best riders.) The concept that a military brat had to be number one at whatever they did, was instilled at a very young age. Many years later, when the Prince viewed the movie 'The Great Santini' with its definitive and explicit portrayal of life in a military household, he found it excruciating and became so agitated, he had to leave the theater. It was as if someone had captured his childhood terror on film.

Every full moon, the club would sponsor a moonlight steeple chase for all its members. The Prince actually counted down the days till its arrival each month, as it was the one thing he absolutely loved.

There was one full moon I'll never forget. The lunar halo was so iridescent the trails were illuminated, as if riding beneath a huge fluorescent bulb hanging from the sky. Usually, during a steeple chase, I would hold Bronson back as we ran the open fields, and then spur him on faster with a nudge of my feet as we would approach the jump. This night I threw all caution to the wind and literally gave him free rein. We had traversed the course many times before, and he knew it better than I did. Galloping full gait beneath that starry veil with its Cuban corona spotlight tracking our every move, we were as one. Flying over the jumps with total abandon I felt more alive than I had ever known before. *

Usually, after completing the steeple chase, everyone would head down the main trail to the beach area where there would be a bonfire and barbecue waiting. This particular night, however, I chose to go by way of the Hanging Moss Trail, which was off limits at night because of being so close to the cliffs. Many people wouldn't even ride that trail in the day time, but I realize now I was testing my own courage.

Guided by the moonglow reflected off the sea, and with the taste of salt kept aloft by the warm Caribbean breeze, Bronson was as sure-footed as he could be. A feeling of fearlessness came over me as the two of us made our way slowly down towards the oceans edge, and the closer we got, the more exhilarated I became. Just then, as I looked towards the heavens, the shadow of a large seagull passed between me and the opalescent moon and I shouted out a greeting in gull language, confident we were equals and he would understand.

Bronson delivered me safely, and after the barbecue, a few people decided to take the saddles off their horses and ride them into the ocean. Keep in mind now, in Cuba there are so many sharks in the waters, that for everyone's protection, they have to enclose the beaches and make a pool. This was accomplished using huge piles of boulders, placed 100 yards or so from the shore in a semicircle, just high enough so the waves could

* Dancing Girl...Awakening Imaginations CD #10

scurry over the top, constantly replacing the water. The middle of the swim area was thirty-five to forty feet deep, and this was where we were swimming around with the horses that night.

I held onto Bronson's mane, as his powerful body pulled me through the tranquil saltwater pool, and as I looked out towards the sea, the reflections of the others against the back drop of boulders appeared to be other-worldly. Then, when I turned back to the shore, I was greeted by a huge bonfire casting puppet-like shadows that danced on the coral cliff and seemed to loom up into the unknown.

Here I was with my best friend, my arms wrapped tight around his graceful neck, while the moon seemed to smile on me, having been the only witness to my first test of courage. I wished that night would never end.

This was the first unconscious attempt by the Prince to prove himself a man. Later, it would become a conscious effort as well, but more about that later.

Jamaican Ganja and Girls

"The young leading the young, is like the blind leading the blind; they will both fall into the ditch."

Lord Chesterfield

Somewhere around the age of fourteen, I read an article about marijuana in Time Magazine, which immediately intrigued me. I could hardly wait for the day when my sea scout troop (similar to the Boy Scouts), was embarking on a field trip from Guantanamo Bay, Cuba, to Montego Bay, Jamaica. The featured article had mentioned that not only could you find cannabis on that island in great abundance, but that it was some of the most potent in the world.

Once we landed, the twelve boys in my troop split up into three taxis, with the one and only chaperon for our entire party, conveniently getting into one of the other vehicles. Since we'd planned this in advance, all the Scouts in our car were in accord and wanted to try out some ganja also. I gave directions to our cabbie to lose the other two taxis, which he managed in short order, and then told him what we were after. He didn't seemed surprised by our request and we soon found ourselves deep in the mountainous jungle terrain of Jamaica.

We all started getting a bit nervous, half an hour into the excursion, when our driver exited the paved road onto little more than a six-foot-wide cowpath. We pulled into a poverty stricken area where the dwellings were nothing more than tin sheets leaning crookedly against each other, looking like a house of cards ready to collapse beneath a good Caribbean breeze. These structures were nothing like the sturdy wood and brick enclaves we were accustomed to back on the military base.

Once we finally came to a halt, our chauffeur/procurer got out of the car and mumbled something over his shoulder as he quickly walked away, having first made sure to put the car keys in his pocket.

We were all alone, and it was obviously a bad neighborhood, though the natives peering in the windows as they walked by seemed more curious than threatening. They probably thought we were midget sailors, as the sea scouts' uniforms we were adorned in were exact duplicates of the U.S. Navy uniform, complete with white swabbie hats tilted cockily at odd angles.

After a few moments (that felt more like an hour), our driver emerged from the sea of tin with a man that looked like 'the wild man' from the bottom of the lake in Robert Bly's, Iron John. He had long matted hair that hung below his waist, resembling a gnarly rats nest, a full gray beard covering his concave chest, and was wearing nothing but a pair of tattered shorts straight out of 'Swiss Family Robinson.' We were sure we were about to be captured by a voodoo witch doctor, as he peered in at us through the closed backseat window.

Though I tried not to show it, I was scared. One of the other boys even started to cry, not realizing we were witnessing our first old Rastafarian with phenomenal dreadlocks *(now a fashion statement)*.

Were we ever startled, as we let out a collective gasp of relief, when our imaginary witch doctor flashed his three remaining teeth in what was supposed to be a smile and offered, "Eh mon, you boys be thirsty?"

Our taxi driver then introduced 'Grok' in faltering ebonics, "He be de man with de plan."

I had wanted to impress my comrades and had envisioned a very cool scene negotiating the deal (much like in 'The French Connection'), but instead handed 'Grok' all our money and, without further ado said, "However much that will buy us."

I know I'm impressed.

Later, after the boys had regained their composure and satisfied their curiosity trying out the ganja, the taxi driver asked if they wanted to go get some girls? After their initial giggling and posturing, the Prince, who was feeling the need to reassert his position among the hierarchy (something all military brats understand), answered for them.

"Sure," as the driver headed towards 'Blueberry Hill'.

Though we were up and coming chameleons (all military brats are), finding a suave medium ground between Cary Grant and John Wayne wasn't something in our respective repertoires' as yet, though you should have seen us rehearsing the remainder of the drive there.

Upon arrival, two of my cohorts chickened out, but since they had double-dog-dared me, I couldn't back down. Nervous, as an innocent in a brothel should be, but determined to see it out to the end, I went through the ritual of scrutinizing my choices before making a selection. All the women there seemed to be so much older than what I had imagined. (*Probably because they were.*)

I might as well have had vestal virgin written across my forehead in florescent day-glow paint, but I was trying to keep a game face and not break into nervous giggles in front of my buddies. The madam of the establishment must have detected my dilemma and gave me a break I'll be eternally grateful for.

"Eh, little mon. You not see a girl to your liking?"

Before I could think of some brilliant repartée she continued in her flowing dialect,
"Not to worry, me have a special one for you."

She sent for her daughter, who couldn't have been any older than I was, and from the looks of her, I'd say she also qualified to be offered as a sacrifice to appease the Gods.

Let me tell you, she was as beautiful to me as that first luxurious spring day after a long icy winter. All my mates stopped snickering immediately. Since prostitution is an honorable profession in Jamaica, and she was wanting to learn her mother's art (or craft, depending on how you look at it), mom must have seen me as perfect for her daughters 'coming out'.

With eyes filled with envy, my peers were busy ogling 'my girl' as I followed her up the stairs to her room. Once there, we fooled around a bit, but since I was really a romantic at heart, it wasn't hard to figure out that a bed covered in newspapers wasn't exactly what I had envisioned. I'm sure

I disappointed her when I told her I had no desire to go through with it. *(As if he knew how!)* Since she seemed eager to earn her wings (so to speak), I convinced her to keep the money and just fake it when we went back downstairs. Then, the two of us just sat there amongst her dolls on the bed and awkwardly talked for a while.

Once I calculated enough time had passed for us to have done the deed, we went back down the stairwell with me knowing my stock was worth considerably more with my comrades than it had been before.

After they returned to Cuba from the Sea Scout trip, the Prince and a couple of the other boys smoked the ganja on a number of occasions, but never really felt its effect. They decided to try it one more time, and if it didn't do anything, then throw it away.

For this final attempt I borrowed one of my dads' corncob tobacco pipes and carried it with me to the sophomore class play practice. There, I rendezvoused with my friend, Bruce, and the two of us stole away to the machine gun bunker behind the school. Since the base chapel was next door to the high school, this particular bunker was primarily used by the Protestant altar boys between services on Sunday as a place to hide out and drink the grape juice they had swiped from the Catholics. Since I was also an altar boy, I knew the terrain well. (We actually tried the communion wafers once, but they were awfully boring, and we couldn't find anything to put on them.)

We smoked and smoked and choked and smoked and still nothing happened.

"This stuff is bogus," I finally said.

"Yea, I don't see what the big deal is about, I don't feel any different," Bruce replied.

We tossed the remainder and wandered back into the hacienda style courtyard of the school where the rehearsal was taking place. A few moments later, one of the actors on stage started shifting around uncomfortably, obviously annoyed by a 'wedgie' (vernacular for when one's under-

garments are unceremoniously wedged in one's crack). Anyway, he was trying to discreetly pull it out right there on the stage when Bruce and I
turned simultaneously to see if the other guy had noticed. That was all it
took, as we both burst out laughing. No one else seemed to know what was
so comical, but after a couple of minutes, other students started getting 'a
contact high', laughing simply because we were doubled over and couldn't
stop. Before long, the entire class had become infected, and it didn't take
the teacher long to spot who the ringleaders were.

After about ten minutes of her trying to regain control, to no avail,
she ran over to me wagging her bony finger while she screamed,

"Leave right this instant."

I managed to get up and lurch a few feet toward the exit before I
had the thought my legs wouldn't work anymore. At that exact moment, I
literally collapsed, still laughing hysterically.

The teacher began screaming even louder, which of course just
made the other students roar even harder. I honestly wanted to abide with
her wishes, but was truly incapacitated. I couldn't figure out how to make
my legs work, and the harder I tried, the more uproarious the situation
became. Finally, using my hands, I managed to drag myself away from her
tirade; my legs still dangling uselessly behind me.

It was the scuttlebutt of the school for days. I came to the conclusion that anything that could inspire forty people to have a thirty minute
belly laugh had to be OK.

*Unfortunately for the Prince, rumor got around the school about the
marijuana and it wasn't long before he was investigated by the Office of Naval
Intelligence and subsequently busted for international smuggling. Talk about
overkill, they sent four agents from military intelligence to secure the contra-
band. (Now you know why they call military intelligence an oxymoron.)
International smuggling?*

*That did seem a bit much to a fourteen-year-old who was simply sat-
isfying a curiosity, but that was just the opening round of his troubles. The
Prince soon found he had been kicked out of the sea scouts as well.*

As if all of this wasn't bad enough, his dad, 'The Captain', also happened to be the base legal officer. (Unspoken military gospel says "if you can't control your own kids, how are you supposed to control your men?")

The Prince didn't understand the big hoopla made over the marijuana, but he did understand 'The Captain's' embarrassment. He tried desperately to make amends, but it was to no avail, and all his attempts fell in vain. It was hopeless. His dad refused to accept his apology, and for the next nine months, didn't speak to the Prince at all.

Not one single word.

That hurt more than the beatings and the restrictions combined. Totally shut out. At first I was devastated and felt incredible remorse. I would have done anything to make things right, but after awhile, my own anger at his harshness took away any possibility we might have had to heal. Any messages between the two of us were relayed by my mother or sister, and all my meals were to be eaten by myself in my room. That part of the punishment didn't really bother me, as mealtimes had become close to unbearable anyway. Having to eat everything on my plate, no matter how bad it tasted, and having to say "thank you that was very good" after every meal, even when the brussels sprouts or collard greens I had forced down were inspiring visions of a toilet bowl, was almost more than I could stomach. Then, not only did everyone have to wait to be excused from the table, but we had to wait until the 'Captain' was through and announced the meal was over. Many were the times I thought he stretched out a meal just to make me suffer. There was a guaranteed sharp reprimand if anyone even started to clear the dishes before he gave the all-clear sign. For this boy, with testosterone pumping and friends waiting outside and phone calls to make, meals had become sheer torture. (Even to this day, I still prefer eating standing up or walking around the kitchen.)

I can still hear the 'sentence' being delivered, "You're not to leave your room for the next three months for anything except school. No television, no music, no radio, no fishing, no horses. Nothing. I want you to sit there and think about what you've done."

It probably wasn't the smartest move I'd ever made when, at that point, I asked 'The Captain' for some clarification.

"Is it OK to go to the bathroom?" I could see my mother roll her eyes, as she knew I was goading him, but by that point, I hated him so much, I didn't really care.

After the bulging veins in his neck receded, he continued, "After three months of room restriction, it will be relaxed to include the rest of the house. Then, for the following three months, if you behave yourself, the yard will be added, and if after nine months you're still behaving, then you'll be allowed to play on the point." (Military talk for the block we lived on).

It didn't get any better the next three years either, as the 'Captain' couldn't forgive or forget, and the air in their house became so thick you needed a machete to cut through. Determined to see it through, the Prince seized his forced isolation and used the opportunity to delve into reading and playing the piano with a vengeance. *

* Burning In Love...Awakening Imaginations CD #3

Defending The Queen

Thunder clappin' it's mighty hands
Everyone heard the crash
Silhouetted up against the blackest night
I saw the jagged flash;
Close to home, I knew at once
No way it could miss
Like a cobra or a rattlesnake
It gave itself away with its hiss.

GWC

*A*s every son of a military man will tell you, there comes a classic time, a milestone, when he finally pulls even with his father and then passes him.

I had fantasized for years how I would even the score man to man, and force him to back down, ending his reign of terror once and for all. When that long anticipated event finally transpired, it wasn't nearly as satisfying as I had imagined it would be.

It wasn't that different from a dozen other fights we'd had. I don't even recall the circumstances, but he was turning me black and blue with a belt. The only difference this time, was that my mother tried to intervene. I'd never seen him touch her before, but when he accidentally shoved her in the midst of the melee and she went sprawling, something snapped inside me. A part of me came out I'd never seen before. It was like a vice had shut down my brain for all those years, but when I witnessed Mom tumble to the ground, the clamp broke and this creature got loose. My fist went flying and connected with his chin, and I knew without a doubt, I could kill if that's what it took to protect someone I loved.

Though I was a good fifty pounds lighter and at least six inches shorter than he, it didn't matter. The years of pent up rage from living in fear finally blew. I only hit him that once, but he was a warrior and knew by the look on my face that the trembling in my body was no longer fear, but pure hatred ready to explode.

I hissed at him one animal to another, "If you ever touch me or my mother again motherf__ker I'll kill you."

He glared at me for what seemed like an hour, but I wouldn't flinch or avert my gaze. He finally backed off and commanded me; "Go to your room."

He never laid a finger on me again. In fact, I don't think he spoke to me more than twenty times the next ten years after that either.

After the initial adrenaline rush wore off, I was discomfited to realize I felt sorry for the guy. My hatred seemed to have been replaced by pity, and the victory I had dreamed about for so long felt hollow and anti-climatic.

Free At Last

"Borrow trouble for yourself, if that's your nature, but don't lend it to your neighbors."

Rudyard Kipling

One of the last conversations I had with 'The Captain', while living under his roof, occurred when I was sixteen. It was just a few months before I was to graduate from High School when he marched into my room and with subdued relish notified me,

"The day after you graduate you're to leave this house and never come back. The only reason I've allowed you to stay this long is because of your mother."

I knew that to be true, but it hurt like hell to hear him say it nevertheless. I didn't say a word or bat an eyelid. I wasn't going to give him the satisfaction of seeing me care one way or the other. I could be just as tough as he could. After all, look who my teacher was.

After leaving home the day after his graduation as was preordained, the Prince headed for Mississippi to spend the summer. He had been accepted at a North Carolina university and would be starting in the fall, but needed a place to stay in the meantime. It was a time of mixed feelings; from trepidation, as to where his life was going next, to exhilaration that he was finally out from under the tyrannical rule of his personal despot. He stayed with different aunts and uncles, as well as his grandparents, and the safety net of the family helped him cope with his father's rejection. (The significance of family and roots was instilled one more time in his young mind.)

September came way to soon for the Prince, as it was time to head off to school. His mom had arranged to have two of his uncles take him to the train station to see him off and to offer any last minute cautionary admonitions and sage counsel as to the pitfalls he might encounter. He might have been disowned by his dad, but a mother's love is one of the most powerful forces in the universe and she was determined he would have a college education.

From an early age, the importance of knowledge and getting an education had been drummed in to him and the Prince had become a voracious reader. Even as a boy, he had spent many days at his grandfather's farm lying out in a field or sitting by the creek with his nose stuck in a good book. Unfortunately, it took him a number of years to discover that knowledge was only half of the equation. Knowing how to apply that knowledge was the other half. Like most of his peers, he was taught what to think instead of how to think; how to regurgitate facts, but not how to arrive at his own conclusions. That's called wisdom.

Knowledge can be forgotten but not wisdom. If I could wave a magic wand and take charge of the education system in America, I would advocate more of a values based education as opposed to a fact based one. I would put at the top of the curriculum how to create healthy relationships and how to love unconditionally; teach children about humility, compassion and how to act altruistically; how to come to peaceful resolution with others; how to celebrate the human body and not be ashamed of it; and how to combine spirituality and sexuality. All subjects the Prince had studied as an adult, but it would have been helpful to start exploring them in his formative years.

Well here I was, getting ready to enroll in an institution of higher learning, but for all the wrong reasons. I was there partly because I didn't have a clue what else to do, but primarily because I didn't want to let my mother down.

I had grown my hair out over the summer and was one of only a handful of up-and-coming hippies on campus when I arrived. Though it was the late sixties, the peace and love movement hadn't moved from Haight Ashbury to North Carolina on a jet airliner, more like a Trailways bus pulling in to every one-stop-light town along the way. I lived in patch pants and tie dye shirts with beaded adornments everywhere, as that was the uniform of the day. My only transportation was a bicycle with a wicker basket on the front for carrying books, as well as paraphernalia. That was all I needed. Everything and everyone in my insulated world was within a scant mile of the dorm.

It wasn't long before I started experimenting with LSD and other psychedelic drugs, as Timothy Leary and his cronies were all in the news with their experiments up in Harvard. I tried other drugs as well, but the mind-expanding ones were really my preference. Beside LSD, I started using mescaline and peyote once I had been introduced to Carlos Castaneda and "The Teachings of Don Juan." Even back then, I was attracted to the metaphysical world he wrote about. I'm not really sure why, other than it seemed to be the only uncharted territory left, and for an adventurous soul that was enough.

I was brought up in the school of thought that hallucinogens were not to be taken lightly, but were a tool that could be used to uncover higher states of consciousness. Before taking a psychedelic I was taught to prepare myself as if I were going on a long journey, which in many respects I was.

First, I would surround myself with my favorite writings, music, and photography for inspiration; make sure my address book was close at hand, in case I needed to talk to someone I loved or in case of an emergency; restring my guitar and make sure I had numerous writing utensils at my disposal. Then, before taking the phone off the hook, I'd call a friend or two who understood the path I was following (*i.e., someone else who took hallucinogens*), make sure they were going to be straight that night, and that they were available in case of a bad trip.

One night while I was 'tripping' (under the influence of a hallucinogen), I had a rude awakening. Shortly after having arrived at ECU I had pledged the Kappa Sigma fraternity (*once again, trying to find a place where he belonged*). I have no idea what I was contemplating at the time, as I had very little in common with anybody there. They all wore shirts with alligators on them, khaki pants, and kept their hair short, while I was evolving from patch pants to bell-bottoms, colorful silk shirts and pulling my hair back in a ponytail. They loved to drink beer, have keg parties, and listen to Pat Boone, while I preferred smoking grass, dropping LSD, and listening to Jimi Hendrix and the Beatles.

This particular night, I wandered over to the fraternity house and watched the plaid sofa drip onto the carpet and listened to a few conversations that all seemed to be centered on beer, cars, or screwing girls. I realized my non-mainstream metaphysical inclinations probably weren't going to fit in and I'd better get the hell out of there before I started to have a 'bummer' (sixties vernacular for having a bad trip.) I de-pledged the fraternity the next day once I came down.

I majored in music, dance, and discovering God through better chemistry, not to mention the opposite sex. This was when AIDS wasn't around yet and sex, well hell, it was the era of free sex and everybody was doing it.

All during the Prince's stay at ECU he was able to explore his fascination with drugs and altered states of consciousness. That, combined with his being born under the sign of Scorpio with all their inherent sexual energy, led the Prince to a new revelation in that arena as well.

One night while searching for a spiritual experience like I'd read about in 'The Adventures of Don Juan', I ingested some peyote and mescaline combined. I wasn't long into the voyage when I got the overwhelming urge to see a woman named Nicole that I'd met in one of my classes recently. We'd gone out a couple of times and I'd found her innocence and naivete' combined with her sense of humor both beguiling and irresistible. She didn't have cover girl looks by a long shot, but I found her red hair and freckles incredibly alluring just the same. I called her dorm repeatedly, but she wasn't in, and I found myself becoming increasingly agitated. I didn't know why; just that it was imperative I see her and knew if I didn't it was going to turn into a long night. *Which of course it would, now that he'd planted that suggestion in his brain.*

Though I could barely see where I was going for all the hallucinogenic colors and trails, I burst from the house, heading for the campus to try and find her. I wasn't half way down the block before she appeared thirty yards away, like an angel coming to my rescue. Somehow she had heard my call. From there on, everything that happened felt like I was being guided.

I took her by the hand and led her back to the house and asked her to sit cross-legged from me with our knees touching. We were both totally dressed (I swear). Next, I had her hold up her hands and placed each of my fingertips against hers while we gazed deeply into each others eyes. I told her it was of paramount importance not to break eye or finger contact (how I knew that I haven't a clue, but it seemed as if I had done it before). If I wasn't so high, I'd probably have been concerned that she thought I was some kind of nut case, but she didn't seem uncomfortable following my lead at all. Nicole wasn't doing any drugs, in fact she never had, which made what happened next even more astonishing.

We sat for nearly 30 minutes, never breaking contact, while the energy flowing between us became more and more intense (like turning up the power on a halogen lamp). After awhile, I heard Nicole emit a soft moan as we both started to tremble. The energy grew and grew until we literally couldn't touch any longer and at the exact instant our fingers separated, we both screamed as a tsunami wave of ecstasy engulfed us.

I immediately left my body and went into a delicious state I can only call Nirvana. It seemed like it lasted hours, but in linear time, it was closer to ninety minutes. Nicole called it 'being in a state of total bliss' as she had experienced it too. Once I could speak again, I looked at Nicole who was still laying on the carpet with her eyes closed. All I could say was,

"Unbelievable."

Later, when I came down from the drug, I asked her to describe what her experience had been.

"There really aren't any words to convey its magnitude", she began. "I crossed a threshold into another world and had multiple orgasms more powerful than any I had ever known, but it was way beyond that."

I knew exactly what she meant. I doubt I'll ever come up with the words to describe it completely, but I know I was guided by a force beyond my control. Call it God, call it life force, call it the power of love, call it whatever you like...I just know that it exists!

Unfortunately, between his untreated ADD and its demand to hyper-focus on things and his already obsessive-compulsive personality, the Prince was to spend much of the next fifteen years trying to re-create that feeling through chemistry. The advice of an elder at this point explaining what had happened, might have helped the Prince integrate the experience quicker and saved him a lot of heartache, and certainly wear and tear on his body.

The Habit Begins

"You'll float below the surface realm
Leave your body far behind
And know your life is so much more
Than the bodies finite mind."

GWC

*O*ne drug led to another (and don't let anybody tell you different), until one day the Prince tried heroin and it was love at first shot. For a little while, all was right with the world. That feeling of contentment he'd sought for so long he found sitting right in his own living room 'nodding out'. The love affair was short lived, though, as his habit increased dramatically over the next three months.

In the beginning I could 'get down' for a dollar, but within a couple of months, I was spending thirty dollars a day to reach the same plateau of numbness. Not only that, I quickly ascertained that doing heroin and getting a college education didn't really mix that well. Maybe Edgar Allen Poe could have a life while being a junkie, but I was finding it increasingly difficult to do anything except focus on where the next fix was coming from. Once I became cognizant of that fact and realized how fast my habit was growing, I stopped doing heroin altogether, though I did continue using "recreational drugs" such as hallucinogens and grass.

After the Prince was able to walk away from the drug on his own, it gave him a false security that his willpower was enough to stop anything. After all, heroin was supposed to be the worst and most addictive of all the drugs. Years later, that misconception would almost cost him his life. (Or rather, almost caused a grave error. Sorry, I couldn't resist.)

It was during this time, I began attending the huge rock concerts that were just coming into vogue once Woodstock had set the standard. I crashed both Atlanta festivals, where I was able to experience Jimi Hendrix, as well as most of the biggest names in rock and roll at the time. I remember hitchhiking in with thirty hits of blotter acid (drops of LSD on a piece of paper), taped inside my glasses as if I had broken ear pieces. I thought I was really clever.

One night, I took an extra large dose, and timed it so I would be at the height of the experience when Hendrix came on. I danced with complete abandon through most of his performance, and toward the end, I actually saw the notes coming out of the amplifiers and the waves of sound started to knock me to the ground. As I was looking for a place to land, a blond diva in tie-dye, who had been swaying behind me, obviously detected my dilemma and appeared at my side inquiring if she could be of service. I had no doubt I was soon to leave my body, as I had experienced this before, and invited her to look after it till I returned. She said "no problem", put my head in her lap and started stroking my head until I made the transition. I thought that was so cool, when I returned three hours later, I asked her to marry me. I'll never forget her answer.

"We'll discuss it when you come down." *Just another day in the life...*

Then there was Love Valley, North Carolina. Though not nearly as large, it will be remembered in lore as one of the best and certainly most intimate rock festivals ever held.

Once I hiked into the site through the oldest foothills in the world, I was enchanted to come upon a town with one dusty street straight from the wild west, complete with hitching posts for your horses and a saw-dust-floored saloon. The entrance had the proverbial swinging double doors. They could have filmed 'Shoot-Out At The OK Corral" there; it was that perfect. Imagine a band of long-haired nomad gypsies descending upon Robin Hood's Sherwood Forest, only to discover Wyatt Earp's town run by a rock and roll band, and you've got the picture.

The Allman Brothers Band playing daily and there was a huge supply of pure MDA (the love drug) being given away throughout. Now, for the uninitiated, imagine falling in love with everyone you met for an entire week and each time you snapped your fingers, just the physical act of moving your fingers was sheer ecstasy. *The drugs had nothing to do with all the intimacy the Prince experienced, I'm sure.*

The festival that probably had the greatest impact on the Prince took place up in Canada at the Mosport race track outside of Toronto. It was to be a seven-day event, but he had arrived two weeks early as he'd planned on staying in Canada after the festival. He had been busted at East Carolina University for drug possession and his lawyer had told him, since this was one of the first big drug cases at the school, they planned on making an example of him. The Prince chose to not stick around to find out what-all that entailed (like most gypsies, he had a particular aversion to being confined), and headed to Canada with Billy Bob, a school chum who wanted to make a new life for himself as well.

Now Billy Bob was a rather nondescript good-ole-boy, who had the misfortune of a low draft number, and was willing to go to any lengths to avoid The Ho Chi Minh Trail. Gangly in appearance and a bit clumsy by nature, he had a heart of gold and could often make the Prince laugh with his dry wit. (Two very important attributes when choosing a traveling companion.)

Because they had arrived at the festival so early, the Prince and Billy Bob were able to get jobs working as stage security looking after the equipment during the night, in return for backstage passes for the entire festival.

What a gift, being a young musician just getting started, to be able to meet and hang out with half the musical heroes of my time. Meeting Jimi Hendrix was a dream come true, as 'Electric Ladyland' was my favorite album back then. Being a gypsy myself, I idolized him since he was considered 'The King of the Gypsies'. Watching him prowl around backstage in his flowing multicolored robes and scarves reminded me of a big graceful cat, but I was so in awe when we met I was struck dumb and couldn't utter a word other than "hi!"

Not only that, when the performances were going on, I found a way to climb out on the beams directly overlooking the stage. There I had a zoom lens view of not only their playing and moves on stage, but the repartee' between band members as well.

Watching Leslie West and Felix Papalardi of the band 'Mountain' reminded me of synchronized swimming at the Olympics. It was uncanny how they were able to anticipate each other's moves as if they were of one mind. Through their chemistry together they seemed to take the music to a whole new level I never knew existed. I'd never experienced anything like it and swore right then that I was going to learn how to do the same thing!

One night as I was getting ready to head back to my tent, one of the roadies that worked for the band 'Ten Years After', gave me what was supposed to be some fantastic MDA along with the warning, "Don't do it standing up."

I didn't know much about the drug at the time, except that the few times I'd tried it (Love Valley), I'd found I wanted to tell everyone in my vicinity that I loved them and would usually do so in great detail.

Well, the Prince aimed to find out if it was really that good and went back to the tent to prepare an injection, and to share it with Billy Bob.

When I got back to the campsite, Billy had already gotten the fire going and was busy rolling a couple of joints. It was way after midnight and the grounds were relatively quiet. Since we had been among the first arrivals, we had a prime hillside vantage point overlooking not only the stage, but the instant city of a half million people that had come together. I plopped down on a blanket and gazed out over the twinkling campfires that seemed to spread out for miles. "Billy, I think I got something special here. You want to try it?" I proceeded to tell him what I knew about MDA and where this dose had come from.

I already knew his answer. On the drive up from North Carolina I'd queried Billy on what was his favorite drug. When he replied, "Whatever you've got", I knew I'd found a kindred spirit.

I went first and fell into immediate reverie. I lay back on the ground and felt literally as if I was becoming one with the earth. The physical reaction was exquisite. Any movement, no matter how slight, brought on sensations as pleasurable as an orgasm. The waves were becoming extremely intense, and I soon felt like I was leaving my body. Billy was laughing at me (so obviously enjoying myself), and couldn't wait to follow suit. It wasn't long before he was enraptured as well, but rather than go with the waves as they became more intense, he started to get alarmed and then frightened by it's magnitude. His breathing became hurried and he tried to get off the ground, which I tried to tell him would only intensify the situation. Soon he started to plead, "Help me, I think I'm dying."

I wanted to help him out, but by this point, I was unable to even raise my head off the ground. I was also thoroughly enjoying it and answered, "Yea, I think I am too, isn't it great? I'll meet you there." *

Looking back, it was the first time the Prince realized he wasn't afraid of death. Till then, he'd had no problem mentally accepting he was an eternal being, just borrowing this two-by-four body for a while, and that death was simply a transition to another state. Now, after this first close encounter with the death experience, any doubt he might have had left, vanished.

Primarily, because someone had stolen his entire grubstake during the festival, but also because he didn't like the thought of being a fugitive the rest of his life, the Prince decided to come back to the states and fight the drug bust once the festival ended. He decided he would even pay his debt to society, if that was the verdict, though he was not entirely clear why he owed society any debt, when the only person he felt he could have possibly harmed was himself. But, when in Rome...

* Merry Go Round

Fiddle Festivals
and The Bagband

Go beyond your mind
Listen to the rhyme
Divinity

GWC

*T*hroughout the ages, music and rhythm have been used to access the divine; a way to get beyond man's finite intellectual capacity; a way to feel inside something he knows to be true, but can't quite describe. For the Prince, returning to his ancient roots as a troubadour was even more than that. It was the one path open in which he might not only survive, but thrive in this incarnation.*

"Music is great for an avocation, but you can't make a living at it." That was the message my parents instilled in me at a very young age. *A bittersweet message to be sure.*

As a child, I used to be enraptured when the entire family would get together and make music. Mom played the glockenspiel, tuba or organ; dad would get on the clarinet, my big brother handled the trumpet parts, while little sister was usually on piano. I always wound up on either clarinet, bass clarinet or saxophone, depending on what the music called for. There must have been twenty-five different instruments in our house to choose from.

At Christmas time we'd break out the books of carols and everybody would play their part. Since we all played numerous musical instruments and enjoyed different styles, I developed a passion for a wide variety of music by the time I left home.

While I seemed to have inherited my mother's love for classical music and Dixieland, my first musical influences were The Beatles and

Simon and Garfunkel records my brother bought home. Living in the islands also seemed to have a pronounced effect on me, as it opened up an entire new world with its Reggae, Calypso, and Cuban rhythms. I later fell in love with Andrew Lloyd Webber's 'Jesus Christ Superstar' which I had been given as a Christmas present, and must have listened to a thousand times. Shortly thereafter, I developed a passion for Rock 'n' Roll, Ragtime and Mississippi Delta Blues, but the actual first record I ever bought with my own hard-earned money, was by Allen Toussaint playing his style of New Orleans Jazz.

Once I struck out on my own, my love of music continued and I sought it out constantly. I found myself drawn more and more to fiddle festivals in the mountains where people would journey from great distances to camp out, break bread and share their music and stories with one another. Every evening at twilight, people would gravitate toward the campfires, and you could hear music of every color, shape, and variety throughout the night.

It was common to see one minstrel come upon another strolling through the forest, where they would pause for a few moments greeting, and more times than not, break into spontaneous song. Soon others would appear like magic, and before long another campfire would be lit.

Now since I would roam great distances to attend these events, I found myself on the road a lot and had become adept at traveling light. Towards that end, I had a special leather bag made for myself, that served a dual purpose. I had it made the size of a mailman's pouch so I could keep my collection of percussion instruments there. That number always varied between fifty and seventy-five instruments, depending on how many were returned after a performance. It held everything from tambourines, cowbells, wood blocks and maracas, to African finger drums, a juiro from Brazil, finger cymbals, castanets and a set of bones. On the front of the bag, beneath the flap, were twenty-four individual pouches where I would keep all my harmonicas in alphabetical order, ready for quick retrieval. The song could be halfway finished if I didn't have a system in place to instantly find the right key. There was also a strap on the bag itself, which was made out of a thick wooly sheepskin, so the bag doubled as my pillow when camping. Of course, I would always bring my best friend Gildy (a guitar), and wherever the bag would appear, the 'Bagband' would play.

One of the more memorable 'Bagband' performances was when 80 some-odd (and I do mean some very odd) band members came on stage in Shady Grove, North Carolina singing 'May the Circle Be Unbroken.' Dressed in everything from tie-dyed patched pants and saddle shoes, to one guy in a coat and tie, there had to be at least twenty guitarists, fifteen banjos and ten bass players, as well as numerous mandolin, fiddle and harmonica players all jamming at once. It was truly a sight to behold.

There was another incarnation of the Bagband the Prince remembered fondly, of which he loved to tell the tale. With a gleam in his eye and a mischievous grin, he'd launch into the story of the forty or so totally nude band members performing at "The Gathering of the Tribes" in the Arapaho National Forest.

It was a mammoth gathering of over one hundred thousand people (mostly hippies), in the craggy mountains of Colorado. Folks were attracted from all over the world, and many had been camping on the land long prior to the beginning of the week-long festivities. Based on a Native American myth, a white buffalo was supposed to become visible during the celebration signifying something, but for the life of me, I can't recall what.

All I remember, is that I lived under a billowing parachute on the nudist point, alongside a translucent body of water that I believe was called Rainbow Lake. With all the hallucinogens being passed around, who knows?

You're probably thinking, it sounds like a loss of gray matter. You're probably right.

Besides the obvious fun of playing uninhibited music with numerous hourglass shaped band members, while in the buff, I also took delight in learning the art of massage from one of the more comely members who happened to be a professional masseuse. It seems when she wasn't bouncing naked through the woods, she loved sharing her knowledge, carnal and otherwise, with any male of the species that expressed an interest. I expressed an interest. Seemed like a good time to learn to me.

You see, the Prince had a passion for knowledge, among other things, and would go to great lengths to delve into and discover something new.

Clyde – The Wizard
Of Invention

*"Men call imagination a play thing...the dream faculty...when
actually it is the very gateway of reality."*

Neville

*I*t was around this same time the Prince met a mountain man, named
Clyde, at the 'Folk Festival of The Smokies'... fondly remembered in lore as
the 'Smoke Festival of the Folkies.' Little did the Prince know that their meeting would change his life forever. (Don't you find it exhilarating and a bit awe
inspiring to live in a world filled with such wonder that you can have unlimited possibilities at your fingertips with just a moment's notice or a chance meeting?) I know I do.

Clyde was an inventor, a storyteller, a sacred clown from an ancient
Celtic tribe that loved ritual. Though we were close to the same age,
because of his flowing uncut white beard, his rosy cheeks, and the mischievous twinkle in his eyes, he could easily be mistaken for Santa Claus
around the Christmas season. Many were the days I would stop by Clyde's
dwelling only to find him in the woods on his knees with a magnifying
glass, usually collecting specimens for his renowned smoking mixture. Of
the dozen or so ingredients in it, he swore three of them were opiates that
grew wild within two miles of his house. You could never really be sure if
he was pulling your leg or not, as he loved to tell tall tales and would spin
yarns often. If he wasn't traipsing through the forest, odds were you'd find
him in his workshop creating a one-of-a-kind musical instrument or
kitchen accessory.

One day as I was ruminating in his outhouse (which was 40 yards
downhill from the main house), I saw that there was no more toilet paper
and the Clyde prerequisite corncob bin was empty as well. I did see a note

attached to a string, however, that read, "Pull here for T.P. refill."

Well, having no other sanitary choice, as well as being curious to boot, I yanked on the line. Lo and behold, from up under the eve of the main house came a huge wooden puppet astride a hand carved unicycle flying towards me. As it got closer, it dawned on me the blob of white between the puppets knees was a roll of toilet paper sailing down to my rescue. I laughed so hard, I'd have surely wet my pants, if they weren't already down around my ankles and my bladder wasn't already empty.

This was rather typical of the joys and discoveries one might encounter at Clyde's; just another day at the office.

One of Clyde's inventions was a large fourteen string 1-of-a-kind dulcimer (nicknamed 'Dulci'.) The Prince could sure make her sing and had borrowed her on a number of occasions at 'The Folk Festival of the Smokies', at Clyde's insistence.

Clyde created the instrument by taking the sound board from a 100-year-old piano, combined with rare walnut and birds' eye curly maple and then used four different scales (some having dampers on them), to recreate the drone of a sitar. The music that emanated from 'Dulci' could soothe the most jagged nerves, and often people seemed to become entranced. A few months after they met at the 'smoke festival', Clyde gave that instrument to the Prince. 'Dulci' was special, and Clyde trusted the Prince would share her healing tones with lots of God's children.

That was Clyde's way.

He also gave the Prince 'Dulci's' sister, Gordamer; another one-of-a-kind instrument that originated in his fertile mind. This one had four strings on a banjo-like neck with a violin scroll and a dulcimer scale attached to the body of a petrified gourd. This particular gourd had already lived a useful existence for over fifty years as an egg carrying basket for one of Clyde's neighbors. Now, in its new incarnation...who knows.

The Prince nicknamed her 'Gordi', and most often, whenever 'Dulci' came out to play, 'Gordi' would too, as they were inseparable. Together with the Prince, they would bring new meaning to the expression 'making a joyful noise!'

If you ever want to see how truly creative and imaginative a human being can be, go to the museum in Waynesville, North Carolina. There, on display, is another of Clydes' works of art he built for the bicentennial celebration. A huge clock, all hand carved from wood, with wheels the size of automobile tires down to the size of a quarter, all turning in time beneath a large table running an animated colonial village of hand made pieces. Depending on the quarter hour, you'll see the stone mill start grinding flour, a blacksmith shoeing a horse, the potter throwing pots, or even a sawmill cutting lumber. Truly a sight of wonderment.

Anyway, I digress, back to the festival. The Prince and Clyde, having fallen into league making music and dance and telling tall tales deep into the night, had become like brothers. Now that the festival was coming to a close and the time had come to part company, Clyde extended an invitation to the Prince to come visit him once he got weary from his travels. He then drew up a treasure map, so the Prince could find his mountain hide-a-way. They wished each other Godspeed, and the Prince was back on the road again in search of adventure.

The Carnival Of Life

He who cannot laugh at himself, leaves the job to others.
Author Unknown

Now the Prince was torn between his lust for life and adventure, and his desire to please his mom, 'The Queen', who was wanting him to return to school and complete the education he'd started back at ECU. All his life, she and 'The King' had stressed the importance of a college education and hard work, if you wanted to make something of yourself. (The typical Protestant work ethic, you know, shit won't happen if you work harder.)

So the Prince prayed and prayed for a solution to his dilemma, and do you know what God in his great wisdom replied?

"JOIN THE CIRCUS."

He was thrilled; not only could he continue his exploits, but he could earn money for his education at the same time. So that's what he did. Dell and Travers Shows to be exact.

To prepare for my wanderings, I purchased a baby blue GMC bread truck and converted it into a poor man's mobile home, complete with a fold up bed, all my musical equipment, and a small motorcycle in a rack attached to the front grill. Next, I put huge sound speakers in the rear of the van to balance out the front weight of the motorcycle, and between them, made a bed for my best friend and faithful companion, Grendel, the monster. *(His namesake being the dragon in Beowulf.)*

Actually, this was Grendel the Fifth. Except for my first dog Champ, every canine I had ever owned had been named Grendel. This Grendel though, was unique in a couple of ways. First, she was a thirty-pound malamute, which is extremely small for that breed, and second, she was a she, while all of her predecessors had been male.

Grendel was, without a doubt, the most endearing and devoted creature I'd ever encountered, and was instrumental in teaching me about unconditional love. No matter how inattentive or grouchy I might become, I could always count on her waggling tail and slurpy greetings to let me know she never took it personally.

Interesting to note, that soon after they teamed up, the Prince would fall in love for the first time with a creature of the two legged variety. Ah, but we get ahead of ourselves. Back to the circus.

Joining the carnival was good for me, both monetarily and emotionally. For the first time in my life, I felt like I fit in somewhere. *The fact it was with a bunch of misfits, does strike me as a bit ironic.* My craving to belong and feel like part of a family, as well as my wanderlust minstrel urges, were all satisfied for the time being. Since I was the new chameleon on the block, or should I say the new carney on the midway, I wanted to learn the ropes as quickly as possible. Every few weeks, as we caravaned from town to town, I experimented with different games, looking for my niche.

The first game I ran appealed mostly to the male of the species that fancied himself a shark at billiards. Using a couple gargantuan stuffed bears to draw them in, the goal was to shoot one cueball and knock a silver dollar that had been placed on top of another cueball outside of a drawn circle. I found it immensely entertaining to observe human nature displayed in all its splendor. I ascertained quickly my take home pay would be substantially increased, if I made it a point to tell each contestant exactly how to win. The trick was to hit the ball ever so softly (which was a challenge in itself), but on average, nine out of ten players would either think I was lying, or their male egos wouldn't permit them to take my advice and they would try to put some kind of fancy English or back spin on the ball. They would invariably walk away empty-handed, and I a bit richer.

The next game I worked was balloon poker; five darts thrown at balloons with playing cards placed behind each.

"The better the hand the better the prize", I would call out to passersby. Unfortunately, this appealed predominantly to adolescents at an age where they hadn't yet developed their aim or honed their eye-to-hand coordination. I have the scars to prove it.

One of my favorite games, and certainly my entree to the entertainment world, was the 'Birthday Game.' Constantly moving beneath a sea of dangling teddy bears, I was in all my glory running the 16 color 'lay down', represented by 12 months and four holidays. I would bark people in using humor and poetry.

"Put a quarter on your favorite month. Your birthday, your wife's birthday, the month your wife moved out and your girlfriend moved in."

I would then wail on my harmonica to signal the beginning of the next round and call out "all aboard, the trains pulling out of the station". With my chameleon-like ability to read people and adapt, I usually had the grown-ups digging deep for quarters and chuckling in no time. Between my hamming it up, my harmonica playing, and the fact that I was genuinely having a good time, I was soon raking in some serious money. (Well, not really serious money, but if I said funny money, it might give the wrong idea).

Many a smile did the Prince put on a young child's face, whether they won or not, never letting a deserving child or a pretty girl walk away empty handed.

"It's a quarter to play,
It's a quarter to win,
No way to find out till you try.
Spring for a quarter,
Win one for your daughter,
It's one sure way to make the girl high.
Playing at the carnival called life.
You get bonus five if you got the kids and the wife.
You get minus 10 if you hurt someone,
No sense in doing that, it's supposed to be fun.
Playing at the carnival called life."

Even though the Prince put his own slant on the birthday game (using the harmonica to draw them in), it still had been done before. Always the creative one, he longed to invent his own game, something unique, that had never been attempted before; a game that would not only help him reach his college goal, but one that might elicit smiles on others faces, as well as just plain being fun. (Somehow that seems to get lost too readily in this day and age.)

One night it came to me in a dream and I woke up and wrote it down.

"Put toilet seats on the wall and have people throw rolls of toilet paper through them!"

Aha! I wasn't sure if this was another God-shot or not, but I wasn't going to take any chances. It sounded brilliant and certainly appealed to my sense of humor. The next day, I transformed my entire booth. I put four toilet seats on the wall, using a back drop of black velvet-looking material for that touch of class, and then scattered fifty rolls of colored toilet paper around the joint.

One thing I knew for sure. A roll of toilet paper wasn't gonna be nearly as dangerous as a dart once put in a kid's hand. Then I sat down on the steps of my converted bread truck to create the rules and to make up some rhymes to call people in: "You get three rolls for a dollar. You make all three, you get a stuffed one." (A stuffed animal).

"A shot in the pot,
A roll in the hole,
A load in the commode,
They're all the same,
No Shit——that's the name of the game.
No poop——just the straight scoop
When you play over here.
We've got hogs, frogs,
all kinds of dogs
Winnie the poohs and kangaroos." *

* Put Your Money Where Your Mouth Is…Chameleon CD #15

It was an instant hit with belly laughs galore.

For the first time in his life, the Prince felt what it was like to have some measure of success, and received the highest form of flattery when other carnivals copied his idea and 'The Toilet Game' began to pop up on other midways around the country.

First Love

All my life I'd heard
how wonderful love could be.
But love was just a word,
*'Til you said it to me. ***

GWC

*I*t was at the end of a stretch of Canadian towns with names such as Swift
Current, Red Deer, Prince Albert and then Medicine Hat when the Prince's
gaze fell upon the first love of his life, Lady Helena. *

The day was young; the Prince was leaning against the front of his
joint (carney-talk for booth), with his eyes closed, basking in the morning rays,
when he detected a tinkling sound coming ever closer. Always the curious one,
he lazily opened one eye and saw the most alluring maiden he had ever seen
strolling along the midway. Both eyes popped open and almost out of his head
so that the Prince had to laugh at himself.

Between the sunlight bouncing from her thick luxurious auburn curls,
her twinkling fire opal eyes changing color in the sunlight, and her beguiling
mischievous smile, he knew he was beholding his first Princess. Wearing a
sleeveless summer print dress, that left just enough to the imagination, she had
the face of a teenage girl and the body of a woman armed with all the tools nec-
essary to master the art of seduction. A true woman-child, she had on dozens of
necklaces and bracelets of every shape and variety (hence the tinkling sound that
had caught his attention). Being a Princess, of course, she carried herself with
a certain air of aloofness. However, upon seeing our Prince grinning ear to ear,
surrounded by a herd of stuffed animals swinging over his head, with the pearl
colored toilet seats hanging up against the backdrop of black velvet, it was all
she could do to not trip over herself she was laughing so hard. It was love at first
*sight. ***

Knowing instantly he'd met his match, but not wanting to frighten her

* Love Was Just A Word
* You Are My First Love
* First Time Lovers

away by appearing too impulsive, the Prince curtailed himself for at least half an hour into their conversation before announcing,

"I know this probably sounds a little crazy, but I want you to be my girl." *Nothing compulsive about that.*

Playing hard to get till the end, Lady Helena responded,

"I need to think about it,"

She went off to confer with her traveling companion, Carol, as they were in the midst of their own adventure, and came back a half hour later, walked up to the Prince who was busy holding his breath and said.

"OK."

The Prince was ecstatic and kissed her passionately, right there on the midway, while the dozen or so onlookers clapped their hands. She moved into the van that night. *

Our first night together was savored beneath the northern lights, and needless to say, Grendel (much to her chagrin-that is if dogs have chagrin), ended up spending that evening, and many evenings thereafter, snoozing under the Milky Way, because of her annoying habit of licking the salt brought to the surface during the heat of passion.

The Prince found jobs for both Princess Helena and her girlfriend, Carol, and when it came time for the show to pack up at week's end, the Princess decided she was going to head down into the states with her man. Carol, meanwhile, agreed to stay with their VW van, which had blown its engine there in Medicine Hat, and then rendezvous with Helena in New York City in two months.

However, trouble was on the horizon.

One week later, as their traveling show was crossing the Canadian border back into the U.S., Lady Helena thought it would be better if she walked across the checkpoint on her own, since she was a Canadian citizen and had no work visa. The two young lovers parted momentarily, or so they thought. Boy, was the Prince in for a rude awakening.

Four hours later, he was finally waved across the border, as the blue bread truck had attracted more than a bit of added scrutiny, as did his gypsy

* Destiny

looking appearance. (The fact 'Follow Your Dreams' was emblazoned across the back of the van with a 6-foot effervescent rainbow, had nothing to do with it I'm sure.)

Meanwhile, the U.S. border patrol had refused the Princess entry, having seen her alight from the van on the Canadian side and deducing she was going to be working illegally.

Not knowing what else to do, and with tears streaking her face, Helena had caught a ride and was hitchhiking back to Medicine Hat hoping Carol might still be there. Her plan then was to cross over at another border checkpoint and come find the Prince in North Dakota.

I was unaware of any of this. In fact, the only thing I knew was that Helena was originally from Vancouver and I had neither an address or telephone number to reach her, as we had not anticipated being separated. After one of the border patrolmen let it slip that she had been turned away a couple hours earlier, I ran across the border back into Canada, frantically looking for my Princess. Ignoring the warning shouts of the border guards and heedless of the danger I was in, I ran a quarter mile back into Canada, as fast as I could, until I came across a local resident and asked if he had seen her.

"The pretty blond, eh? She was here, you just missed her. She got a ride on a semi, fifteen minutes ago."

Broken hearted, I ran back to the border and literally begged the guards to let me return in the van and look for her. "I don't care about the show, I'll quit the show. I just want to be with my girl."

The guards, discerning real anguish when they saw it, agreed to let me drive to the last town, twenty miles back, but warned me, "Be back within an hour or we'll come looking for you."

Hoping against all odds she'd gotten off at that first town, I raced back as fast as I could, but no one there had seen her. After posting notices up at the bus station, town hall, and local cafe; crestfallen and heavy hearted, I reluctantly turned the van around. There was nothing else I could do. I was crushed.

Barely able to make out the road for all the tears I was spilling, I'd never felt so helpless in my life, as I did on that lonely ride back to the border. I'd literally lost the only girl I had ever loved.

Finding Princess Helena became my only goal in life. * The next four days, back at the fairgrounds, I barely ate or slept. I went through the motions with my job, but alone with my thoughts, I was inconsolable. At least Grendel was happy. Sensing my dejection, she was constantly licking my face delighted, by the increase in salt she was finding.

The fourth night, I awoke from a dream remembering that the VW place in Medicine Hat might at least have an address or phone number where Helena could be reached. Barely able to contain myself, I got up and paced the grounds till dawn, waiting to dial the phone number I'd already gotten from information in the middle of the night.

Morning finally broke, and I nervously dialed the only chance I was sure I would ever have at happiness. After a few seconds of trying to explain to the mechanic what I was after, he told me to "hold on." Three seconds later, the voice I was afraid I might never hear again, floated across the line.

I let out a holler that startled even Grendel, who was used to my enthusiastic outbursts by then.

It seems Carol hadn't made it out of Medicine Hat before the van developed more mechanical problems and she had been forced to put it back in the shop. Princess Helena had caught up with her three days earlier, and the two of them had just walked out the door, after paying their bill. A minute later and they would have been gone, as they were just climbing in their van when the phone had rung.

Call it fate or destiny or just another one of the many miracles that seemed to always be close at hand when the Prince needed them, whatever else, it was definitely a godsend. The story doesn't end there.

*After the Prince told Helena where the show would be going next, they exchanged addresses, just to be safe, * and made plans where to meet before getting off the phone. Unbelievable! Before the girls had gone two hundred miles,*

* You're Everything To Me
* For You

their VW van blew yet another engine. Not to be denied, they jumped on a bus and were finally able to cross the border. Only problem was, they were met at the stateside bus station in Detroit Lakes, by the local border patrol, and told, "Sorry, we believe you're planning on working illegally in the states and you're going to have to go back."

Thank God, one of the officers saw their tears of frustration and felt sorry for them. He agreed to let them at least come to the fairgrounds and stay the night, but only if they promised to take the first bus back to Canada the next morning.

Keep in mind, the Prince is oblivious to these new troubles and was eagerly awaiting their arrival. When they showed up, depressed and still in tears, he had a confrontation with the patrolman who had driven them and was really the one decent guy in the bunch. After calming down a bit, the Prince decided to go back to the station to plead his case.

"We'll leave the show right now. You can even escort us out of town, but please don't send them back again."

When that didn't work, I tried a different tact.

"Do you know who my father is? What's your badge number?" *It didn't matter if his father wouldn't speak to him, they didn't know that.*

I kept it up, to the point of almost getting arrested, but it was to no avail. They were adamant. If the girls weren't on the early bus the next day, there would be an all-points bulletin put out on them, as well as the van. We'd all be arrested, the van would be confiscated, and Grendel would be put in the pound.

With no options left, the Prince went back to the fairgrounds to tell them the bad news. He was still overjoyed just to have found her again, and didn't want to waste what precious time they had left at the police station.

After talking the situation over, they came up with a plan. Carol would go back and wait for their van to be repaired and then continue on to New York City, where she and Helena would rendezvous later. Princess Helena, meanwhile, would try yet another border crossing, as she was determined to stay with her Prince. Once over the line back into Canada, she would change buses and cross at a different border and then come meet him in Gaithersburg, Maryland, where the show was heading next. This was hopefully far enough away from any prying eyes.

After driving them to the bus station the next morning, and purposely disturbing the border patrolman's Victorian sensibilities with numerous passionate embraces (still thumbing his nose at authority figures), the two lovers parted once again, this time beseeching the Gods that it wouldn't be for long.

This time their plan worked.

Yodeling At The
Mountain Love Nest

Nature is a most jealous God, for she will not whisper her inspiring revelations to you unless you are absolutely alone with her.

Walter Russell

*T*he Prince, true to form, hadn't really thought too far into the future other than knowing, whatever it was to be, he wanted it with his new love. Now that he had Helena in his life, and a fair size nest-egg saved, it opened up all kinds of possibilities. It was then, that the Prince remembered the treasure map to his friend, Clyde's. As soon as Helena arrived in Gaithersburg, the Prince asked her what she thought of getting off the road awhile to go explore the oldest mountains on the planet.

"I know a wizard there I think you'd love to meet, and I know he'd be enchanted to make your acquaintance as well."

Being a word-smith, the Prince would sometimes get carried away with his own loquaciousness, but Princess Helena never seemed to mind, and without a second's hesitation, she said,

"I'd love to. When do we leave?"

So off they went; the Prince, Lady Helena, and Grendel the monster in search of adventure.

Just as the Prince had foretold, Clyde and Helena took to each other like twins separated at birth. Helena adored the old wizard and was enchanted with the mystical Blue Ridge mountains immediately, and of course Clyde, having fallen under her spell, was charmed to say the least.

As fate would have it, in a truly abundant universe, within a week, the Prince had found he and Princess Helena a nesting spot less than two miles from Clyde's, where two lovebirds could hole up for the winter and coo.

The house was a mile up a long, winding canyon road called Liberty

Hollow, with their closest neighbor over a half mile away. Surrounded on three sides by Pisgah National Forest, they had virtually a million acres they could call their back yard.

Not only that, the first water coming down from the Eastern Continental Divide ran directly through the front yard. They could not only watch and listen to the rippling brook from the front porch, but the water was so pure they could even walk down and take a sip from the tin dipper the Prince kept hanging from an oak tree at the waters edge.

The house itself was just a basic three room cottage, without indoor plumbing or running water, but the Prince believed he could turn it into a veritable palace, and that was enough for Helena. *

Inspired by her love, I went right to work, and in short order, had run a gravity line 300 yards up the creek for fresh water. Since no one lived between us and the national forest, I brought the hose directly into the sink in the kitchen. It couldn't have been more perfect, except after a storm when waiting awhile for the water to clear, and even that was perfect.

Next, I found a large Warm Morning wood burning stove at a farmer's market, and hauled it up to the house to keep us snug in the winter months ahead.

One day, I totally surprised Helena with a beautiful A-frame outhouse I built out of slab lumber, complete with reading material; *a design borrowed from Clyde, of course.* Helena was delighted no end. *No pun intended.*

That entire summer was truly magical, as we spent many afternoons making love by the creek and running around leafless under the noonday sun. (This relationship was instrumental in my throwing off the sexual taboos and inhibitions I had been brought up around. I was finally able to see sex as something natural and wonderful).

In the evenings, we would either make music on our front porch, or over at Clyde's, where you were apt to meet all kinds of folks. Even Grendel fell in love that summer, with an English setter, and before long was expecting her first litter.

* With Your Love

Before they knew it, the leaves had turned and the forest took on all the hues of the rainbow, signifying it was time for Princess Helena to go meet Carol in New York City, as they had prearranged. From there, she was going back to Vancouver, British Columbia, to spend Christmas with her family; then pack her belongings and make it back to her Prince and their new home, in time to bring in the New Year together.

The following couple of months, while she was away, passed quickly for the Prince, as he was intent on completing his version of Shangrila before Helena's return. Except for the occasional trip to town to buy supplies, or one of the rare times when Clyde would drop by, the Prince would often go four to five days at a time without encountering another living soul. This being his first extended experience with real solitude (no TV, radio or newspaper), he was pleasantly surprised to find he not only enjoyed it, but relished the time alone.

First thing I did to prepare for my lady's return, was to chop enough wood to last us a winter, meanwhile getting an education about soft and hard woods; which ones to use for kindling, which ones burn the longest and hottest, etc. Then I bought some bee hives, once the bees became dormant, so we'd have honey to look forward to the following spring. Next, I mulched, then tilled the garden under, so the soil would be ready for the spring planting.

I would work on the house throughout the day and then each evening would write 7-10 pages to my love, saving them up till weeks-end when I would mail the entire package off to Vancouver. * The letters consisted of seventy or eighty pages of prose, as well as two or three love songs I had composed and recorded on a cassette player during that week.

The most ambitious of my projects, was to floor the entire loft, make a stairway leading up to it, and cut a hole in the roof where I installed a sky-window that opened up to the stars. I then dragged a huge waterbed up the stairwell, and placed it beneath the sky-window, so we could lay together and gaze out into the universe.

In fact, one crisp evening that winter, we actually opened the sky-window and made love while standing up, with the snow falling all around

* Living A Life Of Love

us. *Not to be tried by lukewarm lovers, as pneumonia could be the result.* It began as a therapeutic massage, to work the kinks out of her shoulders. I had her lie face down, while I made circular motions with my thumb and forefinger up and down her spine, but before long I lost my concentration and was using my fingernails to gently stroke the under side of her arm, where it folds.

That's not true. It had actually begun earlier that afternoon, when I had come home and found her with black smudges on her face from cleaning out the woodburner. Not saying a word, I walked over, cupped her face with both hands, and kissed her gently on the mouth while gazing into those eyes I adored. Then I said her three favorite words,

"Let's go shopping." *Jeez, just kidding. Telling this part of the story is hard enough. Give the kid a break.*

Sorry about the rude interruption, but I warned you about 'Merlin's' humor. Anyway, back to the story. After I told Helena "I love you," you'd have thought I had given her a diamond ring, as tears welled up in her eyes and she threw her arms around my neck. That's when it really began, and continued on into the night.

That evening, after stroking her arm for awhile, I noticed each time I did, she would shiver. By then, her silk gown had ridden up her leg, so I reached down and started doing the same gentle stroking behind her knee. She literally trembled with pleasure, which totally erased any more thoughts I had about therapeutic massage. I continued the gentle fingernail touching, now doing long strokes from her feet up along her thighs, making a point to not linger too long on the inside, where it might drive her crazy too soon. I began imagining I was painting my 'Mona Lisa' and worked on my masterpiece for a long time. Finally, without saying a word, I gently tugged upward on the hem of her gown, and she did the rest, revealing the divine curves that would lead me to heaven.

That thought inspired me to look up and open the sky window, letting in the night air. As I did, Helena pulled the draw string on my shorts and I stood up so they could fall away. With half my body exposed to the elements, I reached out my hand for her to join me. Because of the immense amount of heat rising from the stove downstairs, forcing it's way out of the sky-window *(as well as the obvious heat being generated)*, we were oblivious to everything, except our love for each other. *

Many other stories, too numerous to mention, came out of this time, but it should be noted it was while preparing their lovenest in the mountains, that the Prince learned to yodel.

Now to the neophyte, that might not seem like any great shakes, but believe you me, it's like getting your first blue note or train sound on a harmonica. You can never go back, once you've had your first taste. Just as some people prescribe to the theory that an orgasm is the closest thing to experiencing God in the human body, the Prince set forth the idea that a good yodel is as close as you can get in a human sound.

"The sensation in one's head cavity is truly extraordinary! *

Now, keep in mind, he also believes the Chinese theory that a good sneeze should be included in the list of bodily climaxes, along with a bowel movement, and of course the obvious, though he's still undecided if a yawn should be included or at least given honorable mention. But, once again, we digress.

One night, that first winter in the wee hours before dawn, I was up doing my early morning ritual of stoking up the wood burner. Helena had taken a job waitressing in the nearby town of Black Mountain, and since she was on the early shift, needed to be there by five a.m. Knowing she disliked the cold, I would arise around three-thirty and get the fire roaring, so the house would be toasty when she climbed out of bed. Then, I would drive her into work in the van and join her for a cup of 'joe' before her shift began.

This particular morning was exceptionally beautiful, as it had snowed during the night, camouflaging everything except the winding indigo brook, which appeared black in contrast, and I thought to myself,

"If for no other reason, I have a purpose in being alive; just keep-

* Practice Makes Perfect Love
* Yodel Away...Rainbow CD #8

ing this angelic being warm and comfortable is enough for me." *

He meant it with all his heart and soul. The Prince had just discovered it was the simple things in life that made it worth living, and being of service was it's own reward.

The next year, Princess Helena had to return to Vancouver, as she had promised her parents she'd attend college. Knowing this would be a long separation, she and the Prince agreed they would both be free to date other people, but had made a pact that when it came time for marriage and children, they would wait for each other.

After a few years, Helena found she was ready to start her family, and had been proposed to for the third time. The Prince, meanwhile, had just signed on to his first big limousine/lear jet circuit playing music, and was ready to jump into the ocean.

Through all the ensuing years, whether together physically or not, the Prince had always known that she was his girl, and vice versa. Their relationship had evolved into an unconditional love, and since they both wanted the other to be happy and their every dream fulfilled, they agreed it was probably best to move on and let each other follow separate paths. Intuiting the enormity of their decision, neither the Prince nor Helena wanted to break their pact over the phone or in a letter, so the Prince flew to Vancouver.

Both Helena and I had told everyone we dated during those ensuing years about our pact, so it came as no surprise, and probably a huge relief, to the man who had proposed to her that I was finally coming to Canada. At last he would know where he stood.

She insisted her fiancee make other living arrangements, as he was living at her house at the time. She told him she would call him with her decision after I left, and to please respect our desire to be alone. I thought that was so classy of her, but I've always wondered how I'd have felt if I had been the other guy.

Once I arrived in Vancouver, it was like we'd never been apart. We laughed and cried and made sweet love * for an entire week, and when it was time for me to depart, we ended our pact with a ritual we had written

* Angel Of Pure Love…Chameleon CD #3
* Sweet Sweet Darling Angel Divine

ourselves. In it, we released each other with unconditional love, and the desire for each of us to have our every dream come true. Then taking two roses, whose stems were intertwined, we separated them and gave each it's own vase. Finally, I took one of the petals from my rose and offered it to her, first placing it against my heart, and then against hers. She did the same for me, and when both of our tears started flowing, I drew her close and whispered, "Thank you for being. I'll always love you." *

Whenever the Prince would look back in the years to come, he felt tremendous gratitude for God having given him * such a gift. His first taste of love had been filled with such wonder and magic, and most of all, he now knew what love not only looked like, but felt like, and he knew he could never settle for less. This was also the first time the Prince recognized and experienced the power of ritual.

* That's The Way To Create Pure Love

First Mentor

"Religion is for people who don't want to go to hell, while spirituality is for people who have already been there and don't want to go back."

Author Unknown

*T*hroughout the Prince's exploits, there seemed to be a spiritual thread that connected them all and often even led him from one adventure to the next. Whether seeking God through better chemistry or working towards a more evolved type of relationship, it was becoming a constant theme in his life. That spiritual quest really began in earnest, while living with Princess Helena in the mountains of North Carolina. There, the Prince was introduced to a deeper level of God and spirituality than he had heretofore experienced.

One day as the Prince was hitchhiking, he got a ride with an old gentleman who told him at great length of the Bahai' Faith. He told the Prince someone could have been a Bahai' all their life, and never even heard the name of their teacher, Bahaullah. The basic premise is that all the masters; Jesus, Buddha, Mohammed, Krishna, Zoroaster etc. were perfect for their times and that in essence, they all were saying the same thing. He went on to say that Bahaullah was just the most recent master to incarnate on earth. It sounded interesting, and the old man was as delightful as he could be, but the Prince quickly forgot about it. (As he was wont to do, being blessed with Attention Deficit Disorder.)

Early one morning, less than a week later, the Prince was at Helena's restaurant having driven her to work, when he overheard two people chatting at the counter. It seems there was a gathering to take place that very evening up on Black Mountain where, coincidentally, the speaker would be giving a talk on the Bahai' faith. Believing in synchronicity, the Prince decided to go and explore it further. It was there the Prince first encountered Jim Goure.

Though Jim wasn't the speaker that night, and wasn't Bahai, he had offered his home for the occasion. After the meeting was over, he and the Prince *were introduced. Jim invited the Prince to drop by on Friday morning at ten a.m., as Jim would be teaching a class of his own. That's where it all began. As they say, when the student is ready, the master appears. Who is "they" anyway?*

Jim was charismatic and very distinguished looking, with a silver lining along his temples and a perfectly coiffed Van Dyke upon his chin. Dressed in a charcoal grey suit with a soft cream-colored shirt that enhanced his piercing eyes, his famous gaze was known to penetrate the walls of the most-stoic. Upon his feet were a pair of black wingtip shoes with a spit-shine; a carry-over from his Navy days as a nuclear physicist. He was the epitome of conservative elegance.

When we first shook hands and he looked me in the eyes, I felt like he could see right into my very core *(probably because he could)*, but there were no judgements; only kindness and compassion. His eyes had a mischievous gleam, and there was a quiet unobtrusive joy that emanated from him. I felt at ease immediately, and certainly welcome. Vulnerable and yet safe at the same time, I found it most curious that at the end of the evening, I wasn't ready to depart.

Many people believed Jim to be one of the avatars. On that subject, I have no opinion, though I do know Jim was one of the most enlightened beings I ever had the privilege of meeting. I figure if the average man or woman is utilizing eight to ten percent of their brain like they say *(there it is again)*, then Jim had to be in the thirty to forty percent category at least. He'd opened not only his third, but his fourth eye, so both his pituitary and pineal glands were going full blast. Not unlike Edgar Cayce, he had abilities far beyond the average man. One of Jim's qualities I most tried to emulate, was his habit of telling the truth and letting the chips... *well, you know the rest.*

The Prince found combining that ability with tact and subtlety was a challenge, and he was grateful to see it embodied in his mentor, since telling the truth was not a quality much appreciated by those out of integrity.

It was Jim who first taught me how to meditate, and his 7-step effective prayer, became a part of my daily regimen. * Subjects such as clairvoyance, telepathy, and clairaudience were just parlor tricks or baby food to him. I knew I was in the presence of one who has bridged the gap between the temporal and the ethereal worlds, though he wouldn't let anyone put him on a guru pedestal. The wisdom and insight that came through him seemed to be from a deep place, and I always had the sense that there was so much more that he knew, but felt his students weren't ready for yet. He was the first person to tell me, "Throw away the books; all the knowledge you seek is within."

*Not only that, in Jim and his wife Diana, the Prince felt he had found second parents. Since they were ex-military themselves, the Prince felt right at home, only here, he felt the unconditional love and support that he'd been starving for all those years. **

Back before Whole Life Expos, New Age Journals, and Psychic Fairs, there were metaphysical retreats where conscious beings from all over the planet would come together to share knowledge and information. Also, to pray for the healing of the planet. Jim was often invited as one of the keynote speakers, and would sometimes take me with him. He actually put on his own retreats, but called them 'advances'. "We're not going to retreat" he'd say, "we're going to advance".

These events would usually last 5-7 days, and Jim would have me compose an original piece about what had happened during the week long event, and then perform it at the final celebration. * I would also lead people in meditations with my 14-string dulcimer (the unique instrument Clyde had built and given me). On a number of occasions, people told me how they experienced a serenity they had never felt before, while listening to its deep resonance, and some even said physical healing had occurred. My dubious nature always found that a bit hard to fathom, but I knew that being acknowledged by not only Jim, but his peers, was certainly healing some of my own wounds. I was just beginning to discover the healing power in my dulcimer, when Jim told me one evening, after a particularly uplifting performance,

"Who wouldn't like to know they were the best at something?

* That's How It Is
* You Got To Be The Star Of Your Dreams
* Chakra Song...Rainbow CD #1

Since you've been given the only instrument of its kind on the planet, I would call that a blessing." *

Since metaphysics and those seeking higher states of consciousness had not yet become socially acceptable, psychics were looked on with great disdain and thought to be at best 'weird', and by some, 'in league with the devil'. Anyone who admitted having gifts of this nature was routinely ostracized and generally found themselves outcasts from society.

One good aspect of that, though, was I felt I could generally trust any clairvoyants who had 'come out of the closet' during this time. *Unlike this day and age, with so many people hanging out their shingle 'cause it's hip, slick, and cool as well as immensely lucrative. I mean for only $2.99/minute you can call the psychic hotline and not only find out who you're supposed to marry, but what should be included in the prenuptial agreement.*

After a while, I had been given so much proof as to the existence of the metaphysical world and of the psychic abilities of some people, that I just assumed it as fact. There was no doubt whatsoever in my mind.

It was because of this knowingness, that the Prince was surprised at how many of his well-educated friends seemed incredulous at some of his experiences. At this point, he decided to start recording and saving his readings. One story that seemed to leave most of his friends with their mouths agape, was when he told them of having readings years apart from each other, with four unrelated psychics in various countries. They all told him about the same lifetime he had lived. The clincher was when each one told the Prince how he had died, with the exact same details in each reading.

It seems he had been a wealthy maharishi in India, and was riding alongside his best friend on an elephant, when the supposed friend knocked him to the ground and threw a spear through his throat, killing him instantly.

Two people with identical details might be called coincidence, but four? (We think not.)

His life would never be the same after Jim became his first and most influential mentor. Many stories about him have become almost legendary, but one instance that stood out vividly to the Prince, was the time he and a couple

* Peace of Mind...Rainbow CD #9

dozen other people were having an outdoor picnic during a weekend 'advance'.

It was a hot day in late spring, and the flies and ants were out en masse. It was most annoying. You couldn't put your plate down for thirty seconds, before it would be covered with bugs. Finally, Jim loaded up a plate with food, did a little meditation over it, and placed it away from where everyone was eating. Lo and behold, every insect, of both the airborne and earthbound varieties, in the entire area went over and ate off that one plate the rest of the day. *Just another day in the life.* *

---

* Quantum Leap

Dreams Come True

"There is a principle which is a bar against all information, which is proof against all arguments and which cannot fail to keep a man in everlasting ignorance-and that principle is contempt prior to investigation."

Herbert Spencer

*W*hen it came to seeking God, the Prince wasn't choosy. Any path that might bring a person a little closer, he felt was a step in the right direction. Over the years, his curiosity had led him to do at least a cursory exploration of most of the major religions and he'd attended a wide variety of worship services. Though both his parents were raised in the Southern Baptist tradition and he had a number of uncles who had been Baptist preachers, the Prince had never attended a Baptist revival before. Since he didn't want to be accused of 'contempt prior to investigation', he resolved to delve deeper into his own roots.

As a military brat, my only religious choices were Protestant or Catholic services, so when I heard about a one week revival at the High Shoals Baptist Church (just south of the Hobbly Wobbly Mall on Pee Ridge in Henrietta, North Carolina), I decided to go see what I'd been missing.

They were raising the roof singing 'When the Roll Is Called Up Yonder' when I got there, and I slipped into the back pew. The first two days were spent on bended knee, asking God to show me what I was supposed to be doing with my life, as I wanted to be 'about my Father's business.' The evening of the second day, while still in prayer, I heard a voice inside telling me to open my Bible. With my eyes still closed I picked up 'The Good Book' laying next to me, opened it at random and then pointed to the page. Upon opening my eyes, I discovered I had pointed to Acts Nine, Verse Eleven which read, "Get thee to a street named Straight." I remember thinking, "Can't get much clearer than that".

Since I had explored the world of drugs back in college, and had gotten a glimpse of how debilitating they could be, I had decided back then they weren't for me anymore. Now, I knew that sharing my experience of getting 'straight' was to be my testimony, and hopefully my 'witnessing' might be of benefit to others.

The Prince soon found himself led to High Point, North Carolina working for a Christian outreach program called 'God's Farm'. Though he didn't live there for very long, a number of dreams he'd carried for years did come to fruition from his being there.

First, while working at God's Farm, I was asked to be the driver for an old fashioned horse drawn hayride, beneath a full moon. For some reason, driving a wagonload of hay full of laughing kids was something I had always wanted to do. *What? So you've never had a dream that was a little quirky?*

The second dream fulfilled a desire I'd carried since I was a kid and watched 'It's A Wonderful Life', starring Jimmy Stewart. The character he played was one of my early heroes. He was humble and giving, yet fiery and ready to stand up for the little guy. I had always imagined myself being such a man, with many friends, and for the first time, understood what my mother meant about the real spirit of Christmas. Again, the opportunity came thanks to God's Farm, where they had purchased hundreds of toys and gifts to give away to the less fortunate for Christmas. Complete with big belly, a red outfit, bells, and a flowing white beard, I became Santa for the children in one of the poorest neighborhoods in High Point.

One at a time, children of every color, shape, and variety would come sit on my lap. Many had a list already prepared of what they wanted, but some preferred to ask questions about the North Pole and my reindeer. One precious little redhead was concerned because her house didn't have a chimney, but I assured her, in this day and age, that Santa often entered through the front door. She even asked what I liked to eat so she could have it waiting when I got there. The expressions of joy and wonder on each child's face, as I gave them their gifts, was the blessing I got in return. Once again, like the days of waking up early to keep Princess Helena warm, I got to see how being of service was its own reward.

The third dream that came true, was learning to play a mean harmonica. I had been mesmerized by train sounds ever since I got my first H+O train set as a kid, and I especially loved the mournful wails and chuga chugas you could get on a mouthharp. At God's Farm I met and struck up a friendship with Terry Mac, who went on to become one of Nashville's leading session players on the harmonica. Terry taught me many of the finer points of harmonica playing, and the two of us spent many afternoons dueling on harps as we walked around the block in perfect cadence, practicing blue notes and mournful train whistles to our hearts content. Later, Terry would be instrumental (no pun intended) in getting me to Nashville. To this day, when a hungry student asks me to teach him the harp, I invariably start them out practicing while 'walking around the block' keeping time.

Also during this time, the Prince was first introduced to 'A Course In Miracles'. This proved to be a Godsend, as he was finding it increasingly difficult to keep his mouth shut about his beliefs on subjects such as reincarnation and karma. With the help of the 'Course', his metaphysical and Christian beliefs were able to coexist, peacefully within, for the first time.

Lastly, on his list of dreams come true, it was becoming increasingly apparent to the Prince that music was his dharma (calling), and he started dreaming about going to music school. Since he had no money and was still cut off from the family, the odds seemed to be definitely stacked against that possibility.

I began praying for a way to go back to school. As fate would have it, during the time I was working at God's Farm, I was living in a really poor neighborhood. That was all I could afford. There were so many cockroaches in my apartment, I had begun sleeping with the lights on. Even with that precaution, after awhile, they became so bold they would scurry about in the open. One night I remember bolting upright from a deep sleep after two had fallen from the ceiling and landed on my face. After that, I jerry-rigged a piece of plastic to cover the bed, much like a mosquito-net used on safari. To this day, I'm still phobic about cockroaches.

It seems that the state had started a scholarship program to help college age kids, living in the slums, so they could go to university. Half a dozen people from the section of town where I lived were to be selected to go to The University of North Carolina at Greensboro, if they qualified scholastically. Time was running out, when I heard about the program, but there was still one opening no one had applied for.

You can guess the rest. The Prince was on his way to music school, all expenses paid. Just happened to be at the right place at the right time . . . ? Old fashioned good luck? The power of prayer? Call it what you will, it was a miracle.

This is where the Prince was able to fine-tune his art for the first time. He practiced virtually seven to eight hours every day, learning the nuances and subtleties of the various instruments he played, as well as studying the craft of song writing.

One far-reaching realization he had during this time was, "what you don't play is often just as important as what you do. The pauses are just as musical as the notes."

Also, for perhaps the first time, the Prince was able to see how the strictness and discipline in his military upbringing could be put to good use. While many of his fellow students were spending much of their day with extra curricular activities, the Prince was able to stay focused and devote the time and energy necessary to excel in his studies.

Though he didn't consciously think to give his dad any credit for that ability, he started to notice he always seemed to have that little bit of extra desire or willpower, when it was the determining factor.

The next couple of years, I became totally absorbed practicing my art. Whether it was guitar, piano, vocal lessons, or composition and song writing courses, I found I flourished in an atmosphere of brain power.

All during this time, however, Terry Mac kept urging me to bring 'Dulci' and 'Gordi' and my music bag and move to Nashville. * Finally

* Rainbow Blues…Rainbow CD #5

after giving it long and serious consideration, I concluded that standing ovations and a possible recording contract sounded much more rewarding than a piece of paper. I figured it would be diplomatic to stay one more semester, and make the dean's list for the first time, and then it was off to Nashville.

Still trying to make his dad proud of him. Even though he'd found his first mentor, with all the acceptance and unconditional love that entailed, the Prince like most young men had an unconscious need for his father's approval.

Front Page News

"The Chinese use two brush strokes to write the word 'crisis'. One brush stroke stands for danger; the other for opportunity. In a crisis, beware of danger - but recognize the opportunity."

Richard M. Nixon

*T*he Prince, recognizing the move to Nashville as a major decision, want-ed to make it memorable and chose January 1 as the day to depart. After loading up the van with all his worldly possessions (mostly musical instru-ments), he embarked on New Years morning hoping to make it to Nashville by twilight. Just as he arrived at the outskirts of Knoxville, Tennessee, the van blew an engine and he was forced to 'depend on the kindness of strangers'. That added four extra days to his migration, but it turned out to be a blessing in dis-guise, when he wrote about the adventure in a song called 'Tennessee Hospitality' that later brought him good fortune. *

It seems the head of the Tennessee Democratic Women's Convention heard the tune, and was inspired to use it for the upcoming election as their theme. She was convinced it was ideal to take the place of 'The Tennessee Waltz' as the official state song. Working towards that goal, she pulled a few strings, and the next thing I knew, I was booked to be the headliner at their upcoming convention. I put together a 14 piece country-dixieland band for the occasion. The song proved to be quite a hit, and for a while, I had a lot of fun imagining what it would be like having written the state song. But alas, the Democrats lost the election and I never did find out.

With the advantage of hindsight, the Prince can look back and laugh at his folly (thinking any song could replace 'The Tennessee Waltz'), but you've got to admit, the kid's got chutzpah.

Finally, after four days, he arrived in Nashville in the baby blue bread truck with its 6 foot rainbow painted across the back and 'Follow Your Dreams'

* Tennessee Hospitality...Chameleon CD #9

captioned above it. By this point, the Prince had christened the van, 'Lady Helena', and had welded the name across her bow in steel letters four inches high.

*He had a heart full of dreams and a head full of creativity, and was ready for whatever God put in front of him. **

One of my first nights in town, I had somehow talked my way into sitting in on harmonica with Freddie Hubbard (a hot jazz trumpet player), at a club called the 'Exit Inn'. (It was memorable, in particular, as there was standing room only and I was one of maybe five people in the entire club who was of Anglo-Saxon persuasion.) Backstage, we had worked out a down and dirty jazz version of 'Beale Street Blues', and I was definitely strung tight that night, as this would be my first live performance in Nashville. I was to play the opening number of the second set and the plan was to walk on with the rest of the band after intermission. The club was pitch black, except for a solitary blue spotlight casting an eerie glow through the layers of thick smoke (both tobacco and other substances). That was fine with me, since I hoped to slip unnoticed to my microphone before the lights went up. Just as I stepped out onto the stage, that idea was dashed, as some belligerent guy in the front row yelled out, "You'd better be another f_king John Mayall." (Mayall was one of the hottest, and definitely most soulful harmonica players around; also white.)

Without a second's hesitation, I ripped into a dozen bars of John Mayalls' most famous harp solo 'Room to Move', and the audience started to applaud; from there I could do no wrong. That night, as I received my first standing ovation, I knew I'd made the right decision in moving to Nashville.

Earning a piece of paper to put on your wall, that says you are accomplished at something, certainly has its place, but for someone with a compulsive personality, as well as Attention Deficit Disorder, I highly recommend instant gratification.

A few weeks later, I experienced another of my dreams coming true. My favorite guitarist, John McLaughlin, was in town to play at the

* Go Beyond Your Dreams

Exit Inn, and the owner of the club, Owsley Manier, knowing what a big fan I was, asked if I wanted to meet him. Having worn out numerous copies of his 'Mahavishnu Orchestra' recordings over the years, I was thrilled at the opportunity. I brought the dulcimer with me, as Owsley had suggested, and after John heard me play, he invited me to come back that night for the show and sit-in with his new band 'Shakti'. I'm certain I performed with him that night, as I have photographs of us on stage, but I honestly don't remember a thing about the performance (and yes I was sober). The one thing I do recall, was that 'Mr. McLaughlin' was so into the subtleties and nuances of his sound, that he changed guitar strings between every set. *That made quite an impression on the Prince, as he approached all his stringed instruments with that same regard, from then on.*

I later thought it a bit ironic that here I was at a rock and roll club in Nashville, Tennessee (home of country music), playing a sitar-like instrument with one of the greatest jazz guitarists of all time. *

This became the typical evening for the Prince those first few months in Nashville; 'sitting in' with bands by himself, or carousing around town with Terry Mac, playing dueling harmonicas with every blues band they could find. This is also when 'dulci' was given the name dulsitar, that was to stick from then on.

The Prince had gone to Quadraphonic Sound Studios to meet with Gene Eichleberger, the engineer, and then was going next door to meet with Tony Brown (a former band member of Elvis' and an up and coming producer). He had been marking time in the lounge for quite a while, as Gene had been delayed, but it just so happened that there was a Brewer and Shipley recording session going on in the studio that night. Just as the Prince was preparing to leave, another engineer, who knew of Gene's delay, invited the Prince to come and have a listen to the tune that was being recorded.

I was thrilled, since I'd never been inside a recording studio before. The song was an up tempo 12 bar rocker, and as soon as I heard it, I thought, "a harmonica would sure sound good on that." Of course, since I always carried one in my pocket (for walking around purposes), I pulled

* Dulsitar Melding…Rainbow CD #3

it out just to see if by chance it might be the key the song was recorded in. (The odds are one in twelve by the way, since there are twelve notes on the keyboard.) Sure enough, as fate would have it, it was the right key. Having never been at a recording session before, I was totally naive as to studio protocol, and didn't realize, till later, the faux pas I committed when I started playing along quietly in the background. The producer and one of the owners of the studio, Norbert Putnam (formerly Elvis Presley's bass player), heard me tooling along, liked what he heard, and not being one to stand on protocol, said,

"Get out there boy."

Between my naivete and my excitement, there wasn't room to be nervous, and for the first time in my life, I walked into a recording studio to lay down a track. The total silence, when they closed the foot-thick door behind me, caught me by surprise, but not half as much as putting on the headphones. When I heard myself playing with echo and reverb blended in, I burst out laughing. Then the sounds of my own hilarity echoing back at me made me guffaw even more. It must have been contagious, because I saw all the guys in the control booth start chuckling as well.

Fifteen minutes later, I was on my first record, and got paid for it to boot. I even still have the check.

That same evening, Dan Fogleberg and Cat Stevens dropped by, being friends of Norberts', and in town for various projects. I was enchanted to meet them, having long been a fan of both. After the session was over, we were all hanging out talking, and after hearing about my giant dulcimer, of course, they wanted to hear it. The next thing I knew, I was jamming with two of my musical idols, when someone asked what the instrument was called.

"Since it's the only one in the world, it doesn't really have a name," I replied.

Norbert then broke in and said, "I think you should call it, 'The Dulsitar.'"

Caught up in the excitement of the evening, the Prince might have let

that idea slip by, but it seemed there had been a reporter from a local music magazine taking in the entire evenings' happenings. Three days later the story of the session and the Prince's harmonica playing broke in the newspaper. The naming of the instrument was to become the first entry into the Prince's musical scrapbook and he was on cloud nine, but it didn't last long.

The following week, while jamming at the "Exit Inn" again, (this time with Blues master, B.B. King), someone broke into my van, stole both my guitars, my money, and worst of all, 'the dulsitar'. I was wiped out. Distraught would have been an improvement over how I was feeling, knowing 'the dulsitar' was irreplaceable. I cried myself to sleep that night.

Never one to wallow in the problem, the Prince had always followed the adage, 'The instant a problem is created, there's a solution created; you can focus on the problem, or focus on the solution, it's your choice.' So the next morning, he started looking for possible solutions to his dilemma.

I began by calling everyone with clout that had so kindly told me since I moved to town, "If there's ever anything I can do, don't hesitate to call."

I called Norbert Putnam and Tony Brown first (since both had played in Elvis's band, I assumed their connections would be far reaching.) Then I called Francis Preston, head of BMI in Nashville, and Billy Strange who ran Frank Sinatra's publishing company. I called anyone I could think of that might lend a hand. Before the day was over, there was a story about the theft in the Nashville Tennessean newspaper, and Francis Preston got me on the six o'clock evening news where I was able to address the thief, saying, "Whoever broke in my van, please return the 'dulsitar'. It is the only one in the world and now that the story has gone out AP-UPI all over the country, it would be awfully hard to sell anyway. You can keep the money and guitars and tape recorders and everything else; just please return the one instrument, no questions asked." Then I sang 'Tennessee Hospitality' (the song I'd written in the van that first day heading for Nashville). Unbelievable.

Three days later, an anonymous message was left in the middle of the night, at the publishing company I was signed to. It read, "You will find your instrument in the dempsey dumpster, behind the building." With my heart throbbing wildly, I ran to see. Sure enough, it was exactly where they said it would be. I was overjoyed!

The media ate it up. Not only was it the lead story on all the evening's newscasts, but it became the feature front page headline story in the Nashville Tennessean, complete with a picture of the Prince holding the returned dulsitar in his arms.

If that happened today, the odds are an agent would have had him on the talk show circuit and made a small fortune off the exposure. Thank God, the Prince, who wasn't ready for that kind of attention, had ideas of his own, and took all that publicity and goodwill in another direction.

Recording With Nashville's Finest

"A nice thing about being young is that you haven't experienced enough to know that you cannot possibly do the things you are doing."

Author Unknown

*M*onths earlier, when the Prince had first arrived in Nashville, he thought he had worked out an arrangement with a couple of local fellows to help them build a 24-track recording facility in exchange for one free album's worth of studio time.

In actuality, he had been conned by a couple of brothers, with the last name of Cash, who claimed to be distant relatives of 'The' Johnny Cash. The Prince, being our typical naive male (one who believes that everyone is basically honorable and a hand shake will suffice), had fallen for it. Now that the facility was nearing completion, the odds of the Prince actually getting any studio time were looking slim. All that changed with the front page article.

I demanded that they honor their agreement. With my new found fame, the brothers' Cash certainly didn't want to bring any undue attention to the fact they were actually from Detroit, so they lived up to their original agreement.

I then proceeded to call on Nashville's finest musicians, and after introducing myself as the guy from the front page, I would tell them, "I don't have any money, but I've got some good songs and a studio to record them in if you'd like to come play."

As unlikely as this may sound in this day and age of agents, lawyers and what not, every single musician I asked responded with their own version of, "Sure, when and where do I show up?"

I couldn't believe it, here I was recording the songs, inspired by my mentor Jim Goure, with some of the best players in the land. The line up read like a who's who of the recording industry at the time. Kenny Buttrey, Kenny Malone and Larry Loundin on drums. Sonny Garrish, Weldon

Myrick and Buddy Emmons (who played a solo for me, even he thought was one of the best he'd ever played), on pedal steel guitar. J.J. Cale, Mac Gayden, David Briggs, Bucky Barrett, Robert De La Garza, Charlie McCoy, Norbert, even Elvis's back up singers, the Jordainaires, on two of the songs. Then to top it all off, a local arranger, named Earl Spielman, called in some of his own favors and put together twenty-four string players. I had a mini- orchestra backing me up for the first time. I scheduled it so we'd record the basic tracks on five consecutive days; two songs per day.

Normally, when recording basic tracks, there will be four or five musicians on the session at most (bass, drums, rhythm guitar etc.), and then the other musicians come in later to overdub. I decided to try a different approach. First, I would use anywhere from seven to ten musicians on each of the basic tracks, so there would be a lot of energy in the studio; sort of like a live show. I figured the players would enjoy that more and hopefully give me some inspired performances. Next, other than a basic map of where I wanted to go and what sound I was looking for, I decided to pretty much give them free rein and let them figure it out. Hell, I was a novice at this, and I knew it. It seemed rather arrogant of me to try it any other way.

If you've never been in a recording studio before, it's like sitting at the helm of a spaceship with all its blinking and flashing colored lights. There's a feeling of power in the control booth, since you actually have the ability to affect millions of lives, for better or for worse, depending on what you're creating. It can be extremely seductive and so very easy to forget your responsibility to the whole and get caught up in personal and selfish motives. Thank God, all I was thinking about was creating magic, and I knew unconsciously the best way to do that was just get out of the way.

Since my idea was to record seven different styles of music representing the seven colors of the rainbow, my next task was deciding which musicians to use on each session, depending on the particular song. Though a little chaotic at times, the camaraderie and joke telling of the players was the glue, and they played their asses off. One session, there were actually fourteen players live (between the horns and the backup vocals), and the joy we captured that day, literally jumps off the CD at you. ('The Chakra Song' and 'There Ought To Be A Law').

All told, fifty-five musicians, and God knows how many engineers and studios, donated their time and energy to the project. It should be especially noted, that Gary Laney, the engineer, spent more nights than I can remember, from midnight to dawn, to help bring the album to fruition.

I called it "The Rainbow Album", based on the fact there were seven different colors of music; from jazz, to rock, to country, to Dixieland. The unifying theme was the lyrics about angels, divinity and the gifts God has bestowed on us all, and how important it was to look within if we're to make the world a better place. * It was my first work of love.

The Prince, not having a commercial bone in his body at the time, hadn't done it seeking glory, but simply because he needed to express all that he'd learned from his mentor, Jim Goure. Though many people seemed to love the music and the idea behind his concept, it wasn't going to be easy to get it on the air waves, where it could do a lot of good. It was a bit too revolutionary for the record companies, whose typical response was,

"It's a great story and we love the music, but which bin does it go in at the record stores?"

Unfortunately, "New Age" music wasn't around yet, so no one knew quite what to do with it. His idealistic young mind was in for a rude awakening, once he discovered that just wanting to make the world a better place wasn't all he needed to make a difference.

That wounded the Prince deeply. By creating a joyful noise, he had hoped to do just that. Unfortunately, rather than feel the pain of rejection, dealing with it and moving on from there, he stuffed the feelings, and a part of his spirit went into hibernation. For people with Attention Deficit Disorder, it's particularly easy to do, as their attention can be easily diverted. The 'Rainbow Album' just sat.

---

* We're All In This Together

The Gong Show

"Change is the providence of adventurers"

Napoleon Bonaparte

*N*eeding a break from Nashville for awhile, the Prince's next adventure began as a trip to Miami, Florida to visit his older brother. He chose to go by way of Black Mountain, to get the recharge that always resulted from being in the Blue Ridge mountains. He also wanted to see Jim and to get a reading from Veneta Mueller, the elderly psychic mentioned back in the prologue.

Veneta, and her partner of fifty plus years, George, were two of the most delightful people you could ever hope to meet. Very nondescript in appearance, if you saw them at the checkout stand at your local market, you'd be apt to think they were your typical grandparents, and wasn't it inspiring how in love with each other they obviously still were. Wouldn't you be surprised to learn they had been exploring metaphysics for well over half a century and had one of the most extensive libraries on the subject ever collected.

Veneta used to give Arthur Ford his readings (other than Edgar Cayce, the most renowned psychic of the times), and she and George had moved to Black Mountain to be near Jim Goure. I asked her one time to describe what it was like when she went into a trance. She replied,

"There's a spiral from your inner being that begins at your solar plexus and comes out from your third eye. It then goes up and joins another spiral swirling the opposite direction coming down from above, and when the two intertwine, I'm there." *

I remember chuckling to myself the first time I pulled into their driveway. They lived a couple miles from downtown Black Mountain, up a picturesque tree-lined winding road. I passed my favorite cherry tree on the way to their house, and started reminiscing about the last time I'd spent

* There Ought To Be A Law…Rainbow CD #7

my day in its branches. As I turned onto their drive, I passed beneath a portal which had two sets of antlers, as if you were driving into a hunting lodge. It was so out of character for them. I doubt Veneta had so much as stepped on a bug in twenty years, and George was always introducing me to some new stray cat or dog they didn't have the heart to run off. That's what inspired the laugh. Once I stepped out of the van, I was greeted by a panoramic view of a majestic blue ridged mountain range that took my breath away. The house itself was a small bungalow with low ceilings, probably built in the fifties. The interior looked like it had been decorated to resemble the metaphysical section of Barnes and Noble. Literally everywhere you'd look there were books. It usually took ten minutes just to clear enough space from the old plaid furniture so there would be room to sit.

She would give readings there in the living room, and it always amazed me when she would come out of a trance (aided gently by George), how she would have more energy than all the people there combined who were half her age. She would always ask upon returning to her body, "Was it helpful? Did you get all your questions answered?'"

The trip to visit my brother in Florida began on a hilarious note. To save money and also just for the company, the Prince had offered a guitarist, named Daniel, a ride down to visit his parents, who lived in upper state Florida. The Prince and Daniel hadn't known each other long, but their friendship had blossomed from day one. It was based on their spiritual inclinations and the fact they were both musicians who enjoyed the entire spectrum of music.

Daniel had proverbial tall, dark and suavely handsome looks and carried himself with a self assurance that made most men pale by comparison. Most striking of all, were his dark brown eyes, intense, and yet laughing at the same time. He dressed for comfort, and would usually be found wearing kung-fu type shoes and baggy pants. His one bow to vanity, was his perfectly coiffed, close-cropped beard, which the Prince envied, as well as his full rug of chest hair. The Prince had neither, and could only wonder what it was like to greet a member of the opposite sex with the top button of his shirt opened, exposing his obvious masculinity.

Daniel was probably the funniest person the Prince had ever met. He had the ability to keep the Prince in stitches, and could literally inspire a guffaw at will, which he enjoyed doing often. One of his favorite ploys, was to make up names for things others might enjoy, but weren't particularly good for them.

A donut became "a pancreas bomb" and ice cream "a consciousness muffler". He wouldn't hesitate to order "a dead cow and a glass of blood please", just to 'goof on me'. As a reminder that he was a vegetarian, while I still enjoyed eating meat, he would tell me, "I won't eat anything that has a face."

I loved Dan's response whenever he had been called on the carpet for something. Whether he interrupted you, or was late, or forgot it was his turn to take out the garbage; it didn't matter, he would always say the same thing "Sorry man, here's a couple bucks", then utilizing his command of comedic timing, he'd wait before continuing "would you take a check?" It was impossible to stay mad at him for long.

Daniel had mastered the art of just 'being', and seemed content with whatever was going on at the moment. He knew how to be still, and quiet and totally in the moment. I used to love hanging out with him for that reason. His easy going manner was the perfect balance for my ADD eclectic enthusiasm, as well as my tendency to be a human 'doing'.

Now it seemed both the Prince and Daniel had grown up in families where the well timed 'passing of gas' was a source of great hilarity. (How they discovered this fact, I'll leave to your imagination.)

Though the Prince readily admitted there were naysayers who thought it to be a bit warped, he had come to the conclusion early on in life, that 'the breaking of wind' was, in reality, another universal language, just like music. On occasion, he had even considered applying for a government grant to study the phenomenon. (Why not? The government gives out money for everything else.) When queried on the subject, the Prince would say,

"It doesn't matter where you are in the world, or what language you speak, almost everyone laughs at a well-timed petard." (The word his mother preferred he used).

Being the inventive fellows they were, the Prince and Daniel decided to create a contest to pass the time, as well as the obvious. You got one point for each petard, two points if you could stretch it out for 10 seconds or longer, and three points if you could make the other guy roll down his window. Between the hilarity of two guys shooting for three pointers, and the ludicrousness of the entire premise, you've never heard so much gasping for breath in your entire life. (The Prince won by the way, having bought a stash of figs as his secret weapon.) Anyway we digress. (Boy do we ever.)

By the time they got to Black Mountain, the Prince couldn't wait to introduce Dan to Jim and Veneta, as he felt it was truly an honor, and one he offered sparingly.

This being his first introduction into the world of metaphysics, Daniel was a bit skeptical, though he took pride in keeping an open mind and tried to do so here. We had talked at length, and he knew the lyrics of many of my songs which made references to angels and the divine throughout. His reticence didn't last long. The second day we were there, I suggested he go get a reading with Jim and ask about the severe lower back pain he'd been experiencing for the past couple of years. He'd seen numerous professionals during that time, but no one could find anything wrong. Though he was hesitant at first, Daniel figured what the hell, it couldn't hurt.

In the ensuing reading, Jim told him the pain was being caused by someone on the West Coast who was incredibly angry with him, and that he owed that person an amends. Daniel knew immediately Jim was referring to a woman he had lived with in Los Angeles, whose unresolved childhood rage had terrified him. At the time, the only way he felt he could escape her manipulating clutches was to just up and leave, and he had done so, without saying a word. He hadn't spoken with her since. Daniel took Jim's advice and phoned her that very evening. They had a long tearful reunion over the phone, during which she forgave him, and by the time he hung up, every bit of pain in his back was gone. Daniel, and his skepticism were blown away.

Just as I had predicted, Daniel loved my surrogate family in Black Mountain, and the feelings were mutual. He found George and Veneta simply adorable and by the time we left, they were ready to adopt him.

They spent a few more days in the mountains, writing songs, getting readings from Veneta, and meditating with Jim, before continuing on their journey down to Florida. After dropping Dan at his parents, the Prince put the old blue van in gear once more and headed down to see his big brother. His plan was to stay a week or so, then head back to Nashville, but it turned out quite differently.

For the past year or so, I had found I could pick up extra cash competing at gong shows (the current rage in all the clubs), and after arriving in Miami, I heard about one, in particular, at a really posh yachting and tennis club in Fort Lauderdale. Not even knowing what the prize was, I took my harmonicas and went to compete.

As usual, I did my shtick and danced through the crowd playing a boogie-woogie on the harp, while grinding my hips to titillate the heathens. Then, having already picked out my unknowing accomplice, for my grand finale, I got a running head start across the polished floor and came sliding up on my knees, wailing like a train in front of the sexiest woman I could find in the front row. Preferably a judge.

Though I didn't always win the cash prize, I invariably walked away with something, or someone. Often it was the girl who I had ended up on my knees in front of. *(Funny how that works. I wonder if anyone has ever done a study on that phenomenon?)*

This time, however, he won it all, but instead of a cash prize it was a round trip ticket with accommodations to St. Thomas, in the Virgin Islands. By now, you've probably got a good idea what our Prince did next. After parking the van at his brother's, he packed a few clothes, lots of percussion instruments; Dulci, Gordi, and Gildy (his guitar), and he was on his way 'back to the islands'.

Habit Forming Hormones

"Time is the only thing everyone is given equally, yet no one seems to have enough of."

African Proverb

*O*nce the Prince alighted from the plane in St. Thomas, memories from his Cuban days came flooding back; the hot air that could sear your lungs, if you weren't careful, the constant salty reminder of an ocean close at hand carried aloft by 'the trade winds', which made the heat seem desirable, even sensual. He felt welcomed back by the Caribbean, like the father to the prodigal son saying,"we might have had our differences in the past, but I'll always love you".

It wasn't long before the Prince had gotten the lay of the land, as chameleons are wont to do, and started looking for some fun. He soon formed a band with a local musician, named Don Edwards, and they called themselves "Merlin and The Don and the Rast-a-band", (pronounced 'the rest of the band'). In reality, they were a duet, that preferred being musically inclusive rather than exclusive, and encouraged others with talent to join them. Hence the name (rest-of-the-band... whoever happened to be sitting in that night).

Donnie looked more like a tight end from Nebraska than a troubadour, especially when compared to the Prince, with his colorful garb and long hair, but together they made a good team. Being the owner of a successful construction company, Donnie knew a lot of people, which meant they could guarantee club owners a full house, even before they played their first gig. Playing five nights a week at local bars, they soon became a big fish, in a little pond. Their biggest competitor for bragging rights, as local favorite, came from 'The Mighty Whitey' (the first white guy to ever place in the local calypso competitions).

It was about as picture perfect a life as a lad could envision. Scuba diving, * surfing, hunting lobsters and girls in the daytime (not necessarily in that order), and then playing music throughout the night. The Prince rented a sim-

* Rainbow Lights...Rainbow CD #6

ple two bedroom house with wooden shutters and a red tile roof. Its most distinguishing feature was being plopped in the middle of a rain forest overlooking Megan's Bay (considered by many to have one of the ten most beautiful strands of beach in the world). He decided to settle in there for the winter. Time stood still for the Prince.

One day, after scuba diving, someone asked me what the date was. I realized I not only didn't know the date, but wasn't even sure what month we were in. I answered with complete sincerity, "I think it's July." *

Only later, did it dawn on me how luxurious that was. I think I'd give just about anything to be that carefree again. Though I had very little in the way of material possessions, I was as content and happy as I had ever been. What I did have was peace of mind and a day-to-day joy in living.

One night at the club, I met a waif-like beauty, vacationing from New York, named Natalie, whose main goal in life seemed to be to wear as few clothes as possible. Maybe five feet tall in heels, she had more golden blond ringlets than I had ever set eyes on, let alone run my fingers through. That alone would have caught my attention, but she had an irresistible come-hither smile and a provocative way of throwing her mane back like a wild stallion that made you willing to write bad checks, or whatever it took to be able to nuzzle your face into that neck for awhile. Though I know we talked at length *(boy could she talk)*, I only remember two things about her. One, she was studying to be an actress at a college in upstate New York, and two, she had an insatiable sex drive that drove me out of my gourd. (Maybe that's why I can't remember anything else.) I was convinced I'd met my first nymphomaniac. * She had only planned on staying in St. Thomas for a couple of weeks, but once she discovered I had appetites not unlike her own, she promptly moved in. For the next two months!

Until then, I'd never imagined there could be such a thing as too much sex, as my hormones were raging and in complete control of my life at the time. Natalie quickly changed my mind, and that in itself left an indelible impression on me. Like I'd learned the hard way years earlier with banana splits, after four in a row, they no longer looked quite so appetiz-

* Time
* You're Driving Me Crazy

ing in the soda shop window.

The Prince, as I have mentioned, had untreated Attention Deficit Disorder since childhood, and was prone to obsessive-compulsive behavior that could manifest itself in just about anything. His favorites included, but certainly weren't limited to: the opposite sex, alcohol, drugs, food, working out, and reading books; any of which would help him to stay focused (or hyper-focused) for a while, which for anyone with ADD could become habit forming.

I bring this up now, as there will be a bevy of ladies who come and go through the Prince's life, * and if I tried to describe them all, this little book would become a tome.

The day Natalie was to fly back to the mainland, she convinced me to drive her to the airport with both of us wearing nothing but towels draped across our laps. She had it all figured out; while I drove, she planned on getting me prepared for the main event which was to take place in the airport parking lot. Anyone who has ever had sex while operating a moving vehicle will understand when I say there was a lot of speeding up and slowing down before we arrived; everyone else, use your imagination. Most of the drive was on a one lane road, so I wasn't too worried about shocking some little old lady's sensibilities and even managed to rise to the occasion. However, once we got onto the two lane stretch where people in the cars passing by could look in, I started to lose it. In fact, I was laughing so hard by the time we pulled into the airport, we had to start over from scratch. *

Soon after she left, the Prince was asked to have the 'Rastaband' bring in 'Jouvet' weekend (the official start of the Virgin Island version of Mardi Gras, known as 'Carnival'). Though a week long event, 'Jouvet' officially began on Thursday nights around 2 a.m. when everyone took to the streets, and 'The Rastaband' was hired to start off the festivities at 'Sparky's on the Waterfront', the island's most popular bar at the time.

For the occasion, I added bass, drums and an extra lead guitarist. We played plenty of originals, lots of Jimi Hendrix, Cream, and Beatles songs, as well as Crosby, Stills and Nash and, at least twice a night, our ren-

* Women
* Dirty Talk

dition of Leon Russell's, 'Back to The Islands.' It was truly a night to remember.

Flying over with a bird's eye view would have shown hundreds of people dressed in colorful clown outfits, dancing with total abandon, spilling out of a club with all its doors and windows flung wide open, while hundreds more pranced in the streets.

This all led up to two a.m. when the first tram (a rolling scaffold on wheels three stories high, carrying from fifteen to forty steel drum players) passed by. Each tram was powered by the hands of hundreds of bedecked clowns who frolicked and gamboled alongside. There were dozens of trams; each one encircled and propelled by their own entourage.

I had often mused if there were want ads in the local Caribbean papers that read, "Tram pushers needed; no experience necessary." This was during my 'Sambuca' stage, when I always carried a flask of the licorice tasting liquor on me, and kept the remainder of the bottle in the trunk of my car, so I'd never run out. I didn't pass out often, or not remember how I ended up somewhere, but 'Jouvet' night both occurred. I woke up in a lounge chair, half undressed in six inches of sea water as the morning tide had come in. Next to me was a beautiful native clown, and as I peered about to get my bearings, I realized we had somehow ended up at one of the island's finer resorts. Floating beside us was not only the flask, but the empty quart bottle. I'd seen the clown, now sleeping beside me, sitting at the back of the club listening to the band play on a number of occasions, but she'd always left early, and alone, and never gave out her phone number. Since everyone was in full clown regalia with face makeup, the last thing I remembered was teasing her that I was going to wipe that frown right off of her face. From the looks of her that morning, I guess I did. *This was not an anomaly, believe me.*

It was such a simple life, and the Prince had a sense of belonging like he'd never known before. Since the single greatest quest for a military brat is to belong somewhere, that was quite a revelation.

It would have been easy for the Prince to stay there indefinitely (occa-

sionally taking up one of the offers he got to 'play for his keep' while sailing around the world), but the wanderlust was still surging in his veins. (A.k.a. testosterone.)

Soon afterwards, when he got a call from Nashville saying "Waylon Jennings has been looking for you to come and backup his wife Jessie Colter on their upcoming tour", he didn't have to be asked twice. Being a big fish in a little pond was OK, but being a type-A personality, he had to know how well he would do in the ocean with the whales . . . and the sharks.

Waylon Jennings and Lear Jets

"Some men see things as they are and say why? I dream of
things that never were and say why not?"

Ralph Waldo Emerson

*W*hen last in Nashville, the Prince had recorded the dulsitar on a song
for Jessi Colter. Now it seems that song was to be on her new album,
and they wanted the Prince to come perform it with her on her upcoming tour.
Once Waylon and Jessi learned the Prince played not only the dulsitar, but the
harmonica and guitar as well, they asked him to become Jessi's musical direc-
tor and to form a new band for her. When time became a factor, it ended up
simpler for the Prince to simply join 'The Waylors', and they would back Jessi
as well as Waylon.

When I returned to Nashville from the islands, Waylon was in
Texas preparing to celebrate his fortieth birthday. (Immortalized in the
line, 'just turned 40 and still wearing jeans.') A couple of weeks after my
return from the islands, I was directed to put it in gear and get out to the
airport, ASAP, as I was invited to Texas for his birthday bash. The next
thing I knew, I was on a private lear jet Waylon had sent to pick up me and
Hank Williams Jr., and the two of us are getting loaded at 700 miles per
hour heading for the party.

I had rarely listened to country music before the preceding year. At
the time, I was visiting a friend in Atlanta who had sat me down and put
a set of headphones over my ears.

"I know how you love good music" he said, "I want you to listen
to this album, and tell me what you think." It was Waylon's 'Dreaming my
Dreams'.

I listened to it nonstop for the next 10 hours. It became one of my
favorite recordings. Now, here I was one year later, in the band, flying to
meet the man himself.

It was becoming more and more apparent to the Prince that when he quit trying to control everything in his life and would just get out of his own way, his life seemed to work so much better. In other words, suit up, show up, do the foot work, but leave the results up to God.

Waylon treated his boys real well. He told me when I first joined the band, "I don't care what you do to be ready, but when you walk out on that stage at night, I want you prepared to give it all you've got and not have anything else on your mind."

After the gigs, there would often be limos waiting to take us back to the hotel. Since Waylon seemed to attract more than his share of groupies, we were rarely without female company. I found it surprising how many were nurses, bankers or librarians (women I had stereotyped as leading sheltered lives), who would throw all caution to the wind for a night to live out their wildest fantasies. I surmised it was probably because they knew it was a safe bet that no one would ever uncover their secret.

As to my stories with 'Waylon and the boys'; there were many, but the one I recall most vividly was playing at Willie Nelson's Fourth of July Picnic in Tulsa, Oklahoma. We had flown in from California, after performing at the Universal Amphitheater the night before. The flight itself was noteworthy, as the plane was a huge DC-10 filled with nothing but band members from either 'The Waylors' or 'Lynnard Skynnard'; another current hot band.

The stewardesses were nervously walking down the isles carrying trays of cocaine and grass, as if they were soft drinks, and peanuts while the party raged on. Though I had stopped doing drugs years earlier, I had started indulging in spirits after moving to Nashville. I wanted to fit in, and was just starting to feel like a part of the family, having been initiated by the roadies pool side at the Universal Sheraton the day before; even managing to drag a couple of them in the pool with me. With Waylon it was like that. Family, dogs, kids, nannies, you name it everyone went on the road.

The heat was sweltering, over the century mark, once we arrived in Tulsa, and with well over 100,000 people crammed into the fenced-in outdoor venue, it was close to unbearable. Thank God, the stage was at least 10 feet off the ground, so the performers felt what little breeze there was. Playing before that many people, was an awesome feeling, like nothing I'd known before. Between the adrenaline pumping and the testosterone flowing, I thought my feet might leave the ground, and I prayed before we went on that I wouldn't make a fool of myself. That night, someone took a snapshot of me standing between Waylon (in his black leather vest) and Willie (wearing his signature red bandanna), while both had their arms draped across my shoulders.

"This is it, I've arrived" I thought to myself, "it doesn't get any better than this."

Unfortunately, whoever took the photograph failed to send it to him in Nashville. Over the years, with all his other adventures, that was still the one shot the Prince most regrets not having to show his grandchildren. (Of course it might help if he got married and had some children first). So if you happen to have a picture in your scrapbook of a guy in a new cowboy hat, with a shit-eating grin on his face, standing between a couple of the 'Outlaws', do him a favor. Give him a call.

That feeling of belonging, he'd felt while in the band, was short-lived, as Jessi's album wasn't the hit the record company had hoped for. After the tour ended and the Prince found his services wouldn't be needed any further, he acted as if it didn't bother him, but he was crying inside. All his life, he'd sought the feeling of belonging somewhere, and once again, his hopes that he'd found a permanent home were dashed.

Though subconscious, his need for initiation and to find his place in the world had led him to seek it from his peers, instead of from his elders. He sought to find himself in the external, the way most of us do. This was to become a repeated pattern, with the same frustrating results, time after time. Another recurring theme, was seeking initiation from the countless relationships he found himself involved in. Once again, the women would have been only too happy to help, if they could, but it was a job that could only be done by male elders.

A Work Of Love

"We have no art," say the Balinese. "We just do everything as beautifully as we can."

As was his wont, the Prince always had a little trouble coming off the road and readjusting to civilian life. He seemed to feel most comfortable and alive when in the midst of an adventure. Once off the road, all the unstructured time seemed to drive him a little crazy until his inner clock could adjust. For years, whenever someone would ask him what it was that he did, his smiling rejoinder would be,

"I'm a gypsy. God is my employer. I do whatever is put in front of me."

Once back from the Waylon tour, Daniel and I reconnected, and we decided to form a duo. We started playing, four nights a week, at the one and only elegant French restaurant Nashville had ever seen. We called ourselves 'The Gypsies' and would play everything from authentic gypsy music, to Oscar Hammerstein/Cole Porter classics, with many of our original compositions thrown into the mix as well.

I played everything from honky tonk piano, clarinet, slide blues guitar, to the dulsitar and Beethoven's Fifth symphony on my harmonica, while Daniel would play classical guitar, gordamer and the lute. We both dressed up in tuxedos and Nashville's elite society served as our audience. We had a ball.

Whenever I would start to take myself too seriously (which Daniel, in his own inimitable way pointed out was happening more frequently since the Waylon tour), he would float over on stage (usually in the middle of a love song), and start sniffing in my ear like a puppy-dog. His final sniff was always the textbook sharp exhale. I'd try and keep a straight face, but he'd keep it up until I burst out laughing, usually in the middle of a vocal riff. (Often, to the chagrin of the owners, but the crowd seemed to love our irreverence).

The Prince and Daniel were best friends by now, and were spending more and more time together. After a while, the Prince found himself hanging out at a gorgeous home where Daniel was living. It was owned by Saul, a roly-poly Jewish entrepreneur, with a great sense of humor and a big heart, who also happened to be managing a couple punk bands and a reggae act from Jamaica. (Keep in mind, this is Nashville in the late seventies.) Saul had recently been divorced and didn't like spending time alone, so he started letting half the rock musicians in town crash at his house, and Daniel was one of them.

Saul's abode was a split level brick home, set on an acre of perfectly manicured landscape, in one of the more upscale areas around Nashville. Since most of the cars in the neighboring driveways were newer models, it was obvious something out of the ordinary was going on with the constant comings and goings of all the clunkers and beat up looking vans.

On any given morning, you'd have to step across as many as a dozen bodies sprawled out as if turned to stone the night before from looking back at Methusala. One particular morning, I was awake, but hadn't opened my eyes yet, when I overheard Daniel and Saul talking. Daniel (who had an eye for the absurd), was watching everyone come to, and as they started grazing toward the kitchen, like a herd of cattle in search of food, he commented to Saul, "Why don't you just put up a trough and a few blocks of salt?"

On that note, I started to moo. I was quickly joined by harmonizing moos from all over the house, and we all broke out laughing. From there, it spread like kudzoo and it became commonplace to walk in a bar and be greeted by a sick cow from someone in the far corner who had been there that morning. Soon, a cacophony of moos could be heard in half the bars and from half the stages in Nashville. As is human nature, before long, you'd have thought Saul lived at the coliseum for all the musicians that claimed they had been there when it all began. *It was the first trend the Prince ever launched on the masses, and he actually took great pride in his udder brilliance...*

One weekend, "The Gypsies" weren't playing, so the Prince decided to go down to Black Mountain for a recharge. On the way, he decided to stop and hear a talk being given by Hugh Lynn Cayce, son of the renowned psychic, Edgar Cayce.

The talk was illuminating, and afterwards they talked awhile. Then, the Prince pulled out his instruments and played for him. Hugh Lynn loved it, and told the Prince of his fathers' work of healing with colors and sound, and how each of the colors had its own healing properties. This was the same concept the Prince had been introduced to by Jim Goure in Black Mountain.

Hugh Lynn thought that if the songs were done instrumentally (no lyrics), they could be used as a vehicle for taking people deeper in meditation, and would even help people to heal on an emotional level.

I heard him loud and clear, and knew right then what I wanted to do. All during this time with 'The Gypsies', I had spent my days helping yet another studio owner build a hot little studio near music row (once again in exchange for free studio time). I immediately called Daniel and told him; "Let's record an instrumental album of healing music. Each song should represent a different chakra, so that people can listen to them while bathing under the seven colors of the spectrum. They've already built a room at the Light Center, where people are coming to bathe under the colors, so we have a built-in audience. Let's do the music."

The light room I'm referring to is inside a beautiful geodesic dome that Jim built in Black Mountain as a place for continuous prayer. Inside, there are six banks of colored lights set into the walls, which automatically start at the lowest chakra (red), and every five minutes, move up the spectrum till you've been saturated in violet light at the crown chakra. * It reminded me of stepping inside a circular spaceship that was designed to free up the seven chakras. Then, you could fly anywhere in the universe.

Daniel thought it was a great idea, and we got right to work. I made arrangements to use the studio for seven days in a row. Normally, to record an album in that length of time might seem a mighty tall order, but I felt that this was a divine mission, and since all things were possible (*especially when you're on one of those*), I wasn't going to worry about it.

I inaugurated the album on a crisp fall Monday morning and opened the sessions with a prayer for guidance. I then began recording the basic acoustic guitar tracks. I would push the record button in the control room,

* Children's Song...Awakening Imaginations CD #1

run into the studio, grab my guitar, count it off and it was 'a go'. In the evenings, or actually whenever he felt like it, Daniel would show up and together, we would go nonstop till the wee hours of the next day. Occasionally I would call on outside musicians (when the song called for violin, vibes, or some other instrument not within our own arsenal of talents), and it wasn't long before the project began to take on a life of its own.

That week, I experienced tremendous joy. The life force was flowing through us unabated, and knowing the purpose of the music was to help heal others, I knew we were being of service. The most fun was layering the sounds of nature behind the recorded music. The wind, the birds, the ocean, foghorns, crickets, even the children's laughter had to be brought in just right. I began talking to myself on a regular basis; "I need a little more bubbling brook here", or "a clap of thunder there". *

By Friday night, I felt like all the music was there, but just to be sure, I decided to sleep on it and do one last listening Saturday before starting to mix.

That night, I had a dream in which a painter stood before his easel listening to everyone else's opinion on what to paint beneath a spectacular rainbow he had already completed. He tried various suggestions, but none of them did the rainbow justice, and after awhile, when it had turned into a brown blur, he thought to himself, "I wish I'd followed my own intuition and just painted a simple planet earth."*

Come Saturday, the Prince (who was learning to pay attention to his dreams), told everyone to leave him alone for a while, as he knew what he had to do next.

I closed the heavy wooden doors and locked myself in the sound-proofed control room, took all the phones off the hook, and proceeded to just try and stay out of my own way. For the next thirty- six hours, I went on a creative journey I had very little memory of later. I didn't eat or sleep. I felt like I was being guided by a power beyond me, and just sat at the twinkling console painting a picture. Instead of feeling tired, as the hours wore on, I became more and more exhilarated. It was like nothing I'd ever experienced,

* Ocean Song…Awakening Imaginations CD #6
* Nepalese Princess…Awakening Imaginations CD #4

but I knew from the dream, I was on the right track.

When I stumbled out into the glaring sunlight Monday morning, it was with the master in my hand and a contented smile on my face. I felt as if I'd made a real contribution, and had the strangest thought, "If I was to die today, at least the world's a little better place for my having been here."*

That was important to the Prince, as he always felt as though he had something to prove to his father, and since he was still playing under the old rules, i.e., he who makes the most money is a success; anything he could find to be proud of was a plus.

For the next few weeks, the Prince and Daniel basked in that sense of accomplishment you only feel after a job well done. Still playing at the French restaurant in the evenings, they had build up quite a following for the 'Gypsies' and would sell a few copies at their gig. But since the term 'New Age Music' hadn't even been coined yet, this 'work of love' was to be discovered only by word of mouth.

* (Angels) Shine On…Rainbow CD #4

Princess Claire

"What you gonna do when love comes calling?
Whispers in your ear, "Won't you come fly away?"
What you gonna do when love comes calling?
Will you open your heart and let it have it's say?"

GWC

*T*o give you an idea of where the Prince's priorities were during this time of his life, he had been introduced to 'The Urantia Book' (a metaphysical treatise on the nature and creation of the universe as told by angels). It also had a few hundred pages devoted to the life and teachings of Jesus, as told by beings who were supposedly there and witnessed what he said and what he did during all the years that were unaccounted for. The book was thousands of pages long with tiny print, but the Prince had become so mesmerized by it, he found himself wanting to read fourteen to sixteen hours a day. So what did he do? He rented a house, did a quick fixing up of the loft, so he had a place to sleep and hang his clothes, and then he rented out the three downstairs rooms, so he could live rent free. He did nothing but read for the next nine months, until he completed the tome. Nothing compulsive about the Prince! Then feeling inspired, he printed his first-ever calling card that read:

He had just accomplished this endeavor, one week earlier, when he met his second Princess and fell deeply in love (as opposed to being deeply in heat, which seems to be a common mistake in this day and age). *The Prince and Daniel were hanging out at the Exit Inn with Owsley, as was their usual, when from across the room, the Prince saw a bright glow, and the rest of the world stood still.

He saw a face with golden ringlets cascading down, framing the features of an angel. Trite, though it may seem, her smile lit up the entire room.

* New Age Shuffle

Like an angelic ballerina, kindness, compassion, and innocence were in her every move, and most beautiful of all, she didn't have a clue that every woman around her seemed to be a shadow by comparison. He would later understand that what he was seeing, for the first time, was the face of unconditional love.

Trusting my discernment that she was one-in-a-million, and knowing opportunities like this might only come once in a lifetime, I overcame my fear, and as if in a trance, walked over to her table. In front of the other six women sitting there, I not only introduced myself, but stated my intentions and asked permission to come calling. *(Ask any man, wizard or otherwise, that is one of the most feared journeys a man can embark upon.)* *

Lo and behold, she replied, "I'd be delighted."

I couldn't have been any more pleased if I'd been given a million dollars. *(Maybe that's why they say there are some things money can't buy.)* I was smitten and could hardly wait to see her again. The next day, I called her and we made plans to get together for dinner that very evening. I could barely contain myself, and was practically out of breath by the time we got off the phone. I remember yodeling after we hung up, just to release some of the built up energy. The closer it got to our date, the more nervous I became. I knew already she was a Godsend, and so wanted to make a good impression. After getting dressed two hours early, I decided to go out and have a couple of beers to calm myself down.

Bad move.

The policeman who stopped me, after I left 'The 'Goldrush Bar', thought it was more than just a couple, but rather than take drastic measures, the officer said, "You'll need to leave your car at the station, but you can call someone to come pick you up."

You're probably thinking, "Oh no, he didn't?" You're wrong, he did, and when she came to pick him up, and he admitted he was trying to sedate himself because of being so nervous about their first date, she laughed till she almost cried. He couldn't have endeared himself to her any more, if he'd tried. Like Jim Goure had taught him, rigorous honesty is the best policy.

Princess Claire (as we'll call her), took our besotted Prince home and

* Falling In Love Again...Awakening Imaginations CD #9

they talked and played music for hours. The next thing he knew, he found himself waking up on her sofa in the middle of the night. Knowing he was welcome to join her, he walked down the hall to her bedroom and sure enough, she had left the bedroom door ajar, and even turned down his side of the bed. Even though she had only been with one man before the Prince, they both knew from that very first date, they were meant to be together. As soon as he sat on the edge of the bed, she awoke and reached out to draw him near.

I thought to myself, "I must be dreaming, but if I am, God please don't wake me up." Never in my wildest imagination, had I envisioned I would have such a divine creature wanting me by her side. I wasn't going to take anything for granted, and was content just to be by her side. I lay down beside her, still on top of the covers, all the while thinking I would try and fall asleep. By this point, my body was trembling with excitement, as if an electric current was surging through my veins. So much so, that I started to feel embarrassed. Just then she whispered to me, "It's OK, you can climb under the covers with me."

Still trying to be the honorable Southern gentleman, I told her, "I'm not trembling because I'm cold, but because I want you so badly I can hardly stand it." *

Then she said three words I'll never forget. "It's still OK."

To my ears that sounded like being offered the proverbial platinum platter, and it didn't have to be offered twice. I slid gently between her silk sheets and lay my head between her breasts. I could hear her heart pounding through her thin camisole, and only then did it dawn on me that she wanted me as much as I wanted her. Just knowing that, I was able to contain my passion more easily, and I began to slowly kiss every inch of her face. I spent hours brushing my lips over her eye lids, ears and neck, while my fingers explored the rest of her body. She finally couldn't stand it any longer, and kissed me fiercely on the lips, signaling me to stop. Deciding turnabout was fair play, she then made me lay on my back while she started kissing my face and exploring my body as well. Only after I was in a state of desperation, would she stop. This went on for hours, until we final-

* Groovin' On Love

ly couldn't hold back any longer. We came as one, and I literally wept for joy. I finally belonged somewhere.

Afterwards, the Prince held her close and they slept. He had always sworn, "If I ever meet a girl I can hold throughout the night and still have her in my arms when I awaken, I know I've found the one." This was the first time the morning rays hadn't found him on the other side of the bed. They were inseparable from that night on. *

Princess Claire was as rare as they come, but didn't know it, and the Prince felt like he was rescuing a maiden from the ivory tower. It seems she had gotten tipsy on her prom night, and the guy she was dating stole her virginity. Sure enough, she became pregnant, and of course, back then the only recourse was to get married. Unfortunately, the guy happened to be one of the walking dead, as Jim would say. He had been raised in a family with Rockefeller-type money, whose value system was totally warped. Things were much more important than people, and money could buy any 'thing' or anybody in his world. Being so stunningly beautiful on the outside, Princess Claire was just another ornament to him, a treasure he tried to virtually keep locked away, afraid someone would steal her. Her other gifts, such as clairvoyance, clairaudience, and intuition, as well as her ability to commune with angels, were either ignored, ridiculed or went unrecognized.

She had been told she was crazy so often from her jealous, unconscious former husband and his billionaire family, that she had even started to wonder herself. In actuality, they were just trying to build a case to take custody of her two children Shadrack and Constantine. (A little poetic license with the names of course).

The Prince was just what she needed; someone who would cherish her. He was coming to understand that a man's job was 'to protect women, children, and animals, and that they were to be the recipients of his bounty'. No initiated man would have treated her like her husband. To the contrary, her gifts were so extraordinary, that when the Prince saw what was going on, he laughed and said, "You're not crazy, you're just more evolved than the rest of us. Come with me to the Black Mountain. I know someone there you should meet." Sound familiar?

---

* (I Could Be) The Boy Next Door

So off they went.

It was a meeting of spiritual giants. Jim saw what was going on immediately and reassured her that having psychic abilities, communing with angels, and having visions as she did, were blessings and gifts that very few people are given. I had told her the same thing, but coming from a former government nuclear physicist it obviously carried more weight. From then on, Princess Claire was much more comfortable and able to accept her psychic abilities.

One day, a few months later, I came home (we were practically living together since that first date), and I heard this heavenly voice coming from the back of the house. Rather than interrupt, I just sat in the hall and was enchanted for the next half an hour. Finally Princess Claire emerged, but upon seeing me sitting on the floor, she became flustered and embarrassed.

"How long have you been sitting there?" she demanded.

I answered with my own question, "How come you never sang for me before? You sing like an angel." *

I found out she'd been singing like that for years, but only for her daughter. No one else had ever heard her before. I was astonished and asked, "Have you ever tried writing songs before?" I had already read some of her poetry, and thought it inspired and uplifting, to say the least.

"No", she responded,

"Darling, you have sounds that come out of you and thoughts inside of you that are as pure and divine as anything I've ever heard. The world would certainly be a better place if you were to share your gift. I'd love to teach you to put your thoughts to music, if you'd like to learn."

Princess Claire was touched that the Prince thought it valuable, and even more moved he was willing to take the time to teach her. With tears in her eyes, she said, I'd love you to.

Within weeks, she was writing songs the Prince couldn't believe. Discerning the timing was right for her to share her gift, the Prince decided to surprise her and took her to a conference put on by 'The Spiritual Frontiers

* Gypsy Dance

Fellowship' (one of the spiritual retreats where he was to perform with Jim). This particular conference was to be a week long event, with some of the most renowned psychics and conscious beings on the planet in attendance. There would be workshops on every metaphysical subject imaginable. Then, on the last night together, there was to be a celebration at which the Prince was to perform. Hours before it was to start, the Prince pulled Princess Claire aside and said, "I want you to open the show for me."

Princess Claire's reaction was one of shock, and she said adamantly, "No way."

The Prince kept after her, and finally got her to agree to at least sing harmony with him on a couple songs. Once he had her on stage, he asked the crowd if they'd like to hear some of her original tunes. They went crazy and gave her a standing ovation till she had to acquiesce to their demands. There, eleven weeks after the Prince had discovered her singing for her daughter, Princess Claire sang a number of her compositions, in front of almost a thousand people.

She captivated the audience with her beauty and authenticity and literally stole the show. The Prince couldn't have been more proud, and he knew once again he had been of service by introducing Princess Claire to the world. He truly believed in some small way the world was a little better place for it. *

* Dancing Girl

More Discoveries

"Most of us are totally unaware of the fact that our inner conversations are the causes of the circumstances of our lives. A man's mental conversation attracts his life. As long as there is no change in his inner talking the personal history of the man remains the same."

Neville

Living with Claire was the first time the Prince had had the opportunity to spend a lot of uninterrupted quality time with children, and since he was just a big kid at heart, they had quickly become his life. He took pleasure in getting up and making everyone breakfast, especially on weekends, when he'd make pancakes and waffles. (Who does that remind you of?) Taking the kids to school and doing what many people would consider the mundane chores in life, were a source of joy he savored, * like nothing he'd known before.

Feeling like a part of the family, and that he belonged there, was a cool salve being applied to an old wound festering just below the surface. (Though he could relieve the pain, the dull ache seemed to never really go away completely.) Loving children as he did, the Prince found spending time with them was the best pain reliever he'd ever found. Though he didn't recognize it at the time, his ADD brain thrived on the constant activity the kids created, and he found he loved writing songs when they were together.

For Constantines' fourth birthday, I decided to make it one to remember. This little curly haired cherub had stolen my heart. Words like precious and adorable, barely did her justice. She loved to climb up in my lap and fall asleep, while I was reading to her. Even better, she delighted in bouncing around on my knees when I'd let my ADD involuntary twitch go full blast. She'd start giggling and couldn't stop except to shout, "more, more." Within a month of meeting Claire, and much to her quiet chagrin, I should add, both of the kids were mooing, growling, snorting and imitating every barnyard animal imaginable. She drew the line, when I

* With Your Love

started teaching them how to imitate 'petards' on each others mid- riffs.

Armed with the insiders knowledge I'd acquired while working at carnivals, I headed to the Tennessee State Fair, and won three dozen stuffed animals for Constantine, as well as a big teddy bear for Princess Claire. I then arranged them all over Constantine's room, so that when she came home that day, she was greeted by a veritable zoo of 'hogs, frogs, all kinds of dogs, winnie the poos and kangaroos'.

Her squeals of delight and the look of astonishment and joy on her face was priceless, and I was given one of the most memorable hugs of my life.

Another experience with Princess Claire, that begs to be shared, but also explains her need for anonymity, was the lesson she taught the Prince about a higher form of love that was possible and how it could manifest itself in physical reality.

Claire was so tuned into God, that her connection with the Prince was on a level like nothing he had ever experienced. Whenever he desired to please her, he could just reach across the car (or anywhere else for that matter), touch her breast lightly, and within moments, she would have an orgasm. The Prince felt like the greatest lover in the world. ('Captain', beat that.) There was little physical stimulation to speak of, just the mutual yearning to please someone you love, and the willingness to accept that love.

*This awareness, that there was a more evolved form of sexuality, opened up a curiosity in the Prince that over the years was to lead to tantric yoga, the million dollar point, and other realms formerly untouched (no pun intended). ***

I found it hard to believe, at first, that anyone could be that erotic and sensuous, angel or otherwise. After the first time it happened in the car, my skeptical side thought it had to be an aberration, so I began pleasing her everywhere we went. It was for real. Princess Claire got to where whenever she'd see me coming (once again, no pun intended), she'd cross her arms, so as to not give me a clear shot. She actually seemed perplexed that I thought it was such a wondrous thing. I told her it was just one of those guy things.

* Practice Makes Perfect Love

"I mean, I may not have chest hair, but you should see the reaction from my woman."

Unfortunately, nothing lasts forever, and every silver lining has its cloud (or something like that). The Prince's relationship with Princess Claire was no exception. *

Since Nashville was a small town, it wasn't long before word got out about the girl with the angelic voice and face to match. Soon Claire's phone was ringing off the hook, and she was being wined and dined by some of the top 'big name' producers in town.

I tried my best to be cool (and still be excited for her), when she'd come home telling me of the latest offers, but my jealousy started to eat at me. I'd see the 'big shots' pick her up in their fancy cars, and my self worth would drop another notch. When it came to all my spiritual teachings, it was as if I had suddenly developed amnesia.

"She's my discovery!" I thought.

Princess Claire (having just gotten away from a man with incredible wealth), wasn't nearly as impressed with all the trappings as was the Prince. She loved him, just the way he was, and tried to reassure him that what he had brought to her life meant so much more than anything money could buy.

Being clairvoyant, she always knew when I was feeling depressed and would take on my pain, which made me feel even worse.

"Don't you know how much I love you?" she pleaded. "I don't care what kind of car you drive or how much money you've got in the bank. It makes no difference to me. I care what kind of man you are inside and how you treat me and my children."

"Well it makes a difference to me," I weakly replied.

"Don't you get it", she continued, "I had everything money could buy, and it means nothing compared to your love and support and understanding. You've given me hope and brought joy back into my life."

It was to no avail. Because I didn't have the money and the power I had grown up believing were the makings of a real man, I didn't feel I deserved her.

* Fever

After a while, my insecurities turned to anger, and then to rage. I started acting just like my father; something I swore I would never do, and it humbled me to see it. One night she pulled up in a stretch limo while I had been home watching the kids. Even though she was already late, she sat talking in the car for another fifteen minutes. By now I was seething inside and sat peering out the kitchen window. When she finally came in, I tried to act like nothing was wrong. Unfortunately, I didn't have the tools to let my frustration out healthily, and I certainly didn't know how to express the fear and insecurity I had of her leaving me. It wasn't long before I picked a fight. During the ensuing argument, I took my favorite guitar (the one I'd carried through so many adventures), and smashed it against the wall to make the point,

"See, I love you so much I'm going to hurt myself." *(Makes perfect sense to me)*. That was the beginning of the end. *

I find it alarming, how truly destructive much of the old programming is on what makes up a real man. It's so obvious it's time for a new paradigm, and yet, relatively speaking, so few men have tuned in. Therein lies a challenge for men in the new millennium. It took many years, and many other relationships, before the Prince finally understood "If you really love someone, then set them free", was more than just a great song.

Princess Claire had a gift of being able to simply walk into a room and uplift everyone present, whether they knew it or not. I'll always be grateful for the time we shared. It was as if God entrusted me to take care of one of his angels for a while.

He had.

* Off The Hook

The Dalai Lama

"After all, the purpose of life is happiness."

The Dalai Lama

*B*y now, the Prince and Daniel had become best of friends. Long before they met, Daniel had been practicing Buddhism, and other forms of meditation foreign to the Prince, with seemingly good results. Though Buddhism wasn't his brand, the Prince had respect for anyone who diligently sought a relationship with God.

So the day Daniel came home, all excited, saying they were supposed to go play for the Dalai Lama, the Prince didn't think Daniel had lost it entirely, though he did take advantage of the opportunity to poke a little fun,

"Sure and then we'll drop by the Vatican and play for the Pope."

Daniel wasn't to be deterred. He'd just learned that, for the first time in history, the Dalai Lama was coming to the western world and that he'd be visiting the University of West Virginia, which had a large Buddhist studies program. Never one to back away from an adventure, after a few more jokes at Daniel's expense, the Prince said,

"Load up the van, let's go."

We drove through the night and no sooner arrived, and were walking across the campus looking for a bathroom, when there came the Dalai Lama. Surrounded by his entourage, as well as the university dignitaries, there must have been thirty people in all. It wasn't hard to spot who the monks were, since they were all bald and had on ocher colored robes. The Dalai Lama wasn't dressed any differently, at least not that I could tell, and the only way I recognized him, was the deference paid him by the others, once we introduced ourselves.

Bold as we could be, Daniel and I walked right up, stopped the entourage and explained, "We've just driven 1000 miles to come play for His Holiness." *

* Dulsitar Love Song…Awakening Imaginations CD #11

There was one school official there who was obviously not a practicing Buddhist, as he became agitated and flustered by our innocent approach, as if to say, "How dare you walk up without clearing it with me first." I tried to suppress my smile, but I know the monk standing next to the Dalai Lama caught it, as a hint of like-minded amusement crossed his face.

Any other approach would have probably been met with lots of red tape and intermediaries getting in the way, but our request was immediately translated to The Dalai Lama who, without a second's hesitation, replied, "I'd be honored."

I told Daniel after we left, "The look of consternation on that one official's face was worth the drive by itself."

A command performance was scheduled for two days hence, and we were given dorm rooms to stay in till then. When we arrived to give the concert, we discovered The Dalai Lama had brought not only his entire entourage, but had invited numerous others as well. His Holiness obviously enjoyed the yodeling, in particular, as he asked to hear the song 'Yodel Away' a second time. Later, after hearing our latest composition on dulsitar with gordamer accompaniment, he acknowledged us through his interpreter saying, "Your music is the first meeting between East and West in a musical vibration. It will heal many people."

The memory I most cherish, happened during the performance. The Dalai Lama, obviously never having seen a guitar pick before, reached over and picked one off of Daniel's knee while Daniel was finger-picking and I was playing 'The Dulsitar'. He brought the pick up close to his face and examined it for a few seconds, and then put it back where he'd found it.

Apparently, he had not left it exactly like he'd found it, because less than three seconds later, he reached over and turned it ever so slightly, thus creating no karma or (ripples in the pond). Hmm- good name for a song.

Interesting, that over the years many people have asked me, "How did it feel, weren't you in awe, to be in his presence?", and I would usually say "yes", partly because that was what they wanted to hear, but even more because I was afraid they'd think me arrogant if I told them the truth. I actually felt amazingly comfortable in his presence. He radiated a genuine warmth and easy charisma. I even joked with him through his interpreter, and he made me feel very much like an equal; a visiting dignitary come to share a facet of our culture with him.

The Prince and Daniel played for nearly an hour, and after the performance, the Dalai' Lama leaned over to one of the other monks and whispered in his ear. Neither Daniel nor the Prince knew what was going on, but were thrilled when the interpreter told them,

"His Holiness' wants to honor you."

A few moments later, The Dalai Lama called them forward and after saying a few more words about the blending of the East and West, he took two strips of raw silk, the color of alabaster, from an ornate wooden box that was held out for him by an accompanying monk. Then as Daniel and the Prince bowed, he placed the sacred silk scarves around their necks.

Daniel, being a practicing Buddhist, was thrilled, to say the least, and it was all he could talk about for weeks to come. On the way home, he even suggested going to play for 'The Pope' next and wouldn't it be cool if we could bring the two of them together. It would be many years before the Prince realized what an honor they'd been given, but for now, it was enough to think that Jim and Diana Goure, and possibly even his parents, might be proud of him. Jim and Diana were delighted and wanted to know all the details, but it was years before he even bothered to tell his dad. Sure enough, the response might as well have been " The Dolly who?"

Kuwaiti Royalty

"Our present mental conversations do not recede into the past as man believes, they advance into the future to confront us as wasted or invested words. Your idea is waiting to be incarnated, but unless you yourself offer it human parentage it is incapable of birth."

Neville

*B*oy, were Daniel and the Prince ever feeling elated heading back to Nashville. Not only were they going back with memories of 'The Dalai' Lama's blessings, but a local reporter had written a story about their experience, and taken pictures to boot.

Once back in Nashville, while the Prince was thinking it doesn't get any better than this, he got a call from Mitzi, a good friend, who also happened to be his favorite dance partner.

The Prince had actually started off as a dance major in college, but had decided to switch to music, and ended up becoming the music director for the dance company instead. He still loved to dance though, especially when he had a good partner.

Mitzi was a 5-foot version of Dolly Parton, with all the trimmings and the personality to boot. She was charming, as only a southern belle can be, with her effervescent laughter, her playful, yet sensual, demeanor, and her rapt attentiveness, whenever she wanted to turn it on.

That evening, they went to a little after-hours club, just south of the city, and were kicking up a storm. As usual, they had pretty well cleared the floor and were putting on a show. After one especially strenuous twirl around the dance floor, they had gone back to their table to cool off, when to their bemusement, the waitress brought over a bottle of Dom Perignon and a bouquet of roses.

"Compliments of that gentleman over there, he has thoroughly enjoyed watching you all dance", she said in a thick Southern drawl. She then pointed *to a dark, impeccably dressed young man, sitting by himself in a corner booth, with three or four rather imposing looking gentleman standing close by. The Prince nodded a thank you to the stranger, and after a couple more dances, he and Mitzi sashayed over to meet him.*

The gentleman turned out to be a Prince from Kuwait.

Al (as we'll call him), invited Mitzi and me to join him at his table, and before long (over his protestations), Mitzi had him on the dance floor teaching him a few rudimentary steps. Cinderella would have long since turned into a pumpkin, but we were having such a good time we closed the club. Then we all climbed into Al's limousine and headed back to the downtown Hilton to continue partying. (As we were leaving, I noticed no less than a dozen body guards seem to come out of the shadows.) Since last call had come and gone at the Hilton, Al invited us up to his suite. Both Mitzi and I were in awe once we realized that he had rented out the entire top floor of the hotel and the four burly men that greeted us when we stepped from the elevator were more bodyguards. The next day, I learned it required a key just to get the elevator to go that high.

We partied till the sun started peeking his jolly head around the corner, at which time Al said he was going to bed. He told me if I cared to, I was welcome to take the other bedroom in the suite and stay the night (or day whichever you prefer). Mitzi had left a couple of hours earlier and I had nothing on my agenda that couldn't wait, so I said "sure", and went off to bed, with visions of sugar plum fairies and billions of dollars.

When I woke up that afternoon, there was a note next to a two-hundred dollar fruit plate telling me to make myself at home. Al had gone to a business meeting and would be back later.

Well, our Prince was no fool.

I had somehow landed in the lap of luxury, and was in no hurry to leave. So I kicked back, turned on a ballgame, called a few friends to tell them where I was, and generally made myself at home, like I'd been told. When Al returned, a couple of hours later, he surprised me when he asked, "Why don't you move in and go to work for me." *(Nothing impulsive about our Prince, he took at least a full second before he said),* "Sure, doing what?"

"Be my social director. Make restaurant reservations, and keep me supplied with Johnny Walker Red and Dom Peringnon. Keep fresh fruit plates always on hand and basically, orchestrate my free time. During the day, I'll be taking in business meetings looking to buy properties, but in the evenings, I want to party."

The Prince, with a totally straight face replied, "Sounds kind of tough, but I think I can handle it." Al laughed and handed him five one-thousand bills as an advance.

The next day, I went home, packed a few necessities, found a barber to chop off a foot or so of my hair, bought a half dozen suits, got a manicure, and moved into the Presidential Suite before Al got home. He laughed when he got back to the hotel that night and saw my chameleon-like transformation. For the next six weeks, I lived out a fantasy life most people would have a hard time even imagining. Money was no object, as Al was worth somewhere in the vicinity of seven billion dollars. Easily the most generous man I ever met, he thought nothing of leaving a hundred-dollar tip for a good waitress to show his appreciation. For the next month and a half, anything I could think of, we would do, and do it in style. After a few weeks, Al had finished his business there in Nashville and it was time to move on. (It was just as well. By that point, I had bought up every available bottle of Dom Peringnon in Tennessee and was having to have it shipped in from neighboring states.)

I saved close to 20 bottles, during that month, and gave them to my friends for special occasions over the next year. I hated to see Al go, but I was well recompensed for my services, and besides, I was getting tired of wearing suits all the time.

Jamming With Stevie Wonder/The Waiting Game

"Shoot for the moon. Even if you miss it, you will land among the stars."

Les Brown

*M*itzi was instrumental in introducing the Prince to yet another adventure. Knowing what a big fan of Stevie Wonder's he was, she called the
Prince one day to tell him that Stevie was staying at the downtown Hilton. The
Prince figured the odds of reaching him were probably the same as winning the
lottery, but his intuition told him to go ahead, and he was known for being
lucky so, 'what the hell'.

I called the number she gave me and Stevie picked up the phone. I
knew his voice immediately, and it startled me that it had been that easy.
*After the initial shock, the Prince recovered nicely and said, "I just called to say
I love you." Just kidding.*

I introduced myself and told him about the dulsitar, the Edgar
Cayce album, and playing for the Dalai' Lama. Before long, Stevie said
"Bring some of your music and that instrument you're talking about over to
the hotel. I've got a couple hours before our plane leaves."

Now it was Daniel's turn to be incredulous when I called and said,
"Get ready, I'm coming to pick you up. Were going to jam with Stevie
Wonder."

Never one to miss a good joke at my expense (besides he owed me
one after the Dalai Lama), Daniel without missing a beat replied, "Sure, and
then will go jam with the Beatles and drop by and see how Elvis is doing,
while we're at it." (This was when Stevie was at the zenith of his career, having broken all previous sales records with 'Songs In The Key Of Life'.)

We raced across town to the hotel, as quick as we could, and when
we got there, Stevie's brother, Milton, ushered us into their suite. A few

moments later, Stevie appeared with a big grin on his face and his hands outstretched, palms up; his standard greeting. He had on an African dashiki; and his hair was done up in corn rows (pretty progressive for Nashville back then). He must have sensed we were a little overwhelmed, and cracked some joke he'd heard the day before. I was right away impressed with his humility, and he had such an easy going manner, he put Daniel and me at ease in no time.

"So let's hear this instrument you were telling me about," he said.

I started telling him about Clyde and the dulsitar, and as I was setting it up, Daniel start ripping off some hot licks on his acoustic guitar. I could see Stevie's head tilt to one side, as he was obviously listening to us both. When he started grinning from ear to ear, I looked over at Dan and we both started laughing. By this point, Milton had left the room and it was just the three of us and we started to jam.

We must have played nonstop for an hour. Stevie was fascinated with the sound of the dulsitar, and since he was in the midst of recording the instrumental soundtrack for 'The Secret Life of Plants', he seemed to particularly enjoy the 'The Edgar Cayce Album'.

As luck would have it *(especially if you define luck as opportunity meeting preparedness)*, after hearing the 'Cayce' songs, Stevie asked if we had any pop songs recorded. It just so happened I had four songs on tape that I'd recently recorded, so I put those on. He listened attentively through three songs, and before the fourth could begin, he invited Daniel and me to come to LA. * * *

"You guys are good. I want to help you get a record deal."

"You really mean it?" I was dumbstruck.

"No, I was just kidding," he teased. "Really. I'll have my brother give you my numbers in LA and I expect to see you," he said laughing at himself.

We played awhile longer, until Milton came back and told Stevie they needed to get packed and head toward the airport. We exchanged phone numbers and made plans to meet in two months. Stevie then gave us

* That's How Love Should Be...Chameleon CD #4
* Merry Go Round
* Living A Life Of Love

a bottle of wine to celebrate, and we shook hands.

The Prince was blown away. The opportunity to work with Stevie Wonder, whom he considered to be 'the Beethoven of his times', was a no-brainer. The Prince and Daniel decided since money was tight, that the Prince would fly out in January, for a week or so, get the contracts signed, hopefully, an advance of some sort, and then fly back, so the two of them could drive across the country in the van together. Ah, the innocence and naivete of the uninitiated male. If it was only that easy.

Once again, the Prince chose January first as the day of departure and Daniel drove him to the airport. After the typical 'Men Are From Mars' nonemotional farewell, the Prince was off on his next adventure.

'So he packed up his bags and he moved to Beverly... Hills that is...swimming pools...movie stars...'. Hollywood had called and said, 'Let's do lunch', and since he'd never turned down a free meal...

Thinking he would be gone a few days at most, the Prince packed rather light. Big mistake.

I went to LA for a week and never came back. As fate would have it *(and it usually does)*, Stevie returned to LA a full month after having told me he would meet me there. (I was to find out this was rather typical, as Stevie's sense of time was different from the rest of the world.)

He called every few days to reassure me he was on the way and told me, "Just make yourself at home." He had put me up at The Franklin Plaza Hotel; the same hotel where he resided, and since he was covering all the expenses, I was treated like royalty. They put me up in a big suite, with my own kitchen and a view overlooking Hollywood. I was only two blocks from Hollywood Boulevard and four from Sunset. There was a huge stuffed sofa in the living room, in front of the large screen television, and I quickly became a nocturnal animal. My first few days in LA, I was a bit timid and would only take short forays out to explore my new surroundings, but as each day passed, I became a bit more daring.

Having never seen all night TV before, I got addicted to watching 'Movies till dawn' with their Cal Worthington and Fred Federated commercials, and would stay up all night and sleep till noon. 'Fred Rated' (Shadoe Stevens) and I later became good friends, and I was able to find out the inside scoop behind his zany commercials. (He really was loaded during many of them, it wasn't just an act.)

During the day, I would meander the streets of Hollywood, wide-eyed and bushy tailed, excited about being there, and yet anxious from not knowing how to blend in. The occasional liaison, with local girls impressed that I was Stevie's protege (boy did I ever soak that one for all it was worth), became increasingly frequent, as I learned the language of the LA scene. I had arrived in LA painfully shy to the ways of the big city, but it didn't take me long to learn the ropes. Once I discovered the power in dropping Stevie's name to the girls I'd meet, I was like a kid in a candy store. Every flavor imaginable, and all for the asking. I actually went through a phase where I tried to experience in the biblical sense, every nationality on the planet. It was fun for awhile, but it soon got old; like trying to live on cotton candy when you're body's craving a good home-cooked meal.

It usually takes a chameleon a little time to adapt to the colors of his new environment, but by the time Stevie finally returned to Los Angeles, the Prince was starting to blend right in. Stevie had a heart of gold and certainly meant well, but it was important, if you were in his entourage, to go with the flow and to understand the expression 'hurry up and wait'. The Prince soon realized that, due to that heart of gold, Steveland (Stevie's real name), had promised to help numerous other artists as well as himself, and he might as well take a number. Probably, because of his Attention Deficit Disorder, the Prince had always felt like the 'patience thing' was overrated. The Prince called Daniel to try and get him to fly out, but until they actually had a record deal, Dan wanted to stay put, as he'd already paid his dues in LA and much preferred living in Nashville. The Prince didn't get discouraged though, at least not right away, as he saw this as an opportunity to learn song writing and producing from the master himself, and he wasn't gonna waste the chance.

Since Stevie was a nocturnal creature, all of his musicians and engineers had beepers and were on twenty four hour call. Usually, this meant heading to Wonderlove Studios around ten or eleven every night, waiting till midnight or one a.m., when Stevie would finally arrive and then hanging out watching 'the master' record till dawn. I knew early on, he was to be one of my mentors, and this was an opportunity to learn not only about writing music and producing records, but about life, as his world was teeming with it. The studio itself was fantastic, as it had every new fangled electronic gadget known to man. Often inventors and creators of new technology would bring their latest creations to Stevie, so he could try them out and give his opinions. If they were lucky, even an endorsement.

I loved the way he'd shake hands with people with his palms turned up like an offering, instead of vertically extended like most people do. I actually think the world would be a better place if everyone greeted each other that way. For fun and relaxation at the studio, he'd bought an air hockey table and was actually the defending champ. I'd tease him about resting his free arm in front of the hole, as if he had no idea it was impossible to score against him.

Whether leading him around the studio, singing back up harmony, or just driving back to the hotel with him in his Rolls Royce, it didn't matter to me. I was happy just to be there, and it was all a treat. Since practically everyone in 'the business' would drop by to pay homage to the king, I was being introduced to the entertainment world's elite. I felt like I'd finally arrived, when Stevie gave me the hot line (the phone # right to his bedside).

Looking back, it's amazing to me how impressed the Prince would become by people who had wealth or fame, as if somehow just being around them would rub off.

This schedule went on for over a year, and the Prince got to witness the entire creation process for Stevie's new album 'Hotter Than July'. Call it naivete, but the Prince was sure that Stevie would eventually honor his promise of 'helping him get a deal'. (One of the beliefs of the uninitiated male is that everyone is sincere and will do what they say.)

After a year had passed, I figured it wouldn't hurt to help the process along, so I shopped the recordings I'd originally shown Stevie in Nashville.

Almost immediately I got an offer from Casablanca Records. Ecstatic, I called him, expecting him to be thrilled for me, as he would be producing the record, but the response I got was lukewarm at best,

"Do what you want to do," he said.

Noticing the chill in the air, I tried to make things right, and told him, "Look, you're the boss, if you don't want me to do it, I won't. I was only trying to help."

He wouldn't tell me what was bugging him. It didn't matter anyway, as Casablanca Records went out of business a month later and I was back to 'hurry up and wait', only now I felt like I was back to the bottom of Stevie's priority list. The relationship was never the same.

A couple of other things happened about this time that were to portend the beginning of a downward spiral the Prince was to be ensnared in, and which would almost cost him his life. Still the naive boy when he arrived in LA, the Prince had no idea of the jealousy and envy that had been brewing since he came on the scene. The thinking of some people close to Stevie was that anyone who got close to the top in the pecking order was a threat, because obviously everyone else would then be one notch removed from the source of power.

He has since realized that kind of thinking is prevalent among the masses (the walking dead), especially in the corporate world. At the time, though, the Prince didn't relate to it at all. He truly believed that it was a fair world, and if one had the talent and the right work ethic, then they would get their just reward.

*Also for the first time in his life (other than the long-haired days at ECU), the Prince encountered prejudice. One of the good things about growing up as a military brat, was the lack of race consciousness as the hierarchy was determined by rank alone. The Prince had known friends of every race, color, nationality and creed since he was a child, and had dated Asian, Latino and black women, as long as he could remember. ***

Though I didn't realize it at the time, it had not gone over too well when I showed up at the studio late one night with a beautiful black woman on my arm. We had been out for dinner and dancing, and she was dressed

* We're All In This Together

like a modern day Queen of Sheba, in a short tight leopard print miniskirt, spike heels and a lace boustier. She was a high fashion model and had recently been featured in Ebony Magazine. It was pretty obvious that we'd been getting it on, as she wasn't shy about her affections for me. My thinking was I'd be more accepted if the guys knew I dated black women, but it turned out to be just the opposite. Not everyone felt that way, certainly not Stevie, but there was a definite unspoken ripple among some of the brothers, as if to say, "What are you doing dating our women?" *At the time though, the Prince was oblivious to the undercurrents that were happening right before his eyes. (Again due to his lack of initiation)*

The final straw could only be described as ironic, but it would be almost a full year before one of Stevie's oldest and dearest friends, and a mutual friend of the Prince, told him what had happened.

I had found years before that I had healing hands. *(Remember the Gathering of the Tribes in the Arapaho National Forest when the Prince learned to give massages?)* Having studied various forms of massage ever since, I'd accepted it as a gift that I was able to take away people's pain by drawing it into my hands and then discarding it. My specialty was headaches and I would tell people, "I never met a headache I couldn't cure", using accupressure points on the neck, shoulders, and hands to do the trick.

Since we were putting in such long hours at the studio, I saw an opportunity to be of service, as Stevie was always craning his neck to hear things. (Not to mention the way he constantly rocked his neck back and forth with the music.) More and more, I started massaging his neck and shoulders to relieve the tension, as Stevie seemed to appreciate it.

Unfortunately, someone who was obviously jealous of my relationship with him, saw an opportunity to poison it and told Stevie that I was gay.

It wasn't long before a wall went up. No longer was I welcome to come and go as I pleased, but had to call first before going to the studio. I was baffled and hurt, and didn't have a clue what was going on. The next time Stevie's hot line was changed (which he did on a regular basis), I wasn't given the new number, and when I asked him what was wrong, he assured me everything was fine; it was just that he was busy.

I started drinking more, to stuff the uncomfortable feelings of abandonment I was going through. I didn't know what to do with myself and would sometimes spend fourteen to eighteen hours a day in bed. After all, the only reason I had come to LA was to get a record deal, and that seemed to be slipping away.

This was the first time I remember getting really depressed. I'd had my share of setbacks and disappointments from dealing with my dad's silence in high school, to losing close relationships, as well as a myriad of life's other little defeats, but I was always able to rebound relatively quickly. Other insights and emotions would come into the picture and lead me to take responsibility, and then finally, acceptance of the situation as God's will. This time was different, not having a clue as to what had happened. I felt bleak, demoralized and listless, like I'd wasted an entire year of my life. *Not yet able to see the bigger picture; that it's the journey not the destination that is important, the Prince took a dive.*

Mr. Big Shot, who was going to prove something to 'The Captain', and had gone to Los Angeles to record an album with the 'Beethoven' of his generation, was now coming home with his tail between his legs. I didn't think I could face the look of disappointment on my mom's face, and I knew I wasn't going to give 'The Captain' the satisfaction of saying "I told you so." Since I'd been brought up with the erroneous belief system that love and acceptance were based solely on what you did instead of who you were, I started drinking more and more to numb the feelings. That sent me further into a downward spiral and before long, with my defenses down and no support group around, I said 'yes' to drugs again, for the first time since college.

Much later, the Prince learned that, at some point, every mentor has to let you down and that was just a part of the relationship. It was neither good nor bad, just the way it was supposed to be.

Burning Down The House

"When one door closes, another opens; but we often look so long and so regret-
fully upon the closed door that we do not see the one which has opened for us."
Alexander Graham Bell

*I*n some cultures, they believe a boy has to recieve a visible scar as evidence of
his initiation into manhood. In our culture, much of the scarring endured
during the process of growing up is of the mental and emotional order. The
Prince had just experienced his deepest wounding yet, and only time would tell
if those scars would show or not.

A few months after arriving in Los Angeles, I had gotten a job as
an apartment manager, and had been residing there while spending the
majority of my time at the studio with Stevie. It seemed to be an ideal job
for someone who needed a flexible schedule. I should also mention, it was
the ideal job for someone with an up-and-coming drug habit, as there was
lots of cash coming in each month.

The building was a three story red-brick monstrosity, built in the
fifties, with just a little sampling of a lawn and even less landscaping. In
Webster's, you might find a picture of it beside the word ugly. All told,
there were 60- units in the complex, mostly appealing to low income families and actors and actresses with very little moulah, but very big dreams.
All the windows on the ground floor had bars over them, as it was a rough
section of town, just two blocks from Hollywood Boulevard and The
Chinese Theater. It was a rare day on our block without at least one visit
from the police, fire, or rescue squad, but I got free rent and a small stipend
for keeping the place rented and maintained, and for that I was grateful.

Never having spent that much time in the big city, I got a crash
course those first two years after becoming manager. I inadvertently stopped
a rape by knocking on the door of an apartment I heard yelling coming
from; the guy bowled me over when he burst out a moment later. Another

time, I had a gun pointed at my head by a would be robber after chasing him to the back of the apartment complex. Just as I was about to leap onto the fence; he was almost already over, he stopped, turn back around, and while straddling the top of the fence, pointed what looked like a howitzer at me. I immediately held up my hands and said,

"Whoa, have a nice day! Would you like a cool watch?"

He actually smiled, before continuing his getaway, and I exhaled for the first time in several moments.

Having never seen death at close hand, I almost threw up after finding the enormously bloated foul-smelling body of a young actress, ten days after she had overdosed in one of my top floor apartments. I had no way of reaching her next of kin, so she might still be in a missing persons file for some parent wondering how come they never heard from their child and where they went wrong. Nothing would get the stench out of her apartment, and after three vain attempts by carpet cleaners, the owner capitulated and let me order a new one.

In many ways, since I was still a boy with hayseed in my hair, LA was keeping my hands full. I learned quickly a few urban basics such as; when walking around the neighborhood late at night, it was wise to keep hands in pockets to give any would-be muggers pause appearing to have your own gun. I also found out it was wise to cross to the other side of the road long before you passed someone on the streets late at night, and most important of all, I memorized the areas you stayed away from no matter what.

The building I managed, was owned by an old Hungarian gentleman, named Mr. B., who was a class act, if there ever was one. He had escaped after the war and arrived on a Liberty ship with twenty dollars in his pocket and a contract to pick oranges. He washed dishes for a year, learned English, became a chemist and made a small fortune investing in real estate. His greatest contribution, was the son he fathered, who became one of the world's great violinists (as well as my best friend). The old man was very fond of me and had taken me under his wing treating me like a son.

One Sunday morning, about three a.m., one of the many drunks the Prince was continually chasing off passed out on the lobby sofa and dropped his cigarette. It smoldered for an hour or so before it burst into flame. By the time the Prince was awakened by the alarm in his apartment, the entire lobby was engulfed in flame. The Prince, like most young men, had always wondered how he would do in handling such an emergency.

Scared of what I might find, I opened my front door anyway. Since my apartment faced the lobby, an enormous wall of heat and flames came rushing at me, literally singeing my eyebrows, before I could slam the door shut. *(Lesson number one, always feel the door for heat before opening. We'll give him a C- for his opening gambit; brave but dumb.)*

Next, I dialed 911 and gave them the address *(textbook)*, grabbed a fire extinguisher and the building keys, ran to the living room, and jumped through the window (after having opened it of course.) *Now that deserves an A.* Next, I ran to the back of the building where I could bypass the lobby and still sound the general alarm. *Good thinking, another A for poise.*

From there, I came in the back entrance and ran up and down the hallways of all three floors, screaming "fire" at the top of my lungs, while pounding on all the doors. I managed to get everyone safely out of the building, before being overcome by smoke inhalation. *(Looking back, maybe all the practice he had, inhaling foreign substances ended up to his advantage. Let's give him an over all A-).*

Later, after I had been released from the hospital, one of the firemen brought me a souvenir; the phone that had been hanging on the wall at the far end of the lobby. The fire had been so intense, it had melted, and was now 3 feet long. Seeing that melted phone, brought the entire experience back into reality for me. Once I'd opened my front door, I'd gone into automatic mode and it all seemed surreal. The fear I'd felt, but been able to overcome, was now replaced by pride at a job well done.

Oddly enough, the Prince considered the entire experience a gift, as he would never again have to wonder what his natural reaction in an emergency would be. He didn't think of his actions as being heroic, though others did. He was simply taking care of the job put in front of him, and the safety of the tenants in that building was his responsibility. (Now there's something he could definitely give 'The Captain' credit for instilling in him.)

Over the years, he came to believe that wondering how you would handle an emergency was a question most uninitiated males had pondered as well, and he was grateful it had been answered for him.

Who Shot J.R.?/ The A-Frame

"The universe is just a big Xerox machine. It simply produces multiple copies of your thoughts."

Neal Donald Walsch

*I*t was around this same time, that the Prince decided to try his hand as a concert promoter. He approached an eccentric, wealthy businessman with his idea, and they struck up a deal. Since the investor owned a phenomenal house up in the Hollywood Hills, they decided the Prince would use that as his office, to keep the overhead down, while they were getting started. Soon the Prince was spending his days floating around in a pool, high above Sunset Boulevard, with a phone glued to his ear just like he'd seen in the movies.

At first, when I started to feel like a caricature, I'd call Daniel and other friends back in Nashville to do a reality check by making fun of myself. After awhile though, I started to forget it was just a role and started thinking it was really who I was; *an egomaniac with an inferiority complex in the making.*

The first show the Prince put together was a big success. He booked Ray Charles as the headliner at the Dorothy Chandler Pavilion (one of L.A.'s classiest venues), and threw a huge birthday party for Ray right after the show. Many celebrities from the music, film, and political arenas all came to pay their respects, even the Mayor.

I thought my career as a concert promoter was off and running. For the second show, I decided to use my Nashville connections and do a huge country extravaganza at the Long Beach Arena. I booked Tanya Tucker, Asleep At The Wheel, Johnny Paycheck, and Dolly Parton's little sister Stella, with the advertisements announcing a special surprise guest as well. It should have been a winner, but it just wasn't meant to be. Ten days before the show, it was announced that on the very same evening as our concert, 'Dallas' would finally reveal the long anticipated answer to, "Who shot J.R.?"

I knew right away that spelled disaster for us and went to my investor saying, "Let's postpone, take a small loss and reschedule." He wouldn't listen. Two days later, J.R. made the cover of Time Magazine and the largest viewing audience in history (many of them country music fan's) stayed home to watch TV that night.

The concert was a bust, but I made the best of the situation and did what made perfect sense at the time, knocked off a bottle of Jack Daniels with our surprise guest artist, Glen Campbell.

I tell this story, because our naive Prince learned a hard lesson that night. He had signed a hand written contract with the investor that he was to be paid a guaranteed amount against the profits, whichever was greater. He quickly found that the investor had no intention of paying him a cent. The Prince was discovering, the hard way, that everyone in this world wasn't honorable, and that living a life of integrity and ethics wasn't high on the priority list in many people's lives.

Unfortunately, the Prince was coming to other conclusions as well, especially about the entertainment world he was immersed in.

First, was that connections (who you know), were much more important than talent.

Second, that with the right PR and packaging, the public would buy anything 'the powers that be' wanted to shovel out. Third, 'the powers that be' were mostly of the male gender.

And fourth, the three things that influenced and, more times than not, determined their decision making were: Drugs, beautiful women, and money.

Since the Prince didn't have the money, he certainly didn't have the drugs, but the one thing he did have in his life, was lots of beautiful women. For better or for worse, it was the hand he'd been dealt, and he would make the best of it (or die trying).

At first, it was an unconscious effort to surround himself with attractive women. It was just a natural offshoot, for someone addicted to love, to always have a good supply of his drug handy, but after a while, it became a conscious effort as well.

Just as an alcoholic needs his John Barleycorn, or a food addict needs their freezer full of Haagen Daas, a love addict needs to always know there is someone available to validate their self worth and meet their needs.

It got to the point where I had at least two dozen current phone numbers on my person at all times; every race, color and creed imaginable. I'd meet them everywhere; shopping, gas stations, church, walking down the street; it didn't matter as long as I got their phone number. When my stash was getting empty, i.e. running out of new women to call, I would go find a club in Beverly Hills, pick out a half dozen of the most attractive women I could find, and start working the room. On a typical night, I would leave with at least three or four new possibilities in my wallet. It was my security blanket, since I never knew when I might need a fix. At first, it occured most often when I was feeling angry, hurt, insecure or resentful, but after awhile, I found myself calling women just because I was bored and feeling lonely. Insecurity seems to play a major role in most love addicts lives, I know it did in mine.

"If you think I'm OK, then I must be."

One Halloween night, I did my usual and got directions to half a dozen parties friends had said to go and check out during the course of the evening. Little did I know that on my list was an invitation to the now infamous A-frame up in the Hollywood Hills. (A sexual arena I later came to find out was known throughout the world.) After picking up my date for the evening, we headed up Sunset Plaza Drive and walked up to the front door of a rather non descript A-frame house (*duh*). There my date and I were greeted by a beautiful, voluptuous, scarlet-haired ingenue' standing there in all her glory (and I do mean all her glory.)

Either the surprised countenance on my face, or the fact that I was drooling down my chin, prompted her to ask, "Is this your first time here?"

Finding it increasingly difficult to keep my eyes from wandering, I managed to stammer out a "yes ma'am", and felt like a real idiot, but she just smiled and introduced herself to my companion. Now that it wasn't quite so obvious to my date (as I hate to be rude), I was able to admire our hostess more thoroughly, and had the thought, "She really is a redhead."

Just as I was chuckling at my own mental process, she brought her attention back to me and chimed in "Let me show you around the place."

Deciding it was a good idea to let her take the lead *(the Prince could be quick on his feet when he had too),* I followed her, as if hypnotized, for a half dozen steps before remembering I'd brought a date. With a chagrined look on my face, I turned back around and found she was standing there laughing at me.

Our unorthodox tour began there in the foyer/living room where a dozen naked people were hanging out talking, as if at any cocktail party. I did my best not to stare, but was finding it difficult to say the least. Next, she showed us into the community room where there must have been at least forty people, all in various group couplings. Here, it seemed appropriate to just pick out your pile and go climb in. Literally.

Maybe it was my mother's Victorian upbringing, I'm not really sure, but I found the entire scene to be rather sad and said to my date, "I must be a prude. I mean I love sex as much as the next guy, probably more, but this is way over the top."

I kid you not, a scene straight out of Sodom and Gomorrah.

Our Irish tour guide next brought us to a room with porno movies showing and couples having sex where other people could watch. My date seemed to like this room the best and even lingered a few seconds to watch one couple, in particular, that were in a position I didn't even know was humanly possible.

By this point, my ADD brain was on overload, from all the stimuli, and my neck was getting sore from having to move the radar. Then, we came to my favorite room. It was the largest room in the house, and had been broken up into dozens of king size bed cubicles, with only hanging sheets as partitions. You couldn't see who was involved or what was happening, but you could hear everything. *

There was a cacophony of moaning, with the occasional climax that would crescendo over the top. It was at the point of hearing three cli-

* Dirty Talk

maxes in a row, that I teased my date, "Would you like to see what's behind curtain number three?"

The fact that this was our first date hadn't even crossed my mind, and I was a little disappointed when she laughed and said, "No thanks, but you go ahead."

Always the perfect gentleman, the Prince refrained from asking their luscious hostess to join him instead, and picked up on his date's cue that she was ready to leave. The Prince figured that, between his compulsive personality and the fact he really did like his date, it was just as well.

As soon as we got outside, I started apologizing immediately. I was sure my date was assuming the entire evening had been a premeditated ruse to get her in the mood. I assured her this was my very first house of ill repute, and had her laughing hysterically, when I thought again and corrected myself,

"Actually it's my second", and then went on to recount the tale of when I was a freshman in high school, on that ill- fated Seascout trip to Jamaica.

Since there was always a high turn over of people in a place like Hollywood, and since the Prince was managing an apartment complex, he was constantly meeting young women coming to Los Angeles seeking fame and fortune. Naturally, they were the ones that got priority when he had vacancies.

Before long, it got to the point unless the applicants were young and gorgeous, they didn't get into the building. However, since young and gorgeous didn't always equate with dependable, the Prince was constantly having to cover his tracks with the owner to explain why certain tenants were always late or didn't pay at all.

Over the years, many of the Princes' male friends had inquired how he did it, what was his secret? How did he manage to always have beautiful women in his life? He usually answered, "I don't do anything you can't do."

The fact is, quite a few of those friends told him if he should write a book on the subject, it would be a guaranteed best seller. The Prince said he

wasn't interested in devoting an entire book to the subject, but:

"A page or two might be fun to do."

I had developed my own take on the differences between men and women and had been advising my male friends for years,

"Think of it this way. You're a rhinoceros and she's a gazelle- two totally different creatures. If you can learn to appreciate the fact that she can leap gracefully through the woods and not try and turn her into a rhino, and hopefully find a girl that appreciates the horn in the middle of your head and understands that at times, you're going to stand around and plod the ground, you'll be a happy man." *(Simplistic, but certainly accurate.)*

If they wanted more scientific data, I would go into detail about the corpus callosum in the brain to support my theories on the differences between men and women; how women can think <u>and</u> feel at the same time, while men tend to think <u>or</u> feel; how women needed to feel cherished to feel loved, while men needed to feel respected. Usually they'd listen politely for a few minutes and then say something to the effect,

"OK, that's all fine and dandy. Just give me a couple lines that you use."

Depending on the kind of day I was having, and how good a friend it was that was asking, I would either sigh and try and change the subject, or would patiently go into my theories.

"First and probably most important of all, I never use lines. Any woman with intuition *(what woman doesn't have that)*, will see through a line in a second."

"Be real."

"It's always been my experience that your basic "hi" or "hello", in a natural tone of voice, combined with a genuine smile, will get a far better response than anything else."

"Now, if you're a male of the species, you spend the majority of your life in the left hemisphere of your brain, so you're probably thinking, 'What does he mean by natural tone of voice?'"

"Don't read into it. By natural, I mean don't try and sound suave and sophisticated like Cary Grant, just sound friendly. It's amazing the women you can meet with those three little words, 'how are you?', if they're said with sincerity."

"Next, don't go into some pre-planned monologue. Be spontaneous. Talk about whatever is going on there in the moment, such as 'How's the food here?' or, 'Can I get the door for you?', or 'You'd look good in that.' *(Not to be said in the produce section by the way.)*"

"What do you recommend?"

"What's that book you're reading?"

"Can I offer you my seat?"

"What kind of razor do you use?" *(Just a joke. You know trying to stay politically correct in this day and age is a full time job, even for a wizard)*

"Meeting women is really a lot easier than you think, and it all starts with hi! As in so many other things, I've found honesty is the best policy."

"If you see someone that just knocks your socks off, and you've been standing around at a newsstand pretending to be interested in architecture from the Neolithic period, once you catch yourself, go tell her! That kind of honesty can be incredibly funny and disarming at the same time. If you just tell her the truth, that you'd have kicked yourself all the way home if you didn't at least go and say hello, she'll surely think it flattering and even charming, if you're lucky."

"Besides, what's the worse case scenario? She'll say, 'I'm flattered but I already have a boyfriend.'"

"The nice thing about telling the truth, is you don't have to try and remember what story you told to who. Also, if you're frank from the beginning, odds are you can remain friends, no matter what happens."

"Don't get discouraged. If you smile and say a genuine hello to ten women in the course of an evening, half of them will say hello back and leave an opening for a follow up." *(Unless you live in LA of course, where you need to somehow let them think you drive an expensive car. Maybe find some-*

thing with the BMW or Mercedes logo on it. A key ring perhaps, belt buckle,
definitely not, unless you're hanging out at 'Denim and Diamonds').

"Be careful when you're out and about. There are a lot of women who are already spoken for, or worse yet, married, who will flirt with you half the night because they're unhappy with their present situation, or just because it's a fix and they can't help themselves. There is a trick to finding out quickly if they're already involved besides looking for a wedding band or being a student of body language. It's not foolproof; they could certainly lie, but most of the time it works. Somewhere in the first few minutes, after you've let them know you're attracted to them, say something to the effect of, "Shoot (ah-shucks works if you're in the South), you're probably already married and have three kids." At that point they will either assure you they're not or will wave a caution flag such as,

"Well...I have been seeing this guy for eleven years, but it's not serious."

"Caution flags usually begin with well, sort of, not sure, (n-o-o-o-t really drawn out, by the way, usually means really.")

"My advice, if there's any hint of unavailability, believe them! There are an awful lot of available women out there without stepping on some other guys toes and getting involved with someone who is out of integrity anyway. Once you know where you stand and what the possibilities are, you very well might choose to hang out and talk to her for the entire party, but at least you now have the information so you can make a choice." *(You know, maybe I will write an entire book on the subject, this is fun.)*

There was one observation I made which could easily be misconstrued, so I'm going to great lengths to offer it in the spirit of fun and innocence in which it is intended.

For all the men reading this, at least those of you that prefer the company of the opposite sex *(that certainly eliminates half the men of this century),* and you'd like to see the women that come to your home take off their clothes quicker than they have been, then this story is for you.

I discovered it while managing the building in Hollywood. An elderly actress, who had lived in the building for over twenty years, passed away and her family (who lived out of state), called and said they needed certain items and papers, but anything else I found while cleaning out her apartment, I was welcome to keep.

It turned out to be a literal gold mine, though I had to wade through a pig-sty to find it. *(A microcosm of life when you think about it.)*

There were at least two feet of newspapers piled (some as much as twelve years old), and the filth throughout the entire apartment was appalling, until I came to one huge closet. Inside, was one of the most beautiful wardrobes of women's clothes, from the twenties and thirties, I had ever seen.

It seems the old lady had been a high fashion model/actress back in the golden age, and her wardrobe was the one thing she still took pride in. There must have been at least thirty hats alone, all in mint shape, still in their original boxes. The same with the shoes, along with dozens of dresses, feather boas, sweaters, with mink around the cuffs and collars, and the most phenomenal collection of lingerie I'd ever seen.

I took all the clothes back to my apartment and found out, quite by accident, that if I left them out, almost every woman that saw them within minutes was taking hers off. I kid you not. Often they'd call or go get their girlfriends and I would just sit back and watch the fashion show create itself. Usually, they'd start off taking outfits to the bedroom or bathroom for privacy, but after awhile, that would become too much bother, and before long, it felt like being at a photo shoot for Victoria's Secret. Of course, then they all want your opinion on how it looks. After awhile, I'd seen some pretty good combinations, so they'd usually try out my suggestions,

"Oh, I think that blouse over there might look better with the skirt you've got on." *Of course being a Southern gentleman, he'd offer to pull up the occasional zipper or two. That was the least he could do.*

Girls, Girls, Girls

"Imagination is more important than knowledge."

Albert Einstein

*O*ne evening, I got a call from a friend flying in from Canada for a business meeting. He was a well-known television producer, with a number of credits under his belt, and was meeting with a couple of other TV executives about a new series. He asked me if I'd like to bring a date and come join them for dinner later, and if possible, set him up with a blind date as well. I had nothing else planned that evening, so I said, "Sure, we'll meet you downstairs at Carlos and Charlie's", (the current hot spot on the strip that had a dinner club downstairs and a dance club upstairs.)

Feeling a bit grandiose that night, I decided to make a statement and do 'the peacock strut'. I invited four of the most stunning women I knew to join us; making a conscious effort to find an exotic blend. First, there was Monica from Sweden, a blond version of Nicole Kidman, who used her native lilt to make men pray she'd say 'ya' to everything they suggested. Next, I invited Amber, who looked like the scantily clad native girl on the cover of the travel magazines meant to allure you with her perfect bronze body, jet black hair and intense green eyes.

Once I knew they were coming, I had both ends of the spectrum covered; Nordic and Polynesian. I decided next, to find someone with alabaster skin, as I had recently started to appreciate the beauty in a woman whose skin had never seen the sun. That was Melanie. She was a head turner, if there ever was one. Problem was, she knew it. She had always gotten by on her looks and was the proverbial 'golddigger' Hollywood so aptly portrays. I normally didn't like to be around people like that, and actually felt sorry for her, but she had the whitest skin I had ever seen, and for the sake of art...I figured I could put up with her for one night. Lastly, I invited Tina as my date. We'd been going out awhile, and I really liked her; an All-

American smart-bomb, who lived a few doors down from the Reagans. She exuded sex appeal, and had a lot of fun in the process. Built like Marilyn Monroe, she had a brain like a nuclear physicist, a laugh that was contagious, and an authenticity that would intimidate most men. I also liked the fact that she was a trained classical pianist. She was perfect.

The Prince had a highly developed gift of discernment, and was able to attract women that were not only physically breathtaking, but had that angelic sparkle in their eyes as well.

Our sociably late arrival, had just the desired effect I was after; every eye, both male and female, followed us in, as we made our entrance. I noticed more than a few mouths' agape, which isn't easy in a jaded town like Hollywood.

After dinner, we went upstairs to the discotheque for drinks. That night, one of the Saudi Arabian royal family and his entourage were there as well. On three separate occasions, during the course of the evening, one of the Saudi Arabian's lieutenants had asked all but one of the women I had invited to come and join his party. They were sitting in the section of the club reserved for VIP's. On each occasion, he had heard a version of,

"No thank you, I'm with . . . ," and they would point to me. Well, this piqued the Arabian's interest and he asked Tina, "Who is this guy with the three most beautiful women in the place, and how does he command such allegiance?"

Finally, his curiosity got the best of him and he asked her for an introduction. After we exchanged pleasantries, the lieutenant asked me if I'd like to meet his boss.

At this point, I had no idea he was talking about Prince Mohammed Ali Ben Saad (the oldest son, and therefore most powerful of the Saudi Arabian Princes at the time). When we met, I liked him immediately. He had a genuine laugh and carried himself with a certain amount of humility (not a common characteristic among most royal family members). Not only that, his manners were impeccable, and he seemed to be a true gentleman. *(Remember our Prince is originally from the South and appreciat-*

ed such things.)

During the evening, Mohammed asked the Prince to join him the following night for dinner at 'Ma Maison' (one of the premier Beverly Hills 'see and be seen' restaurants). * The Prince responded with his usual, "sure, why not."

The next evening, I invited two of the women that had caught the eye of Mohammed from the evening before, and we were all treated to an incredible four-hour, eleven course meal in the private dining room at 'Ma Maison'. It reminded me of the formal dining room that had been off limits at my grandparents house in Mississippi. It had an antique table made of ebony, sitting upon an ancient looking oriental rug, with Victorian chairs featuring exquisitely designed patterns woven into the tapestry of each backrest. The tablecloth and accompanying napkins were made of white Madiera linen, setting off the sterling silver utensils and candelabras. Waterford crystal sparkled both from the table, as well as above us, in the chandelier which hung directly over the ivory eperne. The paintings on the walls were obviously originals that would have made for a good down payment on a beach-front home in Santa Barbara, or a serious gesture as a non-refundable deposit on a major league baseball franchise. With eight of us taking pleasure in spirits, we must have consumed six bottles of Dom Perignon in the course of the evening, and at the end of our gastronomical excursion, Mohammed asked me, "How would you like to come join me in Spain, next month, for a holiday?" My growing cynicism was learning to take it all with a grain of salt, so I said, "Sure, send me the tickets," thinking it was the alcohol doing the inviting, but I'd at least humor the guy (after all, he was paying for dinner.)

Lo and behold, a couple weeks later, I got a call from Mohammed, and the next day, three first class round trip tickets to Marbella, Spain were hand-delivered. Not only that, enclosed was a couple thousand dollars traveling money, to tide us over till we got there. I was in shock, as were the girls I invited, but none of us had ever been to Spain and we did have round trip tickets, so, what the hell, it sounded like the makings for a good adventure.

I was grateful it didn't 'rain on the plane when we landed in Spain'

* Hills of Beverly

(you get the idea), but it wouldn't have mattered anyway, as we were met on the tarmac by our own limousine. The driver and limo were to be at our disposal for the next month, and the driver informed me that Mohammed was in meetings and wouldn't be able to meet us until dinner.

"Here's some money to take the girls shopping, he'll see you later," and he handed me a thick envelope.

I waited until we got in the limo before counting the money. Both the girls and myself were dumbstruck, as there was fifteen thousand dollars in my hand. Rather than dole it out piecemeal, I figured it was easier just to split it three ways and let them do whatever they pleased. It was obviously a good move, as they both responded by giving me a big smooch.

Our typical day consisted of shopping, going out on one of the yachts or exploring the countryside. I found it interesting that once it became known I had access to 'His Royal Highness', the implications were far reaching, and I started getting offers and gifts from people that wanted an introduction. One real estate agent even offered me a half million dollars finders fee if Mohammed bought a piece of property he had for sale.

In the evenings, we would go out for fine dining, dancing and then the casino. It was typical to spend five grand for dinner and champagne alone. If there were eight of us dining, there would be at least ten waiters surrounding the table. After taking a sip of champagne, I found it nearly impossible to get my glass back down to the table before it would be refilled. Believe me, I attempted it more than once.

I'd never seen anything like it. We stayed at the Puento Romano Hotel in Puerto Banus, right on the Mediterranean Sea. (When I finally get married, that's where I want to bring my love for our honeymoon.)

During the next month, Mohammed and the Prince became such good friends that Mohammed asked the Prince if he'd like to work for him on a regular basis whenever he was stateside. The Prince wasn't sure exactly what this entailed, but he assumed it would be a lot like what he had done for 'His Royal Highness', back in Nashville, a few years back. He answered with what was becoming his new mantra,

"Sure, why not."

Working for Khalid was a privilege. I was living out a fantasy life most people would find hard to even imagine, let alone experience. I was in charge of ordering limousines, Lear jets, making reservations, and, of course, always making sure Khalid was surrounded by beautiful interesting people, both male and female. *The Prince mentioned his new job to 'The Captain', at some point, who responded with,*

"You mean you're pimping for the sheik." *Oh well.*

Khalid loved to entertain, and was a class act, so whenever he wanted to throw a dinner party, I was comfortable inviting both my male and female friends to come share in the bounty. Since most of his friends were male, I found I usually needed to invite, proportionately, more women to keep the numbers somewhat equal. *(Just like any good host throwing a party.)*

Usually, it was only for fifteen to twenty people, but I orchestrated a couple sit-down dinners for over seventy-five people and found I thoroughly enjoyed the challenges that entailed; the right amount of food, the seating arrangement, knowing who drank what and ordering specialty items such as Cuban cigars or rare wines, and, of course, making separate arrangements for Mohammed's dates and/or his relatives that might be in town.

I was good at my job and had no lack of confidence in my abilities. I knew the one thing money couldn't buy was the love of a good quality woman, and that was basically what every heterosexual man wanted to find. Money could buy you trophies and sex partners, but not a woman whose beauty began deep inside and had depth of soul as well. That kind of woman, inspired a man to be his best and could light up a room just by walking in.

The Prince knew that, for whatever reason, he seemed to attract women like that. They trusted him. Probably, because they saw not only a Southern gentleman with a desire to live honorably, but sensed his desire to protect women, children, and animals. They also trusted him, because as he put it, "I'm trustworthy."

I wouldn't hesitate to tell Mohammed or any of his brothers to go change their socks or outfits, if I thought they looked inappropriate for something we were doing together. In many ways, I think they liked my insubordinate attitude, as they were so used to everyone kissing their derrieres.

One time, I organized a weekend excursion to Las Vegas for one of Mohammed's younger brothers who was visiting. I didn't really care for this particular brother, but was doing a favor for Mohammed. We took the Lear jet down and were staying at Caesar's Palace. After taking in a couple shows, early that evening, we ended up at the no limit baccarat table around two a.m. Part of me thought of Las Vegas as the modern day cities of Sodom and Gomorrah; hedonistic, amoral and one of the biggest wastes of resources and energy I had ever seen. But, my ADD brain loved it. The action, the toots, the whistles, the clinking of glasses, gorgeous women everywhere and, of course, being treated like a celebrity by Caesars' because I was there with one of their high-rollers. In the next five hours, I watched this spoiled, obnoxious heir win $975,000.

That, in itself, wasn't so unusual. What made it memorable for me, was that I had climbed up and witnessed the entire spree from the pit bosses' chair, high above the action. Only later, was I informed that my sitting there had been a major 'faux-pas' and breach in casino etiquette, but since I was with one of the royal family, the casino had chosen to overlook my indiscretion.

It's funny, but I became bored rather quickly, watching him feed his money habit at the gaming tables, and spent most of that evening feeding my own habit (watching all the women come and go).

It's noteworthy to mention, that at the end of the evening, Mohammed's brother gave both of the women the Prince had invited a couple of $10,000 chips, but didn't give the Prince a dime. Even though he was a billionaire, with all the power that entails, he was still jealous of the Prince.

He was immersed in a world of hedonism that is hard to even fathom. When money is no object, it's amazing the things people will do. Drugs, sex, and rock and roll; wine, women and song; full speed till the wheels fell off. During this time, the Prince found himself partying constantly with the rich and famous of the entertainment industry and was getting more and more ensnared by the trappings, as well as intoxicated with the power.

At first, it was fun for the Prince, running around with the royal family or the Khashogis, the John Travolta's, and Robin Williams of the world. It was all an adventure. Of all the celebrities he met and partied with, he said,

"Robin Williams was, without a doubt, the most genuine and authentic; the one I'd have been most inclined to introduce to my sister."

One evening, after partying all night at the Bel Air Hotel with an arms dealer, who was supposed to be the richest man in the world, I was doing my best to drive half a dozen women home safely, when I was stopped about 5 a.m. on Sunset Boulevard, for speeding. I immediately thought, "Oh no". The first thing the officer said, after he leaned in the driver's window and got an eyeful was, "You got any alcohol in the car?"

Knowing I was loaded, I figured my best bet was to be honest and hope the officer had a sense of humor. "No sir, it's all in me," I blurted out.

It worked. When everyone stopped laughing, the officer leaned back in the window to say, "That's one of the best answers I've ever been given. I see you've got some precious cargo in there. Go on, get out of here, but take it easy."

Though he seemed to be leading an enchanted life, the Prince was descending deeper and deeper into the gratifications of the material world. He had begun to lose sight of the spiritual side of life he had been blessed with through his first mentor Jim. Though he thought he could stay above it all, there was a certain allure about royalty, and an obvious allure of anyone worth billions of dollars, that could draw just about anyone in, regardless of spiritual, moral, and ethical upbringing.

The Prince was no exception. Starting with his father, he was still trying to impress everyone with what he had, instead of being who he was.

Singing For Heaven

"For what shall it profit a man, if he gains the whole world, and loses his own soul?"

Mark VIII, 36

*T*he Prince managed to keep his obsessive nature under control for a long time, but the day finally arrived, when the Prince could no longer resist the peer pressure. His desire to fit in and be 'a part of', got the best of him once again. It happened at the home of one of the most famous actors of the time; someone the Prince had gone to the cinema to see for years. They had been introduced through a mutual friend, at a party, and hit it off immediately. Later that same evening, the actor had asked the Prince if he wanted to bring his date and come back to his home in Bel Air to continue partying. The Prince was already drunk, so when the invitation to smoke some cocaine (freebase) came later, the Prince didn't have the will power to say no. Rationalizing to himself he said, "Ah, what the hell, I'll only do it this once." (Knowing full well he'd never done anything only once in his life.) Still, this was back when cocaine was considered to be non-habit forming, and was being placed on coffee tables at every party in Hollywood.

Around three a.m., we followed him to a gorgeous condominium, behind security gates, in Bel Air, where the guard just waved us through as if watching a repeat. We hadn't been there ten minutes, when our host called me back to his bedroom and handed me a potbellied glass pipe with a piece of dried-looking spackling in its bowl. Then, while holding on to his six inch tall, all-American looking red and white torch with a blue flame shooting out the end, tells me, "Take a hit."

Well, it was an instant love affair between me and cocaine. * Up until then, I had only smoked it by inhaling it through a straw as the heated oil ran down a piece of tin foil (aka 'chasing the dragon'.) Still, attracted more to the ritual than the drug itself, I knew with total certainty, and

* Habit Forming...Chameleon CD #14

my addictive personality, if I ever smoked it in a freebase pipe where I got a real lung full, I'd be in trouble. Sure enough, twenty seconds after it found my bloodstream, I was addicted. Maybe not physiologically, but certainly psychologically. Fifteen minutes later, I wanted to call my mom to tell her how much I loved her, and of course to tell her whose house I was calling from, but I waited till the next morning.

'See who I know, I must be OK.' (Still seeking his parents approval.)

That was all she wrote. The same type of thinking like my first marijuana experience back in Cuba kicked in (anything that can make forty people laugh hysterically, etc.) Of course, 'only once' turned into three straight days, with no sleep, watching a man who was formerly a brilliant actor turn into a pitiful creature afraid to be alone.

I soon discovered cocaine had the exact opposite affect on me than it had on most people. Rather than want to party, I would get mellow and want to concentrate exclusively on my music and writing. Years later, I found out I was simply self medicating my Attention Deficit Disorder, since cocaine (like the pursuit of women), could connect the synapses in my brain, so I was able to focus for the first time in my life. (Much the way ritalin has the opposite effect on a child with A.D.D.).

I became like a mad scientist with my weights and measures and vials and torches. I became expert at taking powdered cocaine back to it's pure form (an oil base). After cooking it up, I would take the ball of oil, which had hardened like a marble, and throw it up against the wall just to show how pure it was. Pretty soon, I had other users bringing me their powder and turning me on, just so I would cook up their drugs for them. In my arrogance, I would guarantee to knock them off their feet, as if I were doing them a favor. Before long, I had earned the nickname 'The Master Blaster'.

In short order, I was staying up around the clock, writing music and recording it on a little 4-track Teac tape recorder I had set up in the bedroom; two, then three, then four days at a time. After awhile, the goal became to not run out of drugs so I wouldn't have to go to sleep. That was the worst feeling of all, to lay in bed tossing and turning futilely trying to turn off my brain, while every iota of my physical being was craving the endorphins.

Before long, I had put mattresses up against both the windows in my bedroom so no sunlight could get in. I began to lose my sense of reality. One night, around three a.m., in the middle of recording, a gun battle erupted between the police and a couple drug dealers from the building across the street. Intermittent gun shots were par for the course in our neighborhood, but once I heard the additional sound of automatic weapons, with their short staccato bursts, and the helicopters thumping close overhead, I shoved aside the mattress, opened up the bedroom window, stuck a microphone out, and used the sound of the battle as the background for the song I was working on.

Because of the constant darkness, the Prince nicknamed the bedroom studio 'The Dungeon'. Apropos, because of the depths to which he was about to sink, few people have ever been there and lived to tell the story.

Almost all my music, up until then, had been about ideal love, God, rainbows, political statements or songs with humor, meant to make you smile. I had never explored the dark side of my nature, or as Robert Bly refers to it in 'Iron John', my wild man. I think I was really afraid to look at myself, for fear of what I might find. *(Again, rather typical of an uninitiated male.)* I had always been able to conquer my addictions on my own, and felt there was nothing I couldn't accomplish, using my own will power. That all changed, once I started smoking cocaine. Though I managed to control it for a while, before long, it had taken over my life. *Years later, when the Prince saw the movie 'Leaving Las Vegas', it was all he could do to stay in his seat, as it mirrored his own obsessive nature and self imposed exile, only too accurately.*

One evening, I was in Beverly Hills partying with the same brother of Mohammed I had witnessed win the million dollars in Las Vegas. We were staying at the Hilton and were on our fourth day of a nonstop binge. Though we had separate rooms, we were partying in 'His Royal

Highnesses' suite, when one of the women I had invited, had a seizure. She went into convulsions for well over a minute. We were so out of it, we all thought she was putting us on, and laughed at her supposed theatrics, until someone noticed the foam coming out of her mouth and cracked the old joke; "How do you get rid of hoof and mouth disease? You wipe the foam from around your lips."

We were all laughing, before we realized it was no joke, and her body went limp. I ran over, but couldn't find her heartbeat, and frantically yelled out, "Someone call the paramedics!"

I felt awful. I couldn't believe we had all been standing there laughing while she could have died before our eyes.

'His Royal Highness', who had witnessed the entire incident, refused to let anyone use the phone, and instead insisted, "Drag her body down the hall to your room before calling for help; I can't be involved in this."

That moment was a rude awakening for me. First, I was amazed at the callousness and lack of concern for human life he had just exhibited. Secondly, I couldn't believe, that rather than call immediately for help like I knew I should, I dragged her body down the hallway, like I had been told. I felt ashamed of not standing up to him. Lastly, and most frightening of all, after the girl 'came to' a few moments later (thank God), she insisted on continuing to get high and would not take no for an answer, even though it could have easily killed her. Not only that, but when I couldn't talk her out of it, I joined her.

When we'd first met, she was a talented, beautiful woman on her way to creating a rewarding life for herself, and those around her. I saw the drugs turn her into a hateful, greedy, selfish and pitiful excuse for a human being. That night, I realized it was doing the same to me!

The power of cocaine, and what it could do to a person, was unbelievable. Talk about cunning, baffling and powerful!

One of the few times I did manage to get out and attempt a normal activity, was the day my friend, Ernie, convinced me to buy a motorcycle and come out cruising with him and a couple of his buddies. I drove like a wild man. Ernie later said, "It was as if you had a death wish, flying around corners and doing all kinds of crazy stunts. It was only a matter of when, not if, you were gonna wipeout."

Sure enough, five hours after I'd bought the bike, I was flying sixty down Hollywood Boulevard, two blocks from Laurel Canyon, when a car pulled out, did a left hand turn in front of me, and I slammed into it. Luckily, I hit the hood and was thrown right over the car. I flew a good 70 feet through the air, and crashed down on the front lawn of one of the houses along the boulevard.

As soon as I hit the ground, I left my body. There was a loud whirling sound all around me, as if I'd been sucked into a wind tunnel; uncomfortable in its magnitude, as I seemed to be speeding through total darkness at a great velocity. It was the strangest phenomenon, to feel myself going farther and farther away. All of a sudden, I was able to look back and see dozens of people running up and milling around my body. At first, I curiously watched what they were doing, but soon lost interest, as I knew what had happened and was glad to be out of there. By this time, an intense feeling of joy had come over me, as well as a peace and contentment, I had never known before. It's hard to put into dimensional language, as what I experienced next was way beyond anything I'd ever imagined, let alone experienced. All of a sudden, I heard and felt the most beautiful voice say, "You're welcome to stay, but your work isn't completed yet." *

Having no fear of death, I remember thinking at the time, "No way am I going back, it was an accident. I got here fair and square."

The being on the other end of the voice was very gentle with me and didn't say anything else or try and talk me out of it; instead, just let me think for a time about what they had said.

It was one of the most difficult decisions I ever had to make. I could see the spiral leading back to my body, like some etheric tornado, and I knew I could easily let it go if I chose to stay, but I also knew, without a doubt, that both the voice and the contentment would be waiting for

* Pied Piper...Awakening Imaginations CD #2

me when I returned. Besides, I'd always been raised to finish what I started, and I was curious as to what this work was I hadn't completed. *(This
one goes way beyond the call of the Protestant work ethic.) I just wish I could
impart that knowledge to some of the people I meet, especially the elderly, that
are so afraid of what's coming. With me, it's not a question of believing that life
after death is true, but knowing it as a fact. We aren't physical beings having a
spiritual experience, but spiritual beings having a physical experience.*

As soon as I made the decision to stay, I jolted immediately back
into my body and heard a human voice saying, "It's OK, you can come
back now."

Just then, I opened my eyes, and there kneeling over me was a mid-
dle-aged woman with her hands placed around my head. There were a
dozen other witnesses in the background, but she was the only one close
enough to hear me. I told her what had just happened, after I left my body,
and she just smiled at me as if she already knew.

It was the strangest thing. I got up and, other than a sprained wrist,
I didn't have a single scratch. I found out later, she was a psychic healer and
had been driving the car directly behind me and had witnessed the entire
accident. Though we exchanged numbers, I unfortunately lost track of her,
so if you happen to be reading this book . . . call me!

*Unfortunately, the accident barely slowed him down, and other than
relating the out-of-body experience to Ernie and Endre (his two best friends
that both lived in the apartment complex), the Prince quickly forgot about it
and returned to 'the dungeon'.*

It was as if my body had its own built-in safety features, passing out
every seventh day or so, regardless of the amount or how pure the cocaine
that I was putting into my brain. Somewhere between twelve and eighteen
hours later, I would become conscious again, often surrounded by shards
of glass from the pipe that had fallen out of my hands when I passed out.

*Ernie and Endre both recollect having found the Prince in this condi-
tion on numerous occasions. Instinctively knowing that he was reaching a crit-
ical mass, the Prince tried to get help, and flew to North Carolina to see his*

mentor, Jim Goure.

It had gotten so bad, my body had to have cocaine in it at all times, or it would literally pass out on me. Since I needed the cocaine to function at all, I took it with me to LAX International Airport to try and smuggle it on the plane. Fortunately, I got extremely paranoid once in the airport, found a men's lavatory, smoked all I had with me, in the stall, and then, afraid someone was waiting outside to bust me, smashed the pipe into the commode and flushed it. With all that racket, it was no wonder when I stepped triumphantly from the stall, thinking I'd fooled 'them', I encountered half a dozen men eye-balling me, suspiciously, like I was from a different planet. *(The truth be told, by that point, he was.)* Afraid one of them might alert airport security about my odd behavior, I scurried off in the direction of my gate, casting furtive glances every few seconds behind me to make sure I wasn't being tailed.

My plan was to head to Black Mountain, by way of the farm, thinking mom's home cooking, and sitting by the creek, watching it flow, might help. It was almost impossible to hide the fact that I was strung out, with my dead-eyes floating in their sockets like a hooked blowfish being pulled out of the water. The fact was, I was forty pounds underweight, looking like a survivor from a Nazi death camp.

I avoided my parents, as much as possible, since my feelings of being a failure were especially magnified, when reflected in my dad's gaze. I felt pathetic and unlovable; the spitting image of a loser. I could tell my dad knew what was going on, but to his credit, he didn't say a word, just surface politeness. I thought at the time, he probably figured I would just kill myself in short order and he'd be rid of me anyway, so there was no need to rub it in.

After a few interminable days, the Prince made as gracious an exit as possible, under the circumstances, and upon arriving in Black Mountain, drove straight up to see Jim.

I walked into The Light Center and Jim took one look at me and almost wept. I'll never forget the look of sadness that crossed over his face, but what I remember most of all, was the disappointment. That was all it took. I would have done anything to erase or ease the obvious pain I had caused him. He immediately closed his eyes, so I couldn't see his anguish, and did a reading to see how much damage had been done.

He told me that the entire side of my head had been blown wide open, and that my auric field was demolished. "You have less than a month to live at the rate you're going."

It was uncanny, the things he could see just by looking at me. I remember once, years earlier, I'd managed to stay away from marijuana for almost three weeks. Upon arriving at the Light Center, for the first time in a year or so, Jim had taken one look at me and said "I see you haven't smoked any grass in nineteen days."

I sat down and figured it out, and he was exactly right. Soon after that, I stopped smoking grass for good, once he told me the euphoria I sensed, and the crackling noises I heard while holding my breath, were in reality the feelings and sounds of brain cells dying.

After he told me what my life expectancy was, he then got on the phone and called a healer he wanted me to see. The next day, a man I had never met, came to Jim's house and set up a massage table, right in the middle of the living room. I thought that a bit unusual, as massages are usually given in private, but I wasn't gonna argue and started to take off my shirt. The healer stopped me right there and said "This will only take a minute, keep your clothes on, take off your shoes and lay face down on the table."

That seemed a bit odd, but I did as I was told. The healer proceeded to stab his finger into one pressure point on my foot and held it for approximately a minute and a half. I literally writhed in agony, thinking what a sadistic SOB the guy was, but he wouldn't let go or lighten up. Once he finally did, he said, "Relax for a second and then we'll do the other foot."

"Thanks, I can't wait," I managed with a sardonic smile. He just grinned and said, "You think that was uncomfortable, you ain't seen nothing yet."

After he repeated the torture on my opposite foot, with even more resultant contortions on my part, he told me with suitable aplomb, "One hour and fifteen minutes from now, you need to be somewhere you don't have to leave for a few hours. It should have both a toilet and thick walls."

I thought that was a bit ominous, but couldn't get any more information out of him other than I was supposed to come back the next day.

Still not cognizant of how much damage I had done to myself and the terrible shape I was in, I was still taking it all rather lightly, as if all I needed was a couple weekends and a two day follow-up to recover. As usual, I had met a girl my first night in town and made a date. Since she lived in Asheville, I figured I'd better head that way just in case this guy wasn't really a quack.

Big mistake.

By the time seventy-five minutes had passed, I was still a few miles from her place. That's when the first wave of nausea overcame me. I managed to stop the car, open the door and fall out onto some innocent bystander's front yard, while doubled over in anguish. My body then went into convulsions, and I began throwing up this black tar-like substance in between screams of agony. I wanted to die, just so the horrific pain would stop. After a few moments it subsided enough so I could gather what remaining dignity I had left and got back in the car. *(Somehow I fail to see any dignity left in a man whose shirt is covered in putrid smelling bile after performing a scene from 'The Exorcist' on some poor unsuspecting onlooker's front yard. Call me cold and uncaring, but I don't.)*

Within a minute, I felt it coming on again, but did manage to get to my date's house before blowing more strands of licorice. She wasn't home yet, but thank God she had left me the key. *(I'm sure he was a pleasing sight when she got home that evening, but we're not even gonna go there.)*

It lasted for hours; wave after wave of nausea, followed by the most foul smelling bile; a brief respite, and it would all start again. *(Sorry I can't resist: can you imagine what the poor girls' diary must have said, 'Dear diary, I had the most delightful evening last night...')*

I was exhausted, and when reminded by Florence Nightingale, later that night, that I was supposed to go back for another treatment in twelve hours, I managed to croak out one of Daniel's favorite lines, "I'd like to, I mean, I'd really like to. Save my place, I'll be right back."

Not wanting to disappoint Jim, more than anything else, I was able to handle five days of the prescribed seven day treatment, and each day I would throw up less and less poison. To the angel in Asheville, who stuck by me the entire time, "I want to thank you for your kindness and patience. You deserve your own chapter". To the healer who worked on me so many years ago, "Thanks, you saved my life. I only wish I remembered your name, as I've known many people, since then, I could have sent your way."

The Prince had been granted yet one more reprieve. You'd think with all the messages from the universe, and the angels that always seemed to pop up at the right time, that he'd finally get it. Like the voice had said, "Your work is not complete." But the Prince hadn't surrendered completely, as yet, and still had one plan left, forgetting the old expression, "If you want to make God laugh, tell him your plans."

I'm Going To Die A Drug Addict

"Be not forgetful to entertain strangers: for thereby some have entertained angels unawares."

Hebrews, XIII, 2

*O*nce back in Los Angeles, the Prince stayed clean and sober, on his own, for almost seven months. Unfortunately, without some kind of support system in place, it was only a matter of time, before the inevitable emotional upheaval came along that he couldn't resist.

I had invested a lot of money restoring a classic Mercedes coupe, but hadn't insured it as yet. Having spent months fixing it up, the second day, after finally getting it back, I left the engine sitting in the middle of the road, after trying unsuccessfully to straddle a median beneath an overpass. I was so upset with myself that later that day, when someone offered me my 'drug of choice', I couldn't just say no.

As most addicts will do, I swore to myself it would only be that once, and meant it at the time. But soon, it became once a week, then once a day, and then nonstop again, until it was worse than it had been before.

'The dungeon', where I moved my studio and basically lived my last year of using, was in the basement of the building I managed. It was thirty feet long and six feet wide, with water pipes running the length of the ceiling. Every four feet, there was a light socket where I put each of the seven colors of the rainbow, starting with a red bulb at the front door. All the walls were covered with African print sheets, to hide the drab beige cinderblocks, and there were a few remnants of stray used carpet strewn over the cement landing. A floor fan provided the only ventilation in my self-imposed prison. Since it took a blue flame to melt the cocaine, it was necessary to block the air flow, when lighting the torch. For that purpose, I had jerry-rigged a square plastic cushion, using a coat hanger with a cord attached, that I would throw over the water pipe so I could lower it down in front of the fan. As soon as I had inhaled the cocaine, I would pull on the cord, which removed the pillow and allowed the air to circulate. Then I'd pull on another cord which turned off all the lights, grab my guitar, push record on the tape recorder, close my eyes and start playing. Since running out of drugs, and thereby, having to try and go to sleep were the two things that were avoided at all costs, and since my body could go seven to eight days in a row without slumber, my norm was to indulge, until I passed out.

It had gotten to the point, where I was literally recording twenty-four hours a day, and had various rituals I would do. Inspiration from one hit on the pipe could last for ten minutes or two hours. Sometimes, I would work days on the same song, or I might start ten songs in one day. After awhile, I started to notice a pattern.

The first day or so on a binge, I would feel wired, and it showed in the music that came out, as it was even more eclectic than usual. Days three, four, and five were usually the most creative. Between fasting from food, and triggering large amounts of endorphins in my brain, many of the songs and rhythms that came through, have proven the test of time. Usually by days six and seven I would start getting spacey and the music would become less lyrical and more Pink Floydish. Years later, when listening back to the tapes, I could usually tell on which day a song had been written.

By now, I had dropped from one hundred and eighty pounds down to one hundred and ten, and was little more than a walking skeleton. Personally, I thought I was looking pretty good, with that gaunt Mick Jagger just-this-side-of-death-pallor, but I knew I had become a drug addict and was dying. Since I'd tried to stop before and couldn't, this time, I just accepted it as my fate. There towards the end, my friends could tell it wasn't a matter of if my addiction would kill me, but only when.

I told both Ernie and Endre, the only two males that were ever allowed to visit me in 'the dungeon', "I'm a drug addict. I'm going to die a drug addict."

They had tried to reason with me, threaten me, anything they could to help me kick the habit, but they both knew it was a lost cause. No human power could have relieved my obsession, at this point. Towards the end, all they could do was bring me food, so at least I wouldn't starve to death. One time, when I was upstairs in my apartment, Ernie had climbed over the bars and through my kitchen window, after seeing candles burning down, knowing I was inside but probably passed out.

Years later, he reminded me, "I could shake you violently, scream in your ear, I even doused you in cold water, but you were out cold. Your body was there, but there was nobody home."

Finally, Ernie couldn't be around anymore, and moved out of the building. "I just can't watch you die like this," he said. *

Knowing my time was drawing near, I called Endre, the only real friend I had left, and asked him, "Will you see to it that my music gets out to the world after I'm gone? At least I'll have something to show for my life, something I can leave behind."

He cut me off. "Quit talking like that. You'll do it yourself."

I replied, "I don't think so, my body is about to give out on me and I'd hate to think I died in vain." *(Van Gogh, can you hear?)*

Endre had known the Prince long enough to know he was deadly serious, and since he prided himself on being a man of integrity, he reluctantly granted the dying Prince his last wish. The Prince pulled the trigger one more time, in his game of Russian Roulette, this time with a smile on his face.

Here he was, virtually on the threshold of death, and he still wanted to make a contribution. (Though I don't agree that the end justifies the means, I do find that an admirable quality.)

These lyrics came through the last couple days the Prince was using.

Please please somebody please, won't you lend me a hand.
I've been down so down, yeah, the third time's coming round,
(It's) Three strikes you're out I understand.
It doesn't really scare me,
Just didn't think he'd be here this soon.

* Goodbye Blues

I see my angels coming now, I hope they like this tune.
>Don't believe he's knocking, he's standing at my door,
>Unless this S.O.S. is heard, my number's up for sure
>and I'll be singing for heaven,
>I'll be singing.
>Singing for heaven, yes I'm singing.
So I turned to my left, sang, "How do you do?
I hope soon to be an angel too."
Then I turned to my right, she loved to hear me sing.
I asked her then and there, "How did you earn your wings?"
>She said, "By singing, Just by singing."
>So I'm singing for heaven now
>Hear me singing *

By this point, I'd started having heart palpitations, and wouldn't even leave the dungeon to go to the bathroom; instead, relieving myself in empty water bottles and plastic bags. I'd become an animal, and there wasn't a thing anyone could do.

I had become a slave to cocaine's demands, and no amount of will power could bring me back from the precipice I found myself dangling. I felt powerless and would go for days without food or sleep, rarely leaving the dungeon, except to get more cocaine and tequila. There at the end, I literally didn't go to bed once, in the last nine months of my using. I would just pass out on the dungeon floor every seventh or eighth day.

It was in the hands of God, and nothing short of a miracle would do. It came in the form of a phone call. I had paged in an order for more drugs to my dealer, as I was unable to leave 'the dungeon' at all by this point. If I didn't have cocaine in my system, I would be unconscious. Using the codes we'd agreed on, I called my dealer, on a pager, to tell him how much I needed and what time to deliver. There was rarely any conversation on the phone for fear of wiretaps (talk about paranoia), but this time was different. The dealer (who was the only person I knew as strung out as

* Singing For Heaven (Please, Please, Somebody Please)

myself, (i.e. could stay up eight days at a time), called back and said, "Sorry man, I'm in a hospital."

What ensued next, I can only describe as 'my moment of clarity.' I had long since given up any hope of surviving my addiction, but out of nowhere, I heard a voice from deep within me say, "Where are you, and how do you get in?"

I don't know which one of my angels decided to intervene, but I was so surprised, I actually peered over my shoulder to see who had spoken, before I realized the voice had come from inside of me.

I didn't think my request had even registered with my dealer, as he was busy making arrangements for someone to deliver the quarter ounce I had ordered. Obviously, he had heard me, because later that day, I got a phone call from someone he had told my situation to. They informed me that even though I had no money or insurance, there was an empty bed at a rehabilitation hospital in Pasadena where I could stay for a few days till the vacancy was filled.

I then called the owner of the building and told him, "I'm checking myself in a drug rehabilitation hospital and you need to make arrangements so someone else can collect the rents."

I'm sure this was a relief to him, since a few months earlier, during a bout with my conscience, I had already told him of my drug problem saying, "Fire me, I'm a drug addict. Anything that even resembles the color green, I'm going to steal to pay for my habit."

Unfortunately, the old man, who was very fond of me, replied, "Just try and keep it under control."

(Certainly compassionate, but not very wise, as the Prince was already beyond the point of no return. In today's vernacular, I think the word would be 'enabling'.) The Prince was supposed to be at the hospital the next morning, but it took until almost midnight of the next day for him to use up the rest of his cocaine, and there was no way humanly possible he could leave till it was gone.

Talk about insanity; there towards the end, the palpitations had become agonizing heart seizures, every time I didn't exhale the cocaine quick enough, and yet I still had to finish it off.

Trying to make it as memorable as possible, I wrote down the details of the entire last day of my using. Having accumulated a lot of paraphernalia, living up to my nickname 'The Master Blaster', I decided to break my remaining seven glass pipes, in ritual fashion, against the four walls and then the roof and floor of the dungeon. The last one would get me to the hospital. Every few hours, I stood up and, with all the might left at my command, hurled the glass container I'd been sucking death out of while screaming, "Fuck you", or "get thee back Satan," or something to the equivalent.

I averaged one pipe every three hours till I was down to the final one. I then called one of my women friends (I use that term loosely as the only women left in my life, at this point, were addicts like myself), and asked her to drive me to the hospital. I took my final hit at the hospital entrance to give me the courage to continue, smashed the seventh pipe up against the curb of the sidewalk, heaved the torch as far as I could, and walked up to the after-hours door of the hospital. If the policeman hadn't opened it while I had the drug in my lungs, I know I would have backed out.

After blowing that last hit in the policeman's face *(with the arrogance of the damned, still thumbing his nose at authority figures)*, I walked through the entrance. What the intake nurse saw standing there resembled a human being, but just barely.

After that last gesture of defiance toward the policeman, I had no fight left in me at all. When the nurse uncovered the two fifths of 'Gold Cuervo' tequila in my bag, and wouldn't buy my explanation, "It's just to take the edge off", I was too exhausted to fight and just shrugged my shoulders when it was confiscated. I slept almost nonstop for the first four days, being awakened only long enough to stuff huge amounts of food into myself.

On the fifth day, I was taken out of detox, and told I had to start participating in the program like the other patients. That meant going to group meetings, where we all were supposed to share, and then individual meetings with a drug counselor, psychiatrist, and M.D. The doctor that examined me said, "If you hadn't come in when you did, your heart would have given out. You only had a few days left, at most, as it couldn't take any more. I'm surprised you lasted this long."

Each night, we were all herded into a van (where of course I taught everyone to moo), and they would take us to an AA meeting in the vicinity. I didn't relate at first, thinking cocaine was my only problem...not alcohol, until one night we drove a long way and ended up at a Cocaine Anonymous meeting. The program was still in it's infant stage, so there were only three or four meetings in the entire city. That night, I heard a speaker say, "If you're an addict and you're thinking you'll switch from cocaine to alcohol, it makes about as much sense as changing seats on the Titanic; either way you're going down. Whenever you go to a meeting, whatever kind it is, look at the similarities, not the differences."

That was probably the first thing I actually heard that sunk in. I still didn't think I could stop getting high altogether, I just wasn't ready to die quite yet. If they could only teach me how to smoke cocaine socially, I'd be mighty obliged. I gained nearly twenty-five pounds in the eleven days they had the empty bed available, but no one was taking any bets I was on my way to recovery. In fact, the day I was leaving, I overheard one of my counselors bet I wouldn't make it a year. I probably owe him my life, cause I walked out of there thinking "I'll show him". I did write one song while at the hospital, which showed there was still a glimmer of hope. *

AA——it's not a new drug.
It's a place I go when I need a hug.
When my life had gotten out of control,
From too much drugs, sex, and rock 'n' roll.
Well I swallowed my pride, that was hard to do,
But I'd bitten off more than I could possibly chew.
Well lo and behold, you know what I found,

* Tears Of Joy

After choking on my ego, it finally came down.
At AA— it's one day at a time.
It's brought me tears of joy that's what I've been cryin'.
Tears of joy running down my face,
Tears of joy, boy that ain't no disgrace.
Welcome back to the human race.

Knowing that the Prince's pride would see it as a challenge, the counselor, that bet against him, probably let him overhear on purpose. What began next for the Prince, was a long slow road of three steps forward and two steps back. Progress, but certainly not perfection. Learning to live without stuffing his feelings, wasn't going to be easy, but I learned a long time ago, don't bet against him. He has some pretty powerful angels in his corner.

Reprieve

"It's what you learn after you know it all that counts."

John Wooden

*T*he Prince took to recovery like he did everything else in life. Full speed ahead. As soon as he got out of the hospital, he remembered they had said it was good idea to find a meeting first thing every day. "Before your 'stinkin' thinkin' kicks in", was the way he heard it eloquently expressed.

I got out my meeting list and found the address of a meeting, called 'Architects of Adversity', which met every morning at seven a.m, over in West Hollywood. It turned out to be in a log cabin, and as soon as I walked through the door, I was welcomed by some guy who offered me a cup of coffee, which I gladly accepted. I must have looked new *(between his hollowed out raccoon eyes and the fact that he was constantly sweating, I can't imagine why)*, because he asked me, "How many days you got clean?"

"This is my twelfth" I answered suspiciously, not quite sure what this was leading to, or what he was after. *(As if he had something anyone else would want anyway.)*

Just then, the meeting started and I was able to make my escape and went and sat against the back wall. I was surprised that everyone looked so normal. There was a housewife who talked about her last binge and how the look on her child's face finally brought her to her knees. There was a construction worker there that had fallen asleep at the wheel and smashed his truck, injuring some innocent bystander. I also heard a priest, a semi-famous actor and two school teachers, that first day back in civilization. One of the best lines I heard that day, was from the fifteen minute speaker.

"Go to ninety meetings in ninety days. Then if you're still not convinced this is the best deal in town, we'll gladly refund your misery." I couldn't help but laugh, and after the meeting was over, I went up and asked him for his phone number, like they'd told me to do in the hospital. He said, "Sure, you know a few of us go out for coffee after the meeting, if you want to come join us?"

That was music to my ears, as I was feeling rather lonely since losing my best friend, cocaine. I gladly accepted.

I'll never forget that morning. A guy I'd never met in my life spent three hours talking to me, helping me learn a better way to live. I remember him telling me, "You don't want to spend a lot of time by yourself thinking; your mind is like a bad neighborhood, you don't want to go there alone."

He also taught me the acronym H.A.L.T. that I would use from then on. He said I needed to be constantly vigilant and not let myself get too Hungry, Angry, Lonely or Tired. It surprised me, when I realized it went against the grain of everything I had been taught about what a man was. All my coaches in high school had stressed; "I want you hungry! Get mad. Be angry. A real man is a loner. Fight till you drop! Only wimps and sissies show vulnerability."

A little while later, he shared another jewel with me. "Going to meetings is like putting money into a sober bank account; you never know when you might have to make a large withdrawal. The fact is, I only need one meeting a week, but I go to seven; because I never know which one it's gonna be."

After I got done laughing, the old-timer got serious again.

"Look at it this way, you're building the foundation of a house you're gonna be hopefully living in for the rest of your life. You want to build it as strong as you can, so it can withstand those winds and storms in life which invariably come up. Children get sick, parents and friends die, car accidents happen, jobs are lost, bankruptcy looms...that's called life."

What did the Prince do? He went to that same meeting every morning for the next ninety days, and then averaged three meetings a day, every day, for the next four years.

I found I always seemed to hear just what I needed. One evening,

I was feeling awfully low and was sharing about how a new relationship was driving me crazy. After the meeting, an old timer pulled me aside and said: "Just remember, feelings aren't facts, they're just feelings and these too shall pass. You're gonna be OK. Most people call AAA when they get a flat tire, but people like us feel like calling the suicide prevention hotline. You want to go get a cup of coffee instead?"

Over coffee, the old timer continued, "They told me when I first got here twenty years ago, 'You're only as sick as your secrets, and if you want to recover, you need to talk to somebody about what's going on. We're not bad people trying to get good, we're sick people trying to get well.'"

The two of us talked on through the night, and I told him my entire story. At one point, after hearing about my family and all the pain, guilt, and sense of loss I had about my father, the old timer made a suggestion. "You might try watching 'Little House on the Prairie'."

That seemed a bit odd to me, as I'd never seen the show, and when I asked why, the old timer smiled and said, "Just try it."

I was willing to try anything, so the next afternoon, I turned it on and was amazed to find it moved me to tears. The show touched the part of me that so desperately wanted a family and to feel like I belonged somewhere. Seeing a father teach his kids the lessons of life, using love instead of fear, tore me up reminiscing about my own childhood. I had my first good cry in years, and thoroughly enjoyed it. That was more of a surprise than the cry itself, having been raised in the old paradigm where real men don't cry or show insecurity. When I called my new friend back and tentatively told him what had happened, he just laughed and said,

"Wait, you haven't seen anything yet, some of the stories will leave you sobbing."

True to form, the Prince rarely missed an episode, over the next three years. At four p.m. every day, you could count on him to be home glued to his TV set. Michael Landon had the ability to pull on the Princes' heartstrings and the old timer had recognized that there was a tremendous amount of tears that needed to come out. Over the years, his tools have evolved, so nowadays, when he needs a good cry, he pulls out his well-worn copy of 'Field Of Dreams'. Never again would the Prince question when an old timer made an odd suggestion.

After a couple of years of steady meetings, I noticed I wasn't sharing near as much as I had been back in my early sobriety. I had started comparing my insides to other peoples' outsides and was thinking I should be further along than I was. I was uncomfortable in my own skin, but wouldn't tell anybody. Swimming in a morass of self pity because, one more time, someone had told me my music was 'the best kept secret in town', I chose to feel like a victim rather than letting that statement empower me.

As usual, before I could get too caught up in a downward spiral by keeping it all inside, I heard a high powered attorney, with a number of years of sobriety, talking about what a rough time he had been having lately, and how his grandiosity had almost killed him. I remember him saying:

"You've only got two hands, but you've got four cheeks, you can save your ass or save your face, but you can't cover them both at the same time." I laughed so hard I almost cried and then raised my hand to share what was going on.

Over the years, I had often struggled with the question of how to tell the difference if it was God's will or my own. The question came up one more time, when my current relationship wasn't working out, and I was in a lot of pain over what to do. I prayed for the answer and heard what was to become my litmus test. Once again, it was from an old timer over a cup of coffee.

"I start my day off, walk out the front door and down the steps. If I hit a wall, I take a left; I hit another wall, I take another left. It's real simple. That's God's will. In the old days, when I hit that wall, I'd back up and get a running head start and either crash through it, or leap over it, get a shovel to dig under it or dynamite to blow it up. Invariably, I'd land in a sewage system on the other side."

I chuckled, seeing my current predicament in the same light. The old timer continued, "Resentments are the biggest killers of all, and you'd better learn to let them go. I learned a long time ago, having a resentment is like taking poison and expecting someone else to die. Have you heard the story of the two monks?"

I shook my head, so the old timer went on.

"There was an old monk and a young monk. They were walking down a dusty road one day when they came to a stream they would have to wade through, as there was no bridge to cross over. It so happened, there was a prostitute there, as well, who wanted to get across, but didn't want to mess up her finery. Well, the old monk, seeing her predicament, offered to carry her across the stream on his back, which she gratefully accepted. Once on the other side of the steam, he dropped her off and the two monks continued on down the road.

The young monk watched all this without saying a word, obviously agitated, but not quite sure what to think. Finally, after they had walked quite a few miles further along the trail, the young monk could contain himself no longer and burst out, 'How could you touch such a defiled woman as that?' The old monk, looked at him with patience and kindness for a few seconds, and then answered,

'I dropped her off a few miles back. You're still carrying her.'"

I saw that's what I had been doing, and how I had such a tough time letting things go. All these years, resenting my father, what a waste of energy. It was time to start dropping them off. Whether I was dealing with food, sex, cigarettes, anger, money, you name it...it seemed to help to gather with other people, that were like-minded, to share our experience, strength and hope with each other. One night, I heard a housewife from Simi Valley sum it all up and put it in perspective. She said, "I may not be all I'm supposed to be; I may not even be what I want to be, but thank God, I'm not what I used to be. I feel like I'm growing up in public, and the growing pains are just a natural part of that process. I've come to the conclusion that, though the pain is often necessary, the suffering is optional."

The Prince was starting to see how all his experiences, good and bad, could benefit others as he found himself slowly becoming a productive member of society. It was during this time, the Prince heard a story that was so powerful and rang such a sympathetic chord, it was to change the way he looked at his recovery from then on. It went like this:

"When I was born I was perfectly whole, perfectly joyous, and perfectly free. By the time I turned five years old, my life was already shattered into a hundred pieces. My father was an alcoholic and a rageaholic, and my mother a Victorian perfectionist that gave him the silent treatment rather than deal with their issues. I was told I was the black sheep and believed it, after all, they were my parents and were supposed to know everything. There was this elephant living in the living room that everyone just walked around and pretended wasn't there. Sometimes the air was so thick in our house you could cut it with a knife." *

"I've spent my entire life trying to somehow fuse those imploded pieces back together again, but until I found the Twelve Step programs, I had no place to put them. I see the programs as the stand where I get to lay down all the various parts I call my life and look at them. Whether it's therapy, or good nutrition, beating on drums with men in the mountains or doing yoga at 3 a.m. on the beach, whatever it takes; for each of us it's different. Finally, I have a table where I can lay them all down, and the twelve steps are the legs that hold that table up."

The Prince, being very visual, just loved the image and rebuild it he did. Some of the pieces the Prince discovered were the commercial brands that come with every starter kit, but some were a bit more obscure. The Prince followed the old adage and always advised those he worked with: "Take what you need and leave the rest." *(Not a bad rule of thumb.)*

* Uprising…Chameleon CD #16

Salving The Wounds

Peace

If you engage with the Warrior... You validate the battle.
If you observe the Warrior... You understand his strategy.
If you hold compassion for the Warrior... You soften the hard-
ness of his heart.
If you love the Warrior... You melt it.

Phyl Sheridan Bushnell

*S*omewhere around his third year of sobriety, the Prince was reminded once
again how well God could direct the show, if he would do his part and just
stay out of the way.

I had gone back to Carolina to have a talk with 'The Captain', to
try and heal some of the wounds we had inflicted upon each other in the
years gone by.

I had been attending ACA (Adult Children Anonymous) meetings
and had really come to see my part in the disintegration of our relationship, and was willing to do whatever it took, to make things right. I was
more than a little nervous (as military men are not known for discussing
feelings), but I was determined to at least extend the first olive branch.

As soon as I arrived at the farm, I found out that one of my dad's
best friends, from Navy days, just happened to be passing through *(right!)*,
and would be there the next day. *(This was the second time he'd 'just dropped
by' in 15 years.)* He was a fellow military officer who knew 'The Captains'
entire story, since the two of them had done a lot of their drinking and
carousing together.

'The Commander', as we'll call him, turned out to be exactly in the
middle, age-wise, between my dad and me. It seemed he had been sober
for a dozen years and in ACA for three, but most amazing, was the reason

he just happened to be there in the first place.

He was returning home to Kentucky to visit his father and hopefully have the same kind of reconciliation I was there to have with mine. For the next two days, the three of us spent countless hours rocking on the front porch confiding, rhapsodizing, soliloquizing and just plain spouting off, like we never had before. I was able to diplomatically query 'The Captain' on many questions I'd always wondered about. Questions like:

"Are you happy? What are the biggest regrets in your life? Why have you been so angry most of your life? What hurt the most?"

After awhile, I became even bolder with queries like, "What were your feelings about me when I was born? Were you always faithful to mom? What would you do differently, if you had the chance? Do you believe in life after death, or do you think this is all there is?"

I've got to give him credit. Though I could tell many of my questions made him uncomfortable, and often he'd volunteer only one word answers (till the 'Commander' might nudge his memory), he hung in there like a real trooper. (Interesting choice of words.) I made it a point to not lay blame on him, as that would accomplish nothing, and wasn't at all my intended purpose. Yes, he was responsible for a lot of the problems I had encountered over my life, but I was responsible for finding the solutions. I knew already that he'd done the best he could, with the tools he had to work with. My job was to clean up my own side of the street, and just being able to talk like that at all, was healing for us both. Certainly, a far cry from where we had been, just a few short years before.

I later hitched a ride to Nashville with 'The Commander', as he was passing through there on his way to Kentucky. We were able to continue our dialogue even further, and by the time we parted company, we even exchanged addresses. Because of our new friendship I was able to perceive my father in a whole new light. It was the first time I was able to have empathy for him. I'd never imagined him as a guy who had a best friend, or how it might have felt at his age with a couple of small children. I thought about the responsibility he must have felt being the commanding officer of a destroyer, and watching a number of his friends be killed when a Japanese submarine destroyed it. I wondered how that might have felt if it had been me. For the first time ever, I put myself in his shoes. It was quite an eye-opening experience.

On the day 'The Commander' and I headed for Nashville, and we were saying good-bye to the folks on the front porch, I remembered hugging my dad, for the first time ever. It was awkward for us both. I never thought I'd see the day, but I was actually sad to leave.

A few months after the Prince had started the healing process with his dad, he received a phone call informing him that Jim Goure (his first mentor and in many ways, the father he had always longed for), had passed over.

The Prince had become adept at suppressing his feelings over the years, but Jim's death was like a stick of dynamite that blew up the wall around his heart. (Since military brats learned at an early age to not let people get too close, and the Prince had gotten that lesson down pat, this was the first real loss he had ever known.)

I remember when that phone call came, I cried out in anguish, "Oh God no, please don't let it be true."

But it was true, and I wept, inconsolably, for a week. This time, I couldn't ignore the feelings, just walk away, or even numb the pain with booze and drugs. I'd never known such grief before. It hit me like a locomotive, and laid me out flat. Feeling desolate and forlorn, the first two days, I just sat in my room and cried. I think I probably took it so hard because I didn't get a chance to say good-bye or tell him how much I loved him. Also, since I didn't learn of his passing till weeks after the fact, I had no one to share my anguish with. Then I got mad at him, because he had checked out so early in life, which only made me feel rueful for being so selfish. Mostly, I felt alone once again in the universe, as he was the one person that knew me to my very core and loved me because of, and in spite of myself.

Jim had been my most influential teacher and significant role model, as well as my first mentor. Besides my dad, he had been the person I most wanted to make proud, and now that he had passed over, that opportunity was gone forever. That day, I recalled something Jim had told me many years before,

"There is no time like the present, which is exactly what it is-a present. What you have is precious and should be treasured."

Later, at a 12-step meeting, I heard it put another way, "If you've got one foot in the past, and one foot in the future, odds are you're shitting all over the present."

Yes, that's certainly another way of putting it.

This was an important time for the Prince. He was growing up, and finding some of it to be quite painful, but he was also discovering that the pain wasn't gonna kill him, and yes, this too shall pass. Between starting to heal with his dad and experiencing the greatest loss he had yet known, the Prince began spending much more time in reflection. He was starting to like what he saw.

Venice Beach

"Guilt is great. So you screwed up, you got a problem, that's what amends are for. But shame is a different thing all together. Shame means you are the problem, and there's nothing you can do about that."

John Bradshaw

*S*ince coming off of the proverbial pink cloud of early sobriety, the Prince hadn't a clue as to what he wanted to do next to support himself.

For six months or so, I had been working for minimum wage as a tech for the same recovery hospital where I'd sobered up. At first, it was rewarding helping people get sober, but for every one I seemed to help, there seemed to be half a dozen that just couldn't get it. After a while, I began to feel my spirit dampened from watching so many people go right back out and start using again.

The final straw happened after spending two days straight talking about sobriety with an old musician friend, Paul Butterfield. He had checked himself into the hospital and seemed to really want it this time. I took Sunday off, and when I came back to work on Monday, found out he had gone AWOL. When he overdosed a couple of days later, I took it hard, and knew it was time to find a new job.

Since my ego was so wrapped up in my music, I had been advised to put those talents on the back burner for a while. Also, since I had answered yes to the question "Are you willing to go to any lengths to stay clean and sober?", I was prepared to never play music again, if that's what it took. Music though was the only thing I knew I enjoyed, and I was definitely in a quandary as to what else I might try. One day, while discussing possible options with my dear friend, Endre, he asked me what else I liked to do, what really turned me on?

"What would you do even if you didn't get paid?"

It dawned on me immediately. "I'd give massages," I said, "I've been a healer for years."

That was it. I was off and running. I borrowed a friend's massage table and began setting it up on weekends on the boardwalk at Venice Beach.

Venice Beach... where the 'debris meets the sea', as the locals liked to say. There's nowhere quite like it on the planet. Practically everyone that has ever been to L.A. has cruised that stretch of real estate. I figured if I'd only stay still long enough, they'd all come by me. Tucked up beneath an old salt-rotted wooden cabana, I set up my slant board (a type of massage table), and could be seen every weekend either walking up and down on people's backs (using the roof of the cabana for support), or sliding down their buttocks, past their thighs, with all my weight on my knees.

Next, I'd utilize my elbows, knuckles and thumbs, all guaranteed to help work out the kinks from life in the city of angels. Skateboarders, roller skaters and bicyclists cruised by on the bike path, ten feet behind me, while tens of thousands a day walked, sauntered, moseyed, strolled, strutted, and stared, as they passed by in a myriad of disguises. I knew they were all sentient beings, but sometimes, it was hard to be absolutely sure. I loved it. In many ways, working on Venice Beach reminded me of my summers spent in the carnival; sort of like being at a zoo that's inside out, with the animals all walking by looking at the people.

I would wear all white and play my Edgar Cayce album to mellow my clients out. There was an early morning twelve-step meeting right on the sand both Saturday and Sunday, so I'd begin my day there, then give massages till the sun went down. Since you could only request donations and couldn't really refuse anyone, I found it was just what the doctor had ordered.

I printed up cards with my new moniker: 'Mobile Masseur' . . . Have Hands Will Travel'.

Before long, I had attracted more regular clients than I knew what to do with, including the TV show 'L.A. Law'. *(Seems that's usually the case when you're doing something you love.)* I even had a few clients I had known back in the limousine, lear jet days. *That's where the humility factor really came into play. 'Mr. Egomaniac with an inferiority complex', was putting his hands on, and healing anyone that walked by and solicited his help. Experiencing humility, for the first time, was a bit awkward for the Prince, like putting on a new pair of shoes, but he found he had never been happier.*

One of the reasons the Prince was a good healer, was because he would deal with the emotional body as well as the physical. He had come to believe that all unexpressed emotions stayed in the body and actually became prime contributors to many of today's diseases. Many times, while working on someone, he would get intuitive insights as to what was really bothering them and make suggestions.

I would instruct my clients, "Let go of your (anger, sadness, fear, insecurity, remorse, guilt, etc.), you don't need it, it's not necessary any more, and is just holding in your pain."

I'd paint scenarios like, "Remember when you were in love that first time, and when it ended, you were sure your life was over. That's when you began building this wall, I've found here in your back, so you'd never have to feel that pain again. Well, let it go. It's not serving you anymore. It might have protected you then, by keeping out some of the heartache, but now it's keeping the pain locked in."

I borrowed one story from author John Bradshaw. "Remember when you were a child and got separated from mom or dad for the first time? You were probably at the grocery store or the mall, and when you finally found them, it was such a relief, you started to cry. Which, by the way, is a natural and healthy way to get fear out of your system. Unfortunately, mom or dad was embarrassed by all the attention you were bringing them, and stuffed a banana or a piece of candy in your mouth and told you to stop. (Especially the boys who were told crying was for sissies.) Well, that's what this knot on your back is all about. Just let it go, you don't need it any more."

It was truly astonishing what would often occur. Many people would start to weep, right there at the beach, and it was then I knew I'd made a good decision in becoming a masseur; once again finding that being of service brought the greatest reward.

Before long, I retired from doing house calls and would have all my regulars come down to the beach. That way, I could give massages only on the weekends, freeing up the rest of the week to pursue other interests. Unfortunately, that decision cost me dearly, as I overworked my hands and wrists, sometimes giving massages twelve hours in a row without taking a break. A year or so later, I was forced to quit giving massages professionally, as I developed a case of carpal tunnel syndrome. (Once again my compulsivity takes its costly toll.)

About the same time my hands were giving out, I found another missing piece of the puzzle; how to be in relationship with others. I had heard about a Barbara De Angelis seminar called, 'Making Love Work', through a friend that invited me to her graduation ceremony. I became hooked from that very first night.

I observed literal miracles come about as the result of her teachings. I saw military officers and FBI agents (guys that probably hadn't smiled in ten years, let alone cried or told their wives and kids they loved them), come in like walls of granite on Friday night, and by Sunday morning, they were hugging and kissing their wives and weeping with joy.

After witnessing that, on more than a few occasions, plus draining a few hours of tears out of my own system as well, I decided to become an assistant (known as a guardian angel), and volunteered to help with the work. It was a profound experience for me, and I learned tools and techniques on how to create and keep healthy relationships.

It's bewildering to me how schools today stress facts that need to be memorized and regurgitated, yet put so little emphasis, if any, on the most basic questions of life. Like how to have a healthy relationship or how to disagree with someone you love, or how to find your calling in life (dharma). I find it sad how ill-prepared most of our children are for the real world.

I realized that often, in my past relationships, when I was feeling hurt, afraid or insecure, I would show anger, as feelings of insecurity and fear were definitely not appropriate among my peers (especially those male peers from military families). On the other hand, most of the women I had known were raised to believe that nice girls didn't get mad, so that explained why so many of them would cry when anger was really much more appropriate. *With no one expressing their true feelings, it's no wonder relationships seemed so confusing and difficult.*

Relationships finally began to make some sense to me. Realizing that everyone in a family unit was connected by emotional pipes, it was easy to see how if one person was stuffing their feelings, then the emotions would be backed up just like a drainage pipe, until someone else acted them out. If everyone in turn stuffed them, then you'd be apt to see a neurotic family dog expressing all the pent up rage by biting people. As it was, I felt as if I had been the designated dog in my family. *(Just a coincidence, I'm sure, that the Captain's nickname was 'The Bulldog').* I learned that in a functional family, the roles would change, that each person should take turns as the family hero or scapegoat or mascot, even dad. I cried the first time I realized all the years I'd been stuck living out the role of the scapegoat.

Another piece of the puzzle that fell into place, around this time, was 'A Course in Miracles'. I had done the course years before, but hadn't thought about it in over a decade. Now here, years later, I was to meet Marianne Williamson, through my dear friend, Endre. She would reintroduce me to its teachings, and for someone raised a Christian, who also believed in metaphysics, it was a Godsend. I was reminded, once again, that miracles were a natural part of life and were there for the asking.

All these various teachings the Prince was learning; how to create healthy relationships, healing his past, combining metaphysics and Christianity, and of course his twelve step foundation, were all essential to his growth and well being. Yet, there was still one piece of the puzzle missing that he couldn't quite put his finger on. They say when the student is ready the teaching will appear. Well, obviously, the Prince was finally ready.

Robert Bly and Rites of Passage

"You don't give a man a weapon till you've taught him how to dance."

African Proverb

All his life, the need to belong somewhere and to feel accepted had driven the Prince. Usually, into the arms of women, but sometimes his unconscious desire to experience a rite of passage, put him into places he had no business being; usually seeking acceptance from his peers rather than his elders. Once he found the work of Joseph Campbell 'The Power of The Myth', the Prince knew he had uncovered an essential piece of the puzzle that had eluded him. (It's noteworthy that almost all the pieces till then, had come from women.)

I was first introduced to the very real power of myth when a number of men took Mr. Campbell's teachings, and started doing experientially what he had taught in theory. One of their basic tenants being that the old men in our society weren't doing their job of mentoring the young men and initiating them into manhood; that as a society, we were no longer honoring our elders and even worse, our elders were becoming disposable; furthermore, it was this absence that was becoming one of the major contributors to the violence and chaos of our youth.

All this rang true to me, particularly the significance of having mentors, as I recognized what a potent role in my life Jim Goure had played. I was impelled to investigate further.

Since initiation and the rite of passage were almost nonexistent in our society (with the exception of the Jewish Bar Mitzvah), I found these men were adopting ideas and rituals from various cultures around the world to author their own. The idea was to create sacred space for ritual, i.e., a safe environment where a man could grieve the loss of a marriage or a child or the Vietnam war, whatever he needed. A framework in which he could not only express his anger and fears safely, but his joy unabashedly in the presence of his elders as well as his peers.

Before long, I heard about a 3-day gathering of like-minded men taking place in the mountains around Ojai, California, and decided to go. I was surprised to find that nearly 300 men had heeded the call as well. At night, our encampment looked like a scene from 'Braveheart', with Robert Bly, our fearless leader, facilitating the event.

Between sessions, on the second day, I felt drawn to get away from the hubbub and hiked a ways up the mountain to meditate. I hadn't gone a thousand yards, when I came upon Mr. Bly, sitting by himself, on a large boulder. Assuming he had hiked up there in need of quiet, as had I, I didn't want to break his reverie, but as I approached on the trail, he spoke first, "How are you?"

"Wonderful", I replied as I gazed out over the valley, taking in the majesty of it all, "It's a gorgeous day."

"Uh-huh" he nodded his head in assent, "What do you think of the conference so far?"

That was all the invitation I needed and, after a couple more polite exchanges, I boldly went for it, "Can I ask you a question?"

He smiled broadly, and with a twinkle in his eye, as if he had been there before and was only waiting for me to get around to it, said, "Sure, what's on your mind?"

"One of the ideas from your book Iron John that I resonated with was that a young man had to be careful and not show his gold too soon, lest it be squandered away or stolen from him. Hence, the importance of initiation. I feel like I'm at a crossroads, having shown a bit of my true gold earlier in life (performing at the metaphysical retreats, as well as recording 'The Rainbow' and 'Edgar Cayce Albums'), but rather than risking having it stolen, I hid it away behind drugs, women, and the pursuit of fame and fortune. Over time, I even forgot that I owned all this gold, much less where I had hidden it. I'm only now thinking about retrieving it."

At this point, I paused, not sure exactly what I was asking, or if I was asking, or if I should even continue. Robert waited till the silence had become deafening, then said,

"Go on."

I gave him a brief synopsis of my journey, focusing mostly on the highlights of what I believed to be my dharma or calling. (The work the angel at the motorcycle accident told me I hadn't completed as yet.) By the time I completed my story, I felt like I already knew the answers to questions I hadn't even asked yet.

He seemed to read my mind, and when I was done, assured me, "The time is ripe to show your gold. Your conquering your drug addiction was a definite rite of passage."

We spoke awhile longer, until I realized an hour and a half had passed, and it was time to get back to the others.

Not since the days of spending time with his first mentor, had the Prince felt the calmness that descended over him. The act of just sitting, student and elder, side by side, and the acceptance he felt from one that had wisdom of which he was seeking, seemed to heal that gaping wound in his gut through which the wind had so often howled.

Later that afternoon, Robert introduced the Prince to Michael Meade, another one of the facilitators and a storyteller par-excellence. (Michael was soon to have the mantel of leadership thrust upon him, once Robert decided he'd taken enough potshots from the ignorant and uninformed and decided to get off the road for awhile.)

The Prince witnessed a profound scene, that same afternoon, that touched his heart and impressed him greatly. In days of old, the slings and arrows shot at leaders were made of physical materials; much easier to spot than the modern day rhetorical barbs hurled from behind cowardly walls of semantics. On three separate occasions, the Prince noticed these oratorical projectiles being launched towards Robert, on the stage, only to see Michael (like the archangel of lore), act as a shield, protecting his elder and deflecting the blows, so that they disintegrated into the mountain air. The Prince felt that kind of ignoble impertinence warranted a good thrashing, but kept his hands to himself.

From that point on, doing men's work became a passion for me. The rituals, the drumming, the dancing, the expressed anger without violence, the honoring of, and acceptance back from, my elders, these were all things I had been craving, but hadn't realized.

Doing this kind of work eventually led me back on stage again; this time accompanying both Michael and Robert, as well as James Hillman, Malidoma Some', and other leaders of the men's movement at various gatherings. I even found myself willing to play in a band again; this time a trio with Bruce Wallenstein (on gordamer and percussion), and John Densmore (former drummer of the Doors), playing at the occasional men's event or poetry reading. We definitely had our moments where heaven and the earth seemed to come together in our music, playing for the pure joy of it.

The acceptance by his elders, and the respect of his peers, was helping the Prince on his journey to becoming a man. Like so many other things, it's difficult to know you're missing something until you experience it in the first place.

I soon identified my need for a smaller, more intimate men's group that could meet more frequently, and joined a dozen other men that began meeting bi-weekly. It was particularly valuable, because at each meeting a different man was able to experience 'holding the container' (creating and bringing the ritual to the circle.) It was a diverse array, economically and socially, though not racially. Attending, were a doctor, a lawyer for social causes, two college students, a Southern construction worker/mountain man, a painter, a forestry worker, and a couple of guys that didn't really have a clue what they wanted to do when they grew up. I related to all of them.

The first time it came my turn to 'hold the container', I told my life story in mythological terms. I reminded them that, when listening to a myth, what is most important is where you, the listener, connect with the story; what part do you most resonate with. It turned out to be quite a powerful evening, as the recounting of my near death experiences triggered some intense emotions with a couple of the younger men. Just the acknowledging of the story felt good to me. To be seen warts and all, and feel not only accepted, but to bond even closer with men, not necessarily from a twelve step background, was a far-reaching realization. Most of the men were incredulous at the variety of my adventures, but the depths to which I went in my drug addiction, held them spellbound. Afterwards, when we passed the talking stick and each man shared, I detected that the tear in the fabric called the father-son relationship was a constant theme with all of us but one.

For my second turn, a few months later, I decided to 'stir up the pot' a bit and organized a trek in the high desert to a place call Mammoth Pools. There, I had arranged to have a motorboat take us three miles across the lake and drop us off on a secluded beach where we would live for three days in isolation, drumming and doing ritual. I might have stirred up the pot a bit too much, as the hardship aspect caused the group to fraction and tempers to flare. *Try telling a doctor and a lawyer there is no ice to be had on a scorching hot day. The Prince, of course, with his latent codependency issues, took it all personally, since he had planned the trip, and had his own muck to wade through...or rise above, whichever he chose.*

Oddly enough, when I would articulate my passions about men's work with all its inherent richness to other men in twelve step programs, a lot of them just didn't get it and even seemed threatened that I would dare advocate anything but the teachings of Bill Wilson (co-founder of Alcoholics Anonymous). For a while, I caught a lot of flack for expressing my opinions on the subject, but I knew what an intregal piece of the puzzle it had become for me, and felt an obligation to share it as part of my experience, strength and hope.

Something else that convinced me how worthwhile this kind of work had become, were the reactions from the wives and girlfriends of the men who were doing it. Invariably, they would say things like:

"I love it when he's doing this work. He comes home from a week or a weekend with you men, and he's the man I always wanted to marry," or

"He owns his power and is much more content with himself."

"He feels more connected, as if he belongs here."

"He's more loving with the children and gentle with me. Even the sex is better!"

Like anything else in life, the Prince found there was both good and bad to be found under the label 'men's work.' There were groups whose motives were magnanimous, and those that were selfish and had hidden agendas.

After a few years, I started asking myself the question, like Michael Meade and a few others had before me, "Is this men's work or white men's work?" Knowing instinctively it needed to be inclusive instead of exclusive, I found myself increasingly drawn to the multi-cultural men's conferences that were just beginning to make inroads.

One of the more profound and, certainly memorable conferences, took place up in the hills, high above Malibu, at a place called Camp Shalom. It was a rustic Jewish retreat, miles from everything, tucked in amongst the scraggly mountainous trees with a dryed up creekbed running through the middle of the grounds. There were ten cabins, with bunk beds that would sleep up to a dozen men each, and a number of out buildings set up for various activities such as arts and crafts, meditation, and even an outdoor stage. The majority of our time, though, was spent in the main lodge. You could always tell when the next round of activity was beginning, from the intensity of the drumming, vibrating from its walls.

It was a week long event, with fairly even numbers of men of Latino, African, and European descent, as well as a handful of men from both the Native American and Asian communities in attendance. Running the gamut from old hippies in their tie dyes, lawyers from Wall Street, gang-bangers from the inner city, an architect and a politician (both of some renown); to a Hollywood screenwriter, a black fireman from North Carolina, and a Chinese film director, with everything in between. Any man who was drawn to be there could attend, regardless of economic back-ground. There were full scholarships available for those that couldn't afford it and work scholarships for those that were borderline. There were only two rules you had to agree to.

One rule, was to make the commitment of staying through to the end, no matter how uncomfortable it might get. (Very important in keep-ing the energy in the 'container' intact.) And rule two; no physical violence.

Everything else, was not only ok, but welcomed. In fact, some of the paramount sessions of the week occurred during 'conflict hour'. (Usually held between five and six, when the rest of the world was having happy hour.)

There was plenty of poetry reading, drumming, mask making, as well as dialoguing, dancing, and most importantly, the preparing and doing of ritual. All of it was geared toward making community, and finding what we had in common, regardless of race color or creed.

Each one of us had to choose which clan he felt most drawn toward upon arrival. That usually depended on current life issues, and what he hoped to heal while there. The symbols used, were often animals, such as snakes, eagles, fish, etc.; the four elements of earth, fire, water and air. We also used colors such as red, often represented by blood in myth, passion, or even the cunning of a fox; white for purity, wisdom, or innocence; and black, the symbol for the dark side, or going down to sift through the ashes in the dungeon.

Each man was invited to cross a threshold into another world; one where his ancestors may have gone long before him, where every man had been through initiation knew he belonged, and every boy knew when he had arrived. A few men present had been there before, but most hadn't, and would have to trust the men who could bring the entire group back, if somehow we managed to cross the threshold. This could only occur if the 'container' was strong enough, and it took the entire community, working together, in order for it to happen.

It did happen. The fourth day on the mountain, the door opened wider than most of us thought possible, and things were seen and felt that ran the gamut from terrifying and explosive, to enlightening, joyous and truly life affirming.

At one point, the energy in the hall felt so combustible it would erupt at the slightest provocation. The expression 'wailing and gnashing of teeth' comes to mind. I was totally immersed in the experience of the moment and honestly didn't know if I'd get out alive. *(As initiation is meant* to be.) At one point, I was standing there weeping, unashamedly, ready for whatever was to happen next, when a man came over to console me. I pushed him away immediately, knowing I needed to experience all the emotions that were so enormously present. It was a profound experience I'll carry with me for the rest of my life. *

The last night of the conference, I had another experience I'll never forget. During the week, each man had been laboring on his own paper mache mask, and had painted and adorned it as he was so inspired. This being my first mask, I decided to paint my original face, the way I saw myself during my formative years. The right side of my face was black, with a single white tear, while the left side was white, with a solitary black tear. This was my way of expressing that I never felt I fit in any world, black or white. Beginning with the red above my eyes, I painted a rainbow on my forehead. Then, I used a glue gun to attach a huge maple leaf as a crown, seven inches over my head. The rainbow represented the hope I could rise above the world of black and white thinking, and claim my right to the throne of my own kingdom, represented by the leafy crown. (A few years later, at a similar event, the Prince made his second mask, and for the first time, revealed the face of 'Merlin...Alchemist of Sound').

The Prince had been told to bring colorful clothes for the final nights festivities, as there was to be a celebration after they finished the final ritual. Though they had done numerous smaller rituals during the week, they had been preparing for this one all week long, putting in three to four hours labor a day. (In many cultures, the preparing of, and actual doing of ritual was how they spent the majority of their lives, and after that week, the Prince understand why.)

Since many of the men in attendance were in need of healing, the elders present decided they would borrow from an ancient African ritual to facilitate. In this particular ritual, any man who chose to, could cross from the material world over a threshold and descend deep into mother earth, to a place where his ancestors had been before him. There, waiting to help him, would be the elders from his tribe. Intention and being on purpose were key, as they could only accomplish the desired result if all were in agreement.

* I Want to Live Like That...Chameleon CD #18

They divided the labor, so that each of the three clans had a different job to do. One clan was to dig out the cave and build a stone slab stairway leading down to where the elders would be waiting. There they would have huge containers of mud pre-prepared, to a consistency that would stick, so they could apply it to the part of the body that needed attention. The Prince's clan was to build the garland candlelit entrance at the threshold they'd be crossing over, and to turn the fifteen foot section of gully into a cave. This was accomplished by stringing rope across the ravine and propping up tree limbs, tall weeds, and other foliage, until the cave appeared totally enclosed. This resembled pubic hair adorning the mound, leading down to the womb of mother earth. The Prince was amazed by not only the transition, but by the detail. By the end of the week, he actually felt like he was descending into an ancient cave, as each stone had been inlaid into the ground as if trodden upon for hundreds of years. Also, inlaid into the dirt walls of the cave were candles, which gave the exact effect they were seeking. The job of the third clan, was to prepare the hall for reentrance into this dimension, as they were hopefully going to be crossing over to another side. Also, their job was to help each man after he returned from the cave and transport them along the luminaried path back to the hall. There, other men would be playing soft music and reading poetry, to help bring them gently back to this world.

Since the clans had not observed the preparations of the others, it had a startling effect on the Prince when he was half carried into the candlelit hall later and gazed, for the first time, upon the painted cloth mural that draped the entire room and ceiling. Before the ritual began, each man had been told to spend a little time in contemplation, thinking of what he wanted to heal, and then they were to gather quietly at the entrance of the great hall.

That night, having completed my prayers, I silently joined the others at the entrance. We began to sing an African entreaty, calling forth our ancestors. Then, we slowly moved, as one, down the luminous path toward the cave. One by one, each of the men in front of me disappeared until I reached the front of the cave. There, standing on the outside of the portal, were two elders who asked me why I had come and what I wished to heal.

Once I felt ready, the elders, each with one hand on my chest and another on my back, guided me across the threshold. On the other side of the portal was another elder, who guided me down the ancient stairway until I reached the bottom, where yet another ancient one stood, whose job was to apply the thick precious salve to my wounds. I had no hesitancy, and had him pack the mud over my heart first, and then onto my head. At that point, something overcame me, and I almost lost consciousness. The next thing I knew, I had fallen to my knees and was scooping out handfuls of moist earth from the cauldron and slapping it onto my entire groin area, while weeping silently. In the background, I heard the collective male voices raise the drone sound to a crescendo, like some ethereal choir welcoming me back home. I'll never forget looking up the candlelit stairway and seeing the shadows of my tribesmen standing beneath the ancient portal reflected against the face of the moon. I was in no hurry to leave, and when I felt complete, comforting hands seemed to lift me up and out of the pit. There, two other men put their arms around my shoulders and half guided and half carried me back to the hall, where I was laid upon a bed of straw. Someone had begun to wash my feet, when I realized the background music was the sound of my dulsitar being soothingly stroked. I had set it up so I could play it for others, and now had the first experience of hearing it from the other side of the instrument. What a gift, someone had thought to give me. Just as I was beginning to float away on its resonance, a deep baritone voice started to read a 'Rumi' poem, grounding me once again. After slowly coming back into my body, I then took my place at the dulsitar to greet the new men being brought in. When all who felt called had gone into the depths, there was a migration to the showers, and then back to the cabins to change for the celebration.

I hurriedly put on my baggy Jamaican print pantaloons, that tied up at the ankles as well as the waist, a black t-shirt and my favorite African skull cap, and headed out the door as the drums were already pounding with a savage intensity.

A couple of the worlds master drummers, led about twenty-five men playing jimbes, as well as other assorted drums and percussion instruments as the celebration began. It went on for hours. Hypnotic rhythms overlapping each other, weaving in and out, as men in full regalia, wearing hand made masks, danced as birds, coyotes, snakes, lions, and every other imaginable source of inspiration.

Even though I had expressed myself through dance hundreds of times before, never had I experienced the kind of exaltation and wild abandon I felt that night. It was one of the most exhilarating experiences of my life.

I hadn't realized just how far the experience had taken me, until I came back from that world and found myself attempting to navigate the Pacific Coast Highway. I literally was not able to drive faster than ten miles an hour, and even then, I had to stop and walk down to the ocean to try and acclimate myself before I could go any further.

After I returned to my home in Topanga Canyon, I rarely spoke and didn't answer the phone for a week, as we were all advised to do. I took the experience inside, so as to not risk dissipating the energy, and have been savoring it ever since. I came off the mountain a changed man, and it was visible to those who had known me before. That overwhelming sense of loneliness, which used to haunt me, had vanished. I felt complete with myself. The need to have someone or something validate me lessened. My ability to feel and express compassion and empathy was enhanced, as I saw how much we all really had in common. * The job the angel said I hadn't completed, as yet, was becoming clearer to me; to be of service to others.

A huge piece of the puzzle had finally been placed on the board. In fact, with this piece added, for the first time, the Prince got an idea what the entire puzzle was supposed to look like. He had gone to the mountain still a boy in many ways, but an initiation by his elders before his peers had taken place, and he would never be the same. Still childlike at times, but never again childish.

* A U Yah

Back To What I Love

"Music is well said to be the speech of angels."

Carlyle

*D*uring this time, I was finding the missing pieces of my life, and repairing others that were broken, I had played very little music. This was due, in part, to seeking answers and healing myself, but also because some part of me was afraid music would lead back to the incomprehensible demoralization I had known just a few short years before. I was afraid I would fall.

"Not to worry," a number of musician friends with the same affliction said,

"Your playing and writing might take a while, but when it does come back, it'll be just as good, if not better, than before."

Now five years later, I was not only writing and playing again, but had built a hot 24-track recording studio to create in.

The Prince started writing and recording with a passion he hadn't felt in years. Oddly enough, once he overcame the fear of his past, he was able to listen to the music from his dark side, and felt it was actually some of the most inspired work he'd ever done. He euphemistically coined the name 'The Dungeon Tapes', when referring to that body of work.

I was determined to use my gift of music differently than I had before, so after I built the studio, I surrounded myself with positive, conscious people, and kept it a drug free environment. This probably cost me a little business, but it attracted clients such as Louise Hay and her company, Hayhouse, who started doing much of their editing there. Soon, other life affirming people and projects started coming through the doors as well. Before long, I was writing, recording, and producing music full time again.

My first source of musical inspiration, came in the guise of a lanky Englishman, named Ian Ritchie. He was quite well known, in Europe, for his work with Roger Waters and Laura Anderson as a producer/engineer and, was a rare find. I had always been a big fan of 'Pink Floyd', and since rumor had it Roger Waters was the main creative force behind that band, I figured his engineer must have some exceptional skills in the studio. I was right.

Ian was very calm and laid back, two necessary qualities, in my book, and I'd often find him, between sessions, reading Yeats or Wordsworth. He was a perfect balance with my eclectic enthusiasm, and we hit it off right from the start. Before long, Ian had become not only the main engineer at the studio, but the co-producer on a few of my originals as well. Our collaborative effort was described in one of the LA music magazines as "The meeting of Depeche Mode, The Talking Heads and Frank Zappa." *

True to my eclectic nature, the next collaborative musical project was on the other end of the spectrum, but brought me just as much satisfaction. At long last, my dear friend, Endre, and I recorded some of my original compositions. We'd been playing together for years, but now I got to feature Endre on his Stradivarius, while I played the guitar.

Endre is one of the most unique individuals I've ever encountered; a regal countenance and bearing that might give the first impression that he's full of himself. He couldn't be more misinterpreted, as he's an observer and, almost always, a man of few words. When he does speak, he chooses his words carefully, as if he were shopping for the most select morsels available. Endre's word is law, in the universe, and he's the one person I've ever known to demonstrate unconditional love. I've always admired his dedication to his art. No matter how interesting or alluring a plan I might come up with, there was absolutely no way it would entice him from the four hours a day minimum he set aside to practice his violin. It's little wonder why he's considered one of the finest violinists in the world.

Interesting to note that, Endre (who has performed as a soloist with many of the major symphonies in the world), had always played music from the printed page and had never just jammed or played from

* Opposites Attract…Chameleon CD # 13

the heart, until his collaboration with me. The first time he accompanied me on an original composition, I wanted to change all my melodies to the lines he was coming up with. I remember thinking, this must be what it was like to jam with Mozart. I think you'll be as enchanted as I, when you hear him play. *In fact, if his performance in 'Angel of Pure Love' * doesn't move you to tears, I'd go see a therapist, or at least an eye doctor.*

After completing the project with Endre, I felt as though I'd fathered a gifted child into the world. I remembered something Jim Goure had taught me: "If you want self worth, then take worthwhile actions."

Another project that stood out, during this time, took me back to my roots. I'd always considered myself a southern boy, but since I'd left Nashville, I had been immersed in every kind of music imaginable, except country. I did record one tongue-in-cheek country tune, amidst the dungeon tapes, called 'She's My Old Lady', but that was about it. *

My love of a song that could tell a good story; a song that could touch your heart and move you to tears had never left me, and when I wrote the song 'Cowboys and Indians', * I was reminded how much I enjoyed country music. That song, inspired me to form a country band with the same name, using some of L.A.'s premier session players. My thinking was, rather than form a band of pretty boys (which seemed to be the latest rage), I would choose the best musicians I could find, and take them into the studio.

I got lucky. The players I ended up with, had been in a number of the most successful bands of all time, and had played on hundreds of the top records in history. There was a lot of thin hair between them, and what hair they did have, was mostly gray. Two fair sized pot bellies and a third on the way, announced up front our intention wasn't to compete with Garth or Aerosmith. But, when you wanted to hear some of the best musicians alive, who could play with heart, I'd have put these guys up against any band in the world. What came out of those sessions was pure unadulterated magic. Knowing in my gut that this was the real deal, I sent copies to KZLA, the top country station in L.A. They loved it, and began playing

* Angel Of Pure Love...Chameleon CD #3
* My Old Lady
* Cowboys and Indians...Chameleon CD #11

it immediately, even though there was no product available in the music stores.

Knowing Nashville to be an 'old boys' network, I figured it would be best to take the tapes there myself. Since I still had a few connections, and had paid my dues there, I was sure it wouldn't be too hard to come back with a record deal in my pocket. I knew the fact the band was based out of LA wouldn't help matters, but on the strength of the music, I didn't see how we could miss. Boy, was I wrong.

Almost all the record labels in Nashville loved the music, but when they saw the band photos and there weren't a lot of chiseled stomachs and jaws, their enthusiasm waned immensely.

At first, I was incredulous, then I became dismayed, and then I got downright depressed. *The societal epidemic of throwing away our elders had even infected country music, the last bastion against that nefarious plague. The Prince had been sure that the Madison Avenue crowd, with their 'sex and youth is the only thing that sells' mentality, wouldn't have taken over Nashville, but unfortunately, that just wasn't the case. He thought to himself, on the plane ride back to Los Angeles, "Has the whole world gone crazy? We're throwing away one of our greatest resources."* *

Discouraged, I went back to L.A. empty handed, and once again a work of art sat on the shelf. A few copies did get out, as we had an underground fan club, from word of mouth and what little exposure the radio station had given us. As one of my friends, who loves country music said, "If you're a country music fan and you ever come across a recording by a band named 'Cowboys and Indians', borrow it, copy it, steal it, if necessary, you'll be glad you did."

I agree.

* Life As We Know It…Chameleon CD #7

Princess Vivien

"Afraid of being swallowed up, consumed within her fire.
Afraid I'll lose my solitude, she'll quench my great desire.
I must think of what I'm gaining, instead of what I'll lose
'cause freedom becomes bondage if I'm too afraid to choose.

GWC

Not long after moving to LA, I had discovered a place, near the ocean, I called 'my spiritual oasis in the middle of the material desert.' It was called Lake Shrine.

In the beginning, I only went there periodically, usually when I felt troubled or needed to be by myself. But as the years went by, I found myself there more and more often to meditate and just 'be', as the presence of God was quite discernible. My final years in LA, I even found myself there, bringing in the New Year, in meditation.

There were divine gardens, with the most alluring roses I'd ever seen, surrounding a spring fed lake filled with koi, swans, and turtles. Along the garden path encircling the lake, were quotes from the Bible, as well as other spiritual sources that would help one to reflect on the higher nature of things. Along side the windmill, which served as a temple, was the courtyard of religions, where each of the seven major religions of the world was represented. People from all over the planet would come there to pray and meditate, or to just walk the grounds and feel the presence of God. There is even a sarcophagus there with some of the ashes of Mahatma Gandhi.

It was built as a temple for the Self Realization Fellowship, the organization started by Paramahansa Yogananda, author of 'Autobiography of A Yogi'. I had worn out half a dozen copies over the years.

It was there, after a meditation service, that I first saw Princess Vivien. It was truly love at first sight. Words like angelic, stunning and exotic, barely do her justice. It was so obvious to me her beauty came from deep within, that my heart didn't stand a chance. I knew I'd never seen such an exquisite smile in my entire life, and I felt like a total geek, trying to get up the nerve to say hello. I couldn't manage it that first encounter, but did notice her chatting to a friend of mine, an Englishman, named David. As soon as she left, I ran over and asked him, "Who was that stunning creature you were just talking to?"

"Her name's Vivien, she's a children's Sunday school teacher here at the lake" he replied.

"Is she spoken for?"

"I don't know for sure, but I don't think so," David smiled.

"Look, you're gonna think I'm crazy, but promise me, you'll meet me here next week and give me a formal introduction."

"OK, if it means that much to you," he promised.

The following Sunday, I got my introduction and I asked her out for coffee after the worship service. *(That's a lie, in actuality, he shuffled around and pawed the ground like a nervous rhino, mumbled something about why he'd asked for an introduction, and she had mercy on him before he had a heart attack.)*

Vivien seemed to hypnotize me. Just the lilting sound of her voice, over the phone, could soothe my anxieties and bring me peace of mind. I'd never experienced anyone like her. Kind and gentle with the sweetest disposition I'd ever come across; she had long black hair, down to her waist, and a dark perfect complexion, as she was originally from the West Indies. We hadn't been together three hours, and I told her I was going to marry her.

I'm sure she thought I was totally crazy, but told me later I did seem harmless enough, so she agreed to a second date.

Before that second date, I sent her 100 red roses *(nothing compulsive about our Prince)*, and by the end of that date, I stole my first kiss. *
She warned me, that same night, not to fall in love, as there was a good possibility she would be entering the convent, as she'd always dreamed of

* I'd Do Anything

becoming a nun. At the time, I thought amusingly to myself, "Right, and then I'll have another habit to break", but didn't say anything."

I proceeded full speed ahead at winning her heart. During the courting process, Vivien seemed to always be dressed in shapeless clothes, so I never imagined what kind of body she had. *(That's not entirely true, he actually imagined it quite a bit.)* It didn't matter anyway, as I was already smitten, but boy was I ever dazzled the first time I saw her in a bathing suit. I believe my exact words were,

"Oh my God." Then Vivien started laughing, when I fell to my knees in supplication.

She exuded so much love and had such an obvious connection with God, that I found myself enlivened like I'd never known before. There was nothing I wouldn't do for her, and I was thankful God had put another angel in my life. What a relief, to know contentment and not be wondering if the grass was greener somewhere else. *

But, alas, it was to be short lived.

Six months after our first date, I orchestrated a romantic interlude, up the coast to Santa Barbara, where she staggered me with an announcement.

"Darling, I've got something I need to tell you."

I intuitively knew it was going to be bruising news, but I wasn't at all prepared for what she said next.

"I love you so much but . . . I love God even more. I've decided to become a nun, and I don't think I should see you any more."

I was speechless, at first, but as it dawned on me she was sincere, I felt crushed by her proclamation. Over the next couple of weeks, I tried everything I could to change her mind, but it was to no avail. After awhile, I felt guilty even trying. Devastated, I headed for the Grand Canyon to find a cave in which to hide out, while I licked my wounds and lamented my loss. *(Though still addicted to drama, the Prince had cut back considerably, though this certainly might qualify as a slip.)*

I kept thinking to myself "How do you compete with that guy?"

* Love Was Just A Word

For four weeks, I camped on the side of a mountain; my tears flowing like the streams I was bathing naked in. I tried writing, meditating, anything I could think of to let her go, 'with love', as I truly loved her and desired nothing, but her happiness. For the first time in my life though, I was angry at God.

Once I reappeared from my self-imposed banishment, I couldn't get her off my mind and thought about her constantly. She was easily the most divine angelic creature I had ever encountered. I was sure, even if she wasn't meant to be with me, she unequivocally shouldn't be locked away in a nunnery somewhere.

"What a waste," I bemoaned to Endre, who had grown used to my melodramas over the years, and could be counted on to offer some sage advice like,

"Sometimes a cigar is just a good smoke." *Now, there's a pearl of wisdom. Three months passed, but the Prince still refused to let it go. Thank God for the twelve step programs. At least he had a place to dump all his anger and frustration, though he would sometimes call Endre to snivel,*

"If I hear one more person tell me to 'turn it over' I think I'll puke." *(Remember, three steps forward and two steps back).*

Not to worry, Vivien exercised her 'woman's prerogative' and concluded that life as a nun wasn't meant for her after all. The Prince was overjoyed (as I'm sure were all his friends, who had been listening to him lament ad nauseam), and he began to court Vivien again.

A few months later, I decided to pop the question.

Since I'd never envisioned marriage before, let alone ruminated on the question, it was an immense step for me, and I wanted to make it perfect. * I wrote a passionate poem, expressing the love and devotion I felt toward her, and put it on parchment paper, then burned the edges to make it look like an ancient scroll. The end of the poem read:

>Your love is all I dreamed it'd be
>
>Darling — - — -?

At that moment, I hoped she'd look up from the scroll and I'd put

* I Love You

voice to those famous four words. I then placed it in a beautifully ornate hand carved jewelry box I'd had custom made.

Next, I planned an Easter egg hunt, up the coast of California, with each egg having a riddle attached which would lead to the next. Starting in Santa Barbara, then to The Hearst Castle, The Madonna Inn, Carmel, and then 'The Esalen Institute' in Big Sur, where the clue would be discovered overlooking the ocean while getting a massage. The next to last clue was to lead her to 'Julian's Castle', which overlooked San Francisco Bay. There she would find her final riddle, which read:

> We've come so far,
> And you're so dear.
> Right from the start,
> It's been so near.
> Within your grasp,
> A twinkling star.
> To make you gasp,
> Right where you are.

Hopefully, this would move her to look beneath the grass in the riddle repository (a.k.a. Easter basket), that she'd been carrying the entire trip, where she would uncover the diamond ring I had designed and made for her. Before opening it though, she must first look inside the jewelry box which had the ancient scroll declaring my intentions and the big question. *

Well, things didn't go as planned. The California floods hit that same week, and the coast highway was closed down to all, but local traffic. Rather than put the proposal off, and take the chance on getting cold feet, I decided to regroup and make other plans.

I made reservations at one of the most romantic bed and breakfasts in Southern California, drove there and left dozens of roses in the room, as well as hundreds of rose petals on the bed. Then, I made arrangements at an elegant Beverly Hills restaurant to have candlelight and a strolling vio-

* Five Senses

linist, and took the jewelry box with the scroll there ahead of time to make sure and keep it a surprise.

It was a surprise all right. I was ready for every contingency, but one; how I would take it if she didn't say yes.

I knew instinctively what Vivien's response would be, since she didn't have a clue what was about to transpire, and there hadn't been any hints. Sure enough, after she read the poem, looked up, and I said those four gargantuan words,

"Will you marry me?", she was speechless. *

It had caught her totally unawares and it was an agonizing minute, for me, before she said, as lovingly as she could, "You know I love you, but I need to think about it."

What I didn't anticipate, was my reaction to that answer. I tried not to show my disappointment, but once back at the bed and breakfast, it was hard to get into a celebratory mood *(probably because there was nothing to celebrate)*, and we soon went to sleep.

Poor kid, his fear of losing himself in a relationship was akin to walking through the valley of the shadow of death. He'd waited his entire life and overcome his greatest fear to say those words, and now that he had. . .

The next day, I drove her home and went back to my own, where I pulled the covers over my head, disheartened and miserable.

Three weeks later, Vivien did say "yes, I'd love to marry you", but it felt so anticlimactic, I never recovered. Not at all what I had envisioned. I put up my best front and tried to sound enthusiastic, but my response sounded flat, even to me.

"Great, so I guess that means we're engaged now."

Shortly after that, I talked her into going home to Trinidad for awhile, so I could focus on the studio, build up a nest-egg, and also to give myself time to mull things over. We wrote often, and a few months later decided to try again. Unfortunately, we found it was almost impossible to get her back in the States, as she wasn't a citizen and had used up her visa. We tried every legal avenue at our disposal, but it was to no avail, and it

* Children's Song…Awakening Imaginations CD #1

soon became a nightmare of red tape. Finally, after a year of frustration, I convinced her to fly into Mexico, by way of Jamaica, and I would drive down and smuggle her across the border.

The clandestine plan was to meet and cross near the Arizona border, where I assumed the border patrol wouldn't be nearly so stringent as in California. Unfortunately, that wasn't the case. When we reached the border, there was a line of cars in front of us which gave us plenty of time to get nervous. When we finally pulled up and the border patrolman asked us if we were citizens, I nonchalantly replied, "Good ole U.S.A.", but when he turned to ask her and her response began with, "Well...", I knew we were in trouble.

I'd forgotten that Vivien had never told a lie in her life, and literally didn't know how. That quickly ended our first attempt. I couldn't believe she hadn't answered "U.S. citizen" when asked, and I was more than a little exasperated with her, as they had almost arrested me and confiscated my car. I hadn't exactly thought this through with all the possible repercussions.

We were both feeling pretty low, at this point, as we'd gone to all this trouble and failed. I found it hard to stay mad at her, when I thought about it. How can you fault someone who only knows how to be in integrity? The fact she wasn't capable of telling a lie, was one of the reasons I had fallen so madly in love with her in the first place. Thank God, they let me go back into Mexico with her. We decided to have a romantic week together, and then she would fly back to Trinidad.

By this point, I was starting to reconsider getting married. The cultural differences were glaring. She had a Hindu background, and I was steeped in new age thinking. I'd spent the last ten years learning to be emotionally available, communicative, and sensitive, and she wasn't comfortable with a man who could cry. I was coming up with a lot of excuses, but the fact was, I was just getting cold feet. I did, however, feel responsible for her having gone back to Trinidad in the first place, as she had only left because of my urging, and I was determined to get her back in the country, if that was what she wanted. She didn't ask me to; it just felt like the right thing to do.

I decided to drive thirteen hundred miles through the interior of Mexico, and then we'd cross again at the San Diego/Tijuana border. The next couple of days, which could have been a vacation for us, turned into a hyper-focused ADD marathon, as I drove almost nonstop. After our first fiasco at the border, I had become dictatorial with her, as I felt like I was dealing with a child, which in many ways I was. *(Again one of the main reasons the Prince had fallen in love with her in the first place).*

Now, I became obsessed with my self appointed mission, and paid her very little mind, forgetting we hadn't seen each other in well over a year. It didn't help that the air conditioning had broken down and the searing heat and desert dust seemed to follow us everywhere. Determined to do it my way, and not look at any other possibilities, I was no fun to be around, and her cheery disposition just made it worse.

I knew she was feeling hurt by my attitude, but I also knew she wanted to live in the U.S., and by now I was starting to wonder if the only reason she wanted to marry me was to get her green card. I couldn't have been more out of line if I tried, but at the time, those were my thoughts, and I couldn't push them away.

I wasn't cognizant of the danger I was putting us in, till we were far along. We were traveling through rather desolate landscape and I started hearing stories of bandits blocking roads with brush and rocks, and the tourists never being heard from again. Thank God, I could speak a bit of Spanish, and got directions back to the main roads. This would add a few hundred miles to our journey, but at least I wouldn't be taking our lives in hand.

Once we arrived at the west coast, I put Vivien up at a hotel in Tijuana. Then, I drove to Los Angeles by myself to pick up a couple of friends to help. I figured if we all crossed together, we would appear to be two couples down shopping for the day. I then bought two straw hats, a serape, and other south of the border trinkets to throw around the car and had Vivien practice saying "U.S." with a southern accent. Afraid the Arizona patrol had sent our pictures to all the other border crossings, I was more than a bit nervous as we inched forward; towards the land of milk and honey. This time, there was 'no problemo'. Vivien delivered U.S.A. like a Georgia peach.

Feeling like I'd done my duty, I escorted Vivien safely to the door of her aunt and uncle. I just wasn't sure of my feelings anymore, and I was afraid if I took on the responsibility of a wife, I would abandon my other dreams. I broke off the engagement, six weeks later.

The Prince was really in love with love and the romantic notion of riding off into the sunset. The realities of building a partnership, based on friendship and mutual respect for the other's process, was a good idea, but one he didn't have the tools to implement. Learning to see a relationship as an opportunity to become the best that you can be, an opportunity for full self expression, an opportunity to heal every false thought or small idea you ever had about yourself; hell, he'd never even considered those possibilities, let alone discussed them with his beloved.

Later, when pressed on the subject, the Prince admitted not marrying her might have been the biggest mistake of his whole life, though that remains to be seen.

The Earthquake

"Love—two solitude's, that border, greet, and protect each other."
                                                    Rainier Marie Rilke

*S*oon *after the Prince broke off his engagement with Princess Vivien, his life
changed rather dramatically. As usual, it had taken a cataclysmic event to
get the ball rolling, and this time it came in the form of the '94 Los Angeles
earthquake.*

   *Around this same time, the Prince had met a striking nurse, with two
young children, who was just coming out of a bad marriage. She had sworn the
night they met, dancing, she wasn't interested in another committed relationship, but she was lonely and did enjoy his companionship. She also saw how
good he was with kids. The gun shy Prince thought it sounded safe enough, and
since he loved being around children, and he too was feeling lonely, it seemed
like a good match.*

   Her parents had appropriately picked her namesake as the wind.
She had perfectly wild blond hair, that took two hours to create under a
hair dryer, to go with her mesmerizing green eyes. *(They came compliments
of Bausch and Laumb).* Mariah was the classic bombshell, in the mold of
Marilyn Monroe, and she knew it. She had a mouth that made mine water,
and alabaster skin (with a fragrance as sweet and wholesome as mom's fresh
deep-dish blackberry cobbler). She had award winning looks, and would
certainly have won an honorable mention in 'the girl next door' competi-
tion, if your zip code was 90210. * I fantasized, the first night we met, that
undoing the top three buttons on her blouse would reveal treasures unlike
any I had ever seen. I wasn't disappointed.

   We had been dating about three months, the night it happened. I
was deep into dreamland, at Mariah's home out in Newhall (about a mile
from where the freeways collapsed), when the 'quake' struck with the feroc-
ity of a wounded lion backed into a corner. My gut reaction, when the

* (I Could Be) The Boy Next Door

house began to fracture and cave in upon us, was to throw my body over hers as a shield. Once the brutal violence slackened to a tremor, my second instinct, was to lurch from the collapsed waterbed and gingerly wade into the pitch toward the plaintive whimpering of her young daughter. There were nearly two feet of smashed furniture and glass strewn everywhere, but I knew I had to get us all out of the house, as quickly as possible. Navigating the hallway, was the first major obstacle; made even more difficult, as aftershocks were coming every few seconds. It probably took less than three minutes to get us all outside, but it seemed like eternity. Once we were all safely away from the structure, it was a matter of going back in to turn off the gas.

As I moved to go back in the house, my body began to shake. At first, I had acted on impulse and adrenaline, but now we were safe, I realized the precariousness of the situation, and fear started surging through my body. Never before, had I experienced sheer terror, and the physical sensation of being terrified, started to overcome me. Just as I thought I was about to collapse, a voice went off inside my head, as if through a megaphone. *

"Breathe into it. Acknowledge the fear and walk through it. What's the worst that could happen? You could die? So what? You've always looked forward to crossing over to the other side. You spent half your life trying to get there. You know there's no such thing as death. You're just borrowing this body for a while, to learn some lessons."

The fear went away, but I'll never forget that voice. It was just like the day of the motorcycle accident. *Call them guardian angels or ancestors or whatever you want; the Prince had been shown one more time that he wasn't alone on this journey.*

Mariah got a flashlight from her car, as it was still pitch black outside, and I reentered the house. By now, one of the neighbors had stopped by to offer help, so we both went in search of the gas valve. I even stopped to get shoes for the kids and a sweater for Mariah. After checking on the other neighbors and making sure everyone was OK, I started thinking

* Days of Old...Awakening Imaginations CD #8

about my own place and my studio in Studio City. Reports were coming in over the radio that entire blocks had collapsed in my neighborhood, which made me a bit anxious, but with the freeway system collapsed, there in Newhall, I knew I was cut off from the rest of the world for a while. There was no sense in worrying about what might be, so I drove over to the local twelve-step clubhouse to see if I could be of service there.

Months later, Mariah confessed to me, "That one act of covering my body with your own bonded me to you and made me fall so deeply in love, that when you later told me you didn't see us as life partners, I was devastated." *

I found this perplexing, as she had seemed to take our gradual distancing into a friendship in stride. We had connected physically and mentally from the beginning, and I loved her kids, but the spiritual (which I consider the glue that holds it all together), was never even close to a match. We'd both recognized it from the start, so I honestly believed she wouldn't become attached.

"If it's any consolation," I told her, "I feel awful. The last thing I would ever want to do is cause you any pain. I loved you then and I love you now, just not the same way."

Then, as an after thought, I asked her, "Protecting women and children, isn't that what every man would do?"

She could tell I was serious, and pondered my question for a few moments before surprising me with her candid response, "Of all the men I've ever known, I could count on one hand, the ones that really think that way, and one of them was my dad. Believe me, you're a dying breed."

Interesting to note, that one of the Prince's friends did the exact same thing (covering his girlfriend's body with his own), only to find she'd gotten mad at him, because she couldn't get up and run for cover. Go figure.

It would be three days, before I would get back to check on my own place and the studio, and it wasn't a pretty sight. I knew right away, I would need to find another source of income.

The fact is, I had become rather discouraged lately, as the studio

* It's Only a Matter of Time

had begun to seem like an albatross around my neck. My gifts were in writing and producing, and using my discernment to bring the right people together to create magic. I loved the creative side of music, but more and more, it seemed my time was occupied chasing down delinquent clients, trying to keep an eye out so equipment wouldn't be stolen, or making sure some artist didn't carve his initials in the recording console, or use the room as a shooting gallery. This was not how I envisioned spending the rest of my life.

After the quake, I decided to take inventory on what I was doing and started asking myself questions.

"Is this bringing me joy and happiness?"

"Is it uplifting anyone?"

"Am I making a contribution?"

I decided, then and there, to make a change. What it was, I didn't have a clue, but I was willing to try anything.

The earthquake brought a number of revelations to the Prince. He realized that people will still reach out and help each other in times of need. It made him hopeful to hear the countless stories of heroic deeds, and feel Los Angeles actually become a community, even if it was only for a little while.

Secondly, Mariah's comment hammered home, one more time, the importance of initiation for men. Whereas, before, he had only been seeking his own initiation from the elders, he now realized he was becoming an elder himself, and it was his responsibility not only to help on an individual basis, but to tell others of what he'd learned.

Thirdly, being honest with one's intentions is a good start, but it's not enough, when it comes to matters of the heart. Though loneliness might not appear to be a bad reason to get involved, the Prince realized two halves do not make a whole, and if he ever wanted to create magic with someone else, he had to become whole within himself first. Furthermore, he was shown, one more time, that men and women are two totally different creatures when it comes to bonding. Like many other men he could have sex without any type of emotional connection at all; for fun, for release, for sport, even out of boredom. But, the

Prince was finally starting to get it; most women are going to bond once you've been inside them. It doesn't matter what they say, or how honest and well intentioned you might be at the early stages; it's a physiological reaction. Like author, Pat Allen, <u>Getting To I Do</u> says,

"Now girls, don't let those boys penetrate your bodies. He could be the biggest geek in the world, but once he's been inside, he starts to look pretty good." We're speaking in generalities here, of course, there are always exceptions. I just think it's God's way of propagating the species.

The last revelation that came to the Prince, during this time, was the old lesson of 'be careful what you pray for'. He had always prayed to have a world class studio for recording, not realizing the <u>business</u> of music could suck all the creativity right out of him, totally defeating why he'd created the studio in the first place.

Real Money/Esalen

*"The perfect love from up above's upon us now on winged dove
open up your soul unto this rhyme.
Let it flow down deep inside, before the light nothing can hide,
and know throughout your being you are divine."*

GWC

*T*he Prince had no idea what he was to do next, but he had faith that he
would be guided. The earthquake had simply been a reminder of how
powerless he was, and he knew God could, and would, direct the show perfectly, if he'd just stay out of his own way.

First thing I did, was inform all my friends I was in the job market, and even tried a couple temporary sales jobs to prove to myself that I
was willing. About three weeks after my decision, I got a call from a friend
who told me about a nationally recognized company, in the investment
world, that was hiring onto their sales force.

He told me, "Some of their top salesmen make $40-$50,000 dollars a year. I can get you an interview, if you want one." I knew absolutely
zero about the stock market, but figured if my job was simply 'to suit up
and show up, and leave the results up to God', then I had nothing to lose
in checking it out.

The rest is history.

*The second week on the job, the Prince broke the all-time record for sales
in a week. Not by a little bit, but he almost doubled the existing record that had
stood for 10 years. The billionaire owner of the company had predicted to the
sales force, just months before the Prince's arrival, that someone in their department would make over six figures in a year. Everyone had laughed at him.*

*Within nine months, the Prince was not only in six figures, but was tak-
ing two and three week vacations around the world; sending back cards from
places like Maui and Tahiti. He received numerous awards, for outstanding*

achievement, from the owner, who told the Prince during one of the award cer-
emonies,

"When you're ready to move up the corporate ladder, come see me per-
sonally."

Interesting, that right after the Prince had broken the all-time sales
record, and the accolades were pouring in, he was so uncomfortable with all the
attention, that it was all he could do to not bolt out the front door. When he
finally managed to get out of the building that day, he cried all the way home.
Some of the scars from childhood take longer to heal than the others.

It was an exhilarating time for me. I'd never known that kind of
financial freedom before. I'd received large chunks of money in the past,
but had never had the experience of controlling my own destiny in that
regard. Every week, I knew I could add thousands into my bank account,
and since you could travel to anywhere in the world for a week's pay, I
began planning trips to every exotic locale I had ever fancied.

One of the first escapades I planned, was to drive up the Southern
California coast to Big Sur and stay at The Esalen Institute, where some of
the worlds' greatest body workers could be found. I planned on treating
myself to all the massages my body could handle. In all the years, and literally hundreds of massages I'd been given, I had never had the privilege of
saying, "OK, you can stop now, I've had enough."

I always wanted more. *(Even though he had the disease of 'more', he*
thought it would be nice to have it in remission, at least once in his life). My
goal on this journey, was to get so relaxed between the mineral baths, the
massages, and being out in nature, that I would actually feel satiated.

Many years earlier, during a visit to the farm, it had dawned on the
Prince how uncomfortable everyone in his family was about touching.

I realized I had never hugged my father hello, good-bye or anything else, for that matter. At most, there might be a hand shake with "hi
son" attached, and my mother would get stiff as a mannequin, if you tried
to hug her; determined to do her duty, but it certainly wasn't something
she could enjoy.

Once I got on that train of thought, I wondered how in the world I had become so tactile? Why did I so love to touch and to be touched? Then, I remembered. During my childhood summer trips to Mississippi visiting my grandparents, I would spend much of my time at my favorite cousin, Rollo's. Each night, my aunt would come and rub our backs till we fell asleep. (This was a tradition I was glad to see my cousin had passed on to his own children.) Years later, once I realized what a precious gift I'd been given, I went to my aunt and said, "Two decades ago you passed onto me the gift of touch. On behalf of myself, every person I've ever healed, and every girlfriend I've ever had, I want to thank you."

Though she didn't say a lot in response, I could see she was deeply moved and grateful for that acknowledgment. *It's astounding, what a profound effect a kind word can have on another human being, as well as, how such a little action can have such far-reaching consequences on others.*

After deciding to go to Esalen, for the ultimate massage experience, I began making preparations for the trip. First, I went and bought myself a copy of Enya's, "Shepard's Moon" CD, as it had inspired me since the first time I'd heard it, and felt it would be the perfect traveling companion.

Next, I resolved to find myself a better sound system to play music on, and that for a change, money would be no object. One thing led to another, and before I knew it, I had purchased a brand new convertible German sports car, that had a 'killer sound system'. Then I grabbed my guitar and a toothbrush, tossed a few clothes in a bag, put the roof down and was off. *(I just wish the Prince were a little more spontaneous.)*

I was in no hurry and took my time, except along the coast of Big Sur. There, I was inspired to go for all the exhilaration only a world class driving machine can offer, when put through its paces. The beauty of the coast drive was breathtaking, almost surreal, and both the lover and the monk in me were in agreement, for a change. *

I had one of those perfect days. *You know, where you're thinking to yourself, "Life doesn't get much better than this." One of those days where you*

---

* I Don't Know How To Do This

crank up the music at stop lights, so the people next to you can enjoy it as well. One of those days when, even if the guy next to you, in his fancy foreign sports car, shatters your tranquility with loud music you don't relate to, you know the light will be changing soon and you can even humor him with a smile. You know...one of those days.

I arrived at dusk, and decided to walk the grounds. Esalen is one of the original and most famous spiritual retreats, started back in the sixties. The grounds cover acres of ocean front property nestled away in a cheery rain forest. Known, especially, for its hot spring mineral baths that jut out over the sea, guests can stay all night in them beneath the stars, with the sound of the ocean crashing just a few feet below.

It wasn't mandatory to be naked at the baths, but since practically everyone else was, I thought I would stick out if I were the only one with clothes on. *(He was also afraid he might stick out if he had his clothes off. You know, peer pressure.)* The A-frame caper, years before, was the closest thing I had ever experienced to being naked in a group before, and I was a bit worried I might see a beautiful woman, and my attraction might become all too apparent. *(And since he wasn't quite ready yet to become a parent . . .)*

Not to worry; people of every age, shape, size, disposition and religious affiliation were there, and it was no big deal. In fact, on different occasions, having met someone attractive at the main lodge, I would suggest going down to the baths. I was in awe to find it took all the urgency away, when meeting someone like that. *The Prince was delighted to find that, since there were no exterior shields up, there was no need to try and take them down, and you could see the person for who they really were. He had that thought, one day, while soaking in the baths with people from at least half a dozen different countries,*

"If it were mandatory, that everyone in the world had to spend at least a week a year in a place like Esalen, the world would be in amazingly better shape." *I agree with him wholeheartedly.*

No longer did I feel driven to get physical, too soon, once the unknown was taken away. It was quite healing for me, to find that sex had lost its power over me, and for the first time in my life, I found I could take it or leave it.

During the day, the baths were available only to those people staying on the grounds, but between midnight and three a.m., visitors were allowed to come and soak in their healing waters, as well.

One night, I was by myself meditating, down at the baths, after midnight, when someone came and joined me in the tub. I opened my eyes for a second, and there I saw the side profile of a very voluptuous, full-bodied woman, framed against the full moon, like some Greek Goddess. I could have been in any number of my childhood wet dreams. I couldn't see her face, but like those boyhood fantasies, it was the differences in our bodies; the hourglass figure, the perfectly upturned nipples seeking out the moonlight, the sensuality that exuded sheer loveliness, that fascinated me and could drive me to the point of ecstatic explosion. After hurriedly finishing my meditation, I opened my eyes to discover her floating on her back; moonbeams glistening off her face, and then her breasts, as they floated to the surface. Just as I was reminiscing about bobbing for apples as a kid, she looked up and said, "You have a beautiful smile."

I told her of the thoughts that had inspired it, and she laughed. There was a gentleness, a kindness in her face, that bespoke wisdom, as well as authenticity. I surmised she was probably in her late thirties or early forties, though there were no lines on her face pointing in that direction. I looked around and saw none of the other tubs were in use, so I knew she had sought out my company. Sensing she wanted to talk, but her innate shyness was in the way, I broke the ice, and before long, the most amazing story emerged.

It seemed she and her husband had been deeply in love for a number of years. A modern day 'Romeo and Juliet', till one day something changed. She wasn't sure what it had been, and he wasn't talking much. Instead, he had decided to do the typical 'Men Are From Mars' routine of going to his cave to figure things out.

The metaphorical cave he'd chosen, was actually hiking to the top of his favorite mountain, as that was where he found he could do his best thinking. Actually, they both loved to mountain climb and usually went together, but not this time.

"He needed to be alone," as she put it.

She kissed him good-bye and Godspeed, and he was headed for the mountaintop. Two days later, half way down, he called her (the old sound back in his voice), telling her how much he loved and treasured their relationship, and couldn't wait to get home to share with her what he had realized.

He never arrived. He was caught in an avalanche and buried under tons of rubble.

It had happened exactly one year ago, that day, and she had been grieving his death ever since. She had just gotten back from hiking to the top of their favorite mountain, where she had done a ritual scattering of his ashes to the winds.

"It's now time to get on with my life, and I chose to begin here, at the baths," she offered.

The longer we whispered into the night, the more intimately she shared her life with me, and I started to feel this wasn't just a coincidence. Even though I had been practicing celibacy, and had closed that door for a number of months, I felt I should at least leave it open, if that was what she needed to bring her back into the world of the living.

My intuition was right; it was exactly what she desired. We made sweet tender love, under the stars and water both, and I knew I had been of great service. (Great work if you can get it.)

We made love till almost dawn, and I had to resist not asking her for her phone number, as it was perfect just the way it was. In no way, did I want to risk diminishing her memory of the experience, or my own, for that matter. But, that was a while ago, and if you happen to be reading this book and you're still single, the Prince can be reached at... Just kidding.

Tahiti

"Beyond the place of right thinking and wrong thinking, there is a field. I'll meet you there."

Marie Rainier Rilke

*T*he Prince's new found financial freedom allowed another of his dreams to become a reality. It began one Friday afternoon, when on the spur of the moment, he decided to take a trip. He found a copy of the travel section from the Sunday Times, and by Tuesday, he was on his way to Tahiti.

Rather than go a la Club Med, where you could count on getting the homogenized Americana version of Tahitian life, I found a charming bungalow, surrounded by trees, two feet from the sand and twenty from the waters edge. There, I had non-tourists for neighbors, unbelievable wildflowers, of every color and hue, breadfruits, coconuts, mangos, and scantily clad women, all within view of my front porch. It was as picture perfect as I had imagined, except for one thing. *

Rather than go alone, I invited Carol. I had met her at a meditation service at Lake Shrine, but had known after a few weeks of dating, that it probably wasn't a match. The first time I saw her face, she was deep in meditation, and had that glow that only God or phenomenal sex can give you.

On paper, she had seemed perfect, stunningly beautiful, mentally sharp, and spiritually inclined; all qualities I thought necessary in my life partner. *(Certainly, at least good for two weeks in paradise.)* But, perfect matches on paper, don't always pan out in real life.

My primary plan for the vacation, had been to not hear a phone or get inside any motorized vehicle for awhile. I envisioned being as native-like as possible; spearing fish, and picking coconuts, mangos and bread fruit from the trees for dinner. Carol's idea, was to visit every tourist trap and go on every tour available. This was not my idea of a good time. You'd

* With Or Without You...Chameleon CD #5

think two mature adults could navigate through these waters, but it had nothing to do with what we were arguing about. *(It rarely does!)*

Unfortunately, she had never dealt with the anger she felt towards her father, for abandoning her as a child; instead, she would take it out on all her boyfriends. It all came to a boil, while we were there in Tahiti. I just couldn't take it anymore. It was starting to drive me crazy, that we couldn't find solutions to what seemed to be such mundane matters. I even tried to use humor and wrote a song about it. *

Unfortunately, she didn't think the song was funny, so I tried another approach. In therapy, I had learned a great analogy, and passed it onto her, trying to be helpful.

"Imagine you're an orange, and your juice is your emotions, that have been building up since childhood. A lot of that juice is your anger, and from what I understand, you have every right to be angry. What you don't have the right to do, is spew it all over me. I've barely known you a month, and have done nothing that warrants this level of animosity."

That hit too close to home, as she just wasn't ready. She started to cry and told me the story of her father, and how this anger had come up in all her previous relationships. Her honesty moved me, and acted as a temporary band-aid, but the warning flags were up. I'd been in recovery too long and knew she had a long road ahead of her, if she genuinely wanted to heal her wounds. My days of rescuing women were obviously drawing to a close. I could be her friend, but I wasn't going to open up and let her stomp around on my heart. I knew I deserved better than that. Deciding some of her behavior was just not acceptable, I told her I was calling it quits. *(Go figure, travel to the most exotic locale in the world to break up.)*

All was not lost, as we agreed to a compromise for the remainder of our stay. I got my wish of no phones or motor vehicles for four days, and the one tour I did go on, was to a museum of Tahitian art and culture. The museum was considered an authority on the life of the artist Gaugin, whom I saw as a kindred spirit. The tortured artist, the desire to be alone

* Stop Pickin' On Me...Chameleon CD #10

and live like a hermit, his leaving the world behind and moving to a South Sea Island...all qualities I saw in my self and resonated with. Thank God, I was able to incorporate them into my life and not let them overwhelm me, to the point of destruction.

The high point of the entire trip, was seeing how the universal language of music could overcome the language barrier with our non-English speaking neighbors. They were two young Frenchmen that flipped hamburgers in Paris, eight months out of the year, so they could afford to come live in Tahiti the other four. The boys taught me how to spearfish and let me borrow their gear; whenever I liked, and their numerous French girlfriends, that seemed to always be topless; definitely enhanced the local landscape.

Living like natives, in tattered shorts, the boys were as delightful as they could be, but spoke almost no English. I knew no French, other than 'Frere Jacques' and 'Voulez vous coucher avec moi ce soir', which of course got a hearty laugh. What the Frenchmen did understand though, were lots of Christmas songs. (*Who cares if it was March?*)

The final night there, we had a farewell party. I drove down to the local port, as I'd heard from a neighbor that the fishermen there often had fresh tuna you could buy straight off the boat. Sure enough, as I was pulling up in my mechanical vehicle (part of our compromise was renting a car for the second week), a boat was just chugging in, and I could see the tuna fish hanging on board. I bought two, twenty-pound beauties and gave them to the boys. When Carol and I, guitar in hand, returned a couple hours later, they had shishima and tuna steaks, with all the trappings, already prepared. After dinner, some more of their friends dropped by (even one who could translate for us), and we went down and started a bonfire on the sand. We sang Christmas carols till the wee hours.

It was a delightful ending to a somewhat disappointing trip, but the Prince was truly grateful he had gotten out of the relationship in four months instead of four years, and besides, he had gotten a great tan.

The Prince learned he would much rather be by himself than be with the wrong person. It didn't matter how exquisite or ravishing a woman was, if her beauty didn't start from deep within. He planned, from then on, to ask every woman he dated how she felt about her father, as soon as it was diplomatically possible. Knowing it worked both ways, he advised his women friends to ask the same question of their partners.

Deepak and Dharma

"Learning to be an accomplished person staying right sized, now there's a challenge."

GWC

*T*he Prince had believed for a long time, that the mark of a spiritual being was one who could manifest their desires rapidly. When he was younger, he had taken that creative ability for granted, but now that he was sober, he wasn't nearly so confident in himself. The Prince knew it was going to be a challenge for him to be a worker among workers (as the 12 step doctrines had taught him), and still use his gifts to attempt august deeds. The Prince had been dwelling more and more, lately, on how to use these gifts and connections, for the greater good, when the first opportunity arose.

I had become interested in both the stopping of cruelty to animals and the raping of our environment, after reading John Robbins, 'Diet for A New America'. I had been so impressed, I changed my diet drastically after reading how the meat industry, alone, was probably the worst offender polluting our planet.

After meeting John, in person, I was even more impressed. It dawned on me, that the very next weekend I was flying to San Francisco to meet Paul and Linda McCartney, thanks to one of my partners in the studio who happened to be their financial controller. Knowing they were also involved with stopping the cruelty to animals and were doing everything they could to educate the public to other alternatives, I took it upon myself to invite John to come to San Francisco, so I could introduce them. From there, I figured I'd get out of the way and let fate take its course. My job was simply to put them together.

The introduction was smooth and effortless, though I did find at times, during the weekend, it took a conscious effort to keep my thoughts purely altruistic and not try and get in the middle. My ego wanted gratification, in a big way, and in the old days, it probably would have won out. It didn't hurt that my friend, Endre, had come as well, and he could always be counted on to remind me to focus on the greater good and not the individual glory.

Another memorable venture during this time, in fact, probably the catalyst behind my telling this story as a musical memoir, was my meeting and playing for Deepak Chopra.

We were first introduced by a mutual friend at Agape (an L.A. ministry of The Church of Religious Science), who told Deepak about my music and the dulsitar, in particular. I liked him immediately. There was no pretense, as you might have expected of one with his worldwide reputation. A strong ego, to be sure, but a childlike sense of humor, which gets a lot of points in my opinion. He was very intense and focused, yet still accessible to those who wanted a word with him. He gave off the air, though, to not waste his time if you just wanted to glad-hand. He seemed genuine. After we were introduced, Deepak asked if I'd like to come to Long Beach, that same night, and perform at a seminar he was conducting there. I hesitated for a second, then said,

"Sure, I'd be happy to."

I was surprised by my immediate answer, as I rarely brought the dulsitar into public. I would normally play guitar, piano, harmonica, percussion, but not the dulsitar. I saved that for special occasions, and I really knew very little about Deepak, and even less about his teachings. Having had such a conscious being as my first mentor had spoiled me. By comparison, most spiritual teachers since, had seemed like they were serving up baby food. I figured Deepak's was more of the same, just packaged differently. On the other hand, if he were able to bring millions of people to start thinking more consciously, then more power to him.

In truth, the only thing I did know about Deepak, was that a couple of my friends swore by his work, and one of his books had been on the best seller list. I knew, that in itself didn't guarantee quality, but I'd learned to trust my intuition more, and something told me to take the time, break my other plans, and go perform.

At first, I felt rusty, since I hadn't performed in a while, but I did manage to get out of my own way and seemed to move a number of people in the audience. At the end of the evening, Deepak asked me if I'd come join him, a few months later, and perform in San Diego for his big event of the year. This was a week long retreat called 'Seduction of Spirit', where he taught meditation techniques, as well as one of the seven spiritual laws of success each day. This time, I didn't hesitate at all, as I'd heard enough that night to know there was a lot I could learn from the man.

During the next couple of months, as I read more of Deepak's work and saw how many lives had been changed for the better, I became even more impressed. Not only did he carry depth of knowledge, but the clarity with which it was imparted, was profound. I described him to a friend as 'Einstein meets Gandhi'. Just like my first teacher, Jim Goure, had done so many years before, Deepak could take scientific, empirical data, and combine it with the spiritual in a way that made perfect sense.

One of his teachings I most related to, and for years had lived by, was the seventh spiritual law of success. Deepak called it the 'law of Dharma'. It basically says everyone has a calling, and there's something in this life you can do better than anyone else. Your job is to find out what that is, and do it.

This was not unlike Joseph Campbell's tenant of 'Follow Your Bliss', or the Prince's own admonition, written across the back of his van so many years before, 'Follow Your Dreams'.

At long last, the time arrived for me to head to San Diego. Southern California traffic was awful, as usual, and I arrived feeling rushed and out of sorts, just a short time before my first performance. I'd worn a suit, as a sign of respect, but was very uncomfortable, and upon voicing this on stage, was greeted by hundreds of people with the mantra, "Take it off, take it off, take it all off."

This was not the crowd response I had expected at all. I thought I would be leading them in a meditation. If I'd had any inkling it was such a lively group, I would have been better prepared; playing piano and guitar songs, using lyrics and humor, as well as the dulsitar.

My unorthodox greeting broke the ice in a hurry. I later was told I'd been taking myself much too seriously and could stand to lighten up. *Hey, what are good friends for, if not to tell you the truth.*

The crowd seemed to love the performance he gave, and other than his slight discomfort, at being asked to do a strip tease, the Prince enjoyed himself, as well. Afterwards, over a hundred people wanted to buy copies of dulsitar music, but since he didn't have any with him, all he could do was start a mailing list. The fact was, he had no product available at all, and it was becoming quite apparent to the Prince that he hadn't been following his 'dharma'. His gifts needed to be made available. *

Over the next couple days, Deepak taught the group a meditation technique I had never seen before. Moving up the seven chakras, one at a time, he would have us take our consciousness to that designated point, repeat specific words (sutras), and then hopefully go to that place between the thoughts, or what Deepak referred to as 'going into the gap'.

Thoughts of transformation, nourishment, destiny, laughter, intention, discernment, truth and enlightenment, were all part of the journey up the spine. Prior to this, 15-20 minutes was as long as I would feel comfortable in meditation. With this new technique, I found myself meditating an hour at a time, 2-3 times a day, and loving it. I was confounded by how little sleep I needed.

On the third night, around three a.m., I couldn't sleep, and had gone out on the balcony of the hotel to meditate. It was a beautiful moonlit night, and I could hear the waves lapping at the shore as I began to drift deeper and deeper. Soon, I lost all track of time and space.

I had moved my consciousness into my solar plexus region (the third chakra), and was slowly repeating the sutra 'destiny', imagining it as a single raindrop splashing into a quiet pond, and then watching the ripples slowly spread out till the waters became still again. Then, I would

* Dulsitar Melding…Rainbow CD #3

release another drop of destiny into the pool. All of a sudden, the lyrics from 'Nature of our Calling', * one of the songs from 'The Rainbow Album', began coming through. I tried to push them away, thinking they were disturbing this great meditation I was having, but couldn't. They kept coming back into my consciousness. *(The old W.C. Fields line, "Go away kid, you bother me", comes to mind.) The Prince hadn't remembered that particular song in fifteen years, and before that moment, could have no more recited the lyrics than he could George Bush's inaugural speech.*

Then, I remembered Deepak telling everyone to simply allow the thoughts to float by, when they'd show up like that, so I did. Ten minutes later, another song from the 'Rainbow Album' came through the same way. The lyrics from the entire album continued to flow in like that, for over an hour. I felt so energized, I couldn't go back to sleep, and I finally wrote them all down. I could hardly wait, till morning, to get downstairs where I had left my guitar.

Each morning, that week, I had been opening the day's activities in the main hall, doing a little creativity workshop. Using the piano and guitar, as well as the dulsitar, I had been singing songs and then showing people how easy it was to write their own ideas in song form. I welcomed everyone from the conference to come down after their morning meditations and join in.

What they were greeted with, this particular morning, was me singing all the songs from the 'Rainbow Album'. The response was overwhelming, as dozens of people requested copies of the music. I realized that morning, I was so comfortable singing those songs, I might as well have been born on that stage. That, in itself, was a revelation, as I hadn't felt that 'at home' performing in years.

*Not since the days of playing at the metaphysical 'advances', nearly a quarter of a century earlier, had he felt this content. He knew he was in the right place, at the right time, doing the right thing. ***

So many people signed up that wanted copies to send to their friends, as well as copies of the Edgar Cayce album, I was overwhelmed.

* The Nature of Our Calling…Rainbow CD #2
* Merlin's Theme…Chameleon CD #1

The music I had written and recorded, so many years before, had seeming-ly finally come of age. I flashed on a memory of Veneta telling me in a trance reading, two decades earlier, that mine was to be a belated success; that my music was 'ahead of its time' and that it would be many years before people would relate to what I was writing about.

She had told me point blank, "You don't just 'believe' in angels and the divine, you 'know' it to be true. Most people, if they're open to the idea at all, think it to be a mere possibility. They're not ready for you, yet."

At the time, in my naivete, I had thought to myself, "No way, peo-ple will relate."

Now, here I was, all these years later, somewhat wiser and certainly humbled. Veneta had been right. *Next, he wondered if the time would ever be right to share 'The Dungeon Tapes'.*

I not only had no copies of 'The Rainbow Album,' I wasn't even sure if the tapes still existed. Even if they did, I had no idea of the quality of the recordings, as time has definitely been known to take its toll on old acetate. All I could do was pray that they would be OK, once I found them.

The Prince now knew why he'd been led to Deepak's seminar. He'd been ignoring his Dharma for many years, instead of focusing on the gift he had been given, which brought such joy. Instead of owning his own magnificence, he had been listening to that voice from years past, the radio station KF-K, broadcast-ing globally with the power of one million mega-hurts. It was the voice that said he would never amount to anything, and that "music was great for an avo-cation, but you can't make a living at it."

The Prince found it daunting, once he realized how incredibly dam-aging messages like that from a parent could be to a young child. He swore, then and there, that if telling his story might help even one person not have to go through what he had gone through, then it would be worth the telling.

Once I returned from the seminar, the first thing I did, was go and search for the master tapes of the 'Rainbow Album'. I found them easily enough, but then came the unnerving part. I booked the best studio in LA known for taking old analog masters and re-mastering them for digital format. There was nothing left for me to do, but pray.

What a joy to find the tapes not only hadn't deteriorated but were in pristine shape. For an added bonus I unearthed a buried treasure of dulsitar tracks I had totally forgotten about that were as clear as the day they were recorded. From there it was a simple matter of going through them one at a time, using today's technological advancements to enhance the magic that had been captured so many years before.

From then on, whenever the Prince would be feeling lonely or unfilled from not having raised a family like most of his peers, he could listen to those recordings and remind himself that he did have a legacy to leave behind. His songs were his children.

The Old Knight

"Our present mental conversations do not recede into the past as man believes, they advance into the future to confront us as wasted or invested words."

Neville

*N*ow remember, all these current adventures were possible because of the Prince's new career at the investment company. He was still breaking all the records and had caught both the eye and the ear of the owner, and was being groomed to move up the proverbial corporate ladder.

On the one hand, moving into that rarified atmosphere meant I could make seven figures a year and continue to be the 'hero'. On the other hand, I knew this wasn't where my heart or passions lay, this wasn't my 'Dharma'. My dad, though, didn't understand anything about dharma. I wondered if I'd lose some of the hard fought-for love and acceptance I'd finally earned. *(Notice he didn't say given.)*

The Prince had felt uncomfortable with his success, from the beginning, and unconsciously, his lifelong rebellion against authority figures had reared its ugly head. If you've been raised in a dysfunctional family that says you'll never amount to anything, becoming successful makes family not only wrong, but liars. The Prince vacillated for a time, should he or shouldn't he go for the brass ring?

Having been immersed in the corporate environment only a short time, I was naive of the immense weight some people give protocol and going through proper channels. I chose to take the owner up on his offer, and went to see him directly, bypassing both my supervisors and the owner's son.

True to his word, the owner set up an interview with the head of the department I was contemplating moving into. Wanting to look the part, I bought my first Armani suit, with matching power tie, and briefcase, a pair of Cole Hahn wing tips, like my father used to wear, and cut my hair to look like George Clooney; Wall Street short, but with that touch of individuality. *(This is where it gets good).*

The day of his interview, the Prince donned his costume and passed over the moat and through the invisible wall (the nickname for the stairwell between the two departments). While he was waiting for the Duchess of that department to interview him, he ran into the king's #1 knight, who worked in the same wing of the castle.

This knight not only earned more gold than anyone in the company (outside the King of course), but was one of the kingdom's top motivational speakers. He was a distinguished older knight who had been through many wars, and since the Prince had become the new standard bearer, the two of them had previously been introduced at a castle function. The Prince, having recently fought a campaign at the front himself, had enormous respect for the decorated knight, not only for what he had accomplished, but because he was an elder from his same clan. The first time they met, the Prince had alluded to the fact he'd like the older knight to be his mentor, if and when the Prince moved to that wing of the castle.

Now, here they were, meeting again the day of the interview. The Prince, knowing of the older knight's reputation as a motivational speaker, could hardly contain his enthusiasm, when recounting the details of a gathering he'd just attended on the other side of the kingdom. It had been based on the writings of a man named Neville 'The Gift Of Imagination', and the Prince had been literally astounded with the profundity of his work. When he had voiced that opinion to other friends, on the spiritual path, he was perplexed to find almost no one had heard of him. The Prince felt Neville was far more accessible than the work of many pundits that were currently being lauded across the kingdom.

"Neville crossed over twenty years ago, but his writings on how to manifest ones' dreams are extraordinary, and certainly applicable to this day and age." *

I went on and on, in great detail, telling the old knight about Neville's teachings, and when I was through, the most extraordinary thing

---

* Play Along

happened. He looked me straight in the eye and, with a gleam in his own, his voice dropped a register, so that I had to lean forward.

"Neville?" he paused, "without a doubt, the single most important influence on my entire life."

The Prince got chills, his jaw dropped, and then came the goose bumps. It turned out that not only had the old knight been good friends and comrades with Neville, but had accompanied him to many of his lectures across the kingdom years before. Furthermore, he was in possession of a number of unreleased manuscripts and tapes that had never seen the light of day. What a gold mine!

The old knight, having a sense of their historical value, later asked the Prince if he would take all the old manuscripts and tapes and put them onto a digital format (a recent invention in the kingdom) for posterity's sake. The Prince felt honored to be entrusted with such an illustrious task.

Then, it dawned on him. This was the reason he was there interviewing in the first place. His record breaking performances and getting the ear of the king, was all just a prelude to his encounter with the old knight. (Synchronicity can surely thicken a plot.)

The interview with the Duchess went great. In fact, they talked for almost two hours. Later, when the Prince mentioned to the King's son how compelling he'd found the Duchess to be, and alluded to how long the interview had lasted, the king's son (who hadn't yet shown his true colors) retorted with a petulant,

"Really? I made her acquaintance ten years ago, and the longest she's ever engaged me, was 20 minutes."

The Prince should have seen the hieroglyphics on the proverbial (castle) wall, but being guileless to the knavery of the corporate kingdom, he didn't have a clue as to the deep well of jealousy from which some men drank. He was about to find out.

Throughout this entire period, I had been continuing with my multi-cultural men's work and was preparing for a week long retreat entitled 'The Absence of Elders, the Violence of Youth.' It was to be held back at 'Shalom Gap', and my intuition told me something pivotal would occur while there. Sure enough, while on the mountain, I bonded with two writers I had great respect for. One happened to be an elder, and unknowing mentor to me, years earlier. He had been an enormous influence on my early sobriety. We ended up not only being in the same clan, but cabin mates as well.

During the week, I was able to show my gratitude to him for being the first old timer, around the 12 step programs, who advocated how imperative it was to verbalize your feelings if you desired deep healing. (Many, from the older generation, championed the attitude 'Just put a plug in the jug; screw feelings.')

Now, it was my turn to be of service. He had never been to this kind of conference before, and I took it upon myself to show him the ropes. As usual, the assembly proved to be a life-enhancing encounter for all, or as I heard one man put it, as we were leaving,

"We spent a year together, one week."

The other writer, I met that week, told me about a course designed to lead people to higher levels of creativity. This piqued my interest, as I had been praying about where to go next with my music, and the more he talked, the more my gut instincts told me I should attend. It wasn't to begin for eight weeks, but I had a premonition I was supposed to be there, and marked it on my calendar. The next few weeks passed ever so slowly, as my heart was no longer where my body was. Since the Deepak Chopra conference, I had become only too aware that I was not being true to my muse, and had become increasingly disenchanted, spending so much energy in the corporate world. Unfortunately, I was too afraid to walk away from that much money. *(The Protestant work ethic strikes again.)*

The day the course was to begin, finally arrived, and I had to decide if I was going to take the entire week off or just leave early that evening. I was vacillating, because of my desire to finish out the month, so I could win yet another award, and get my name emblazoned on a plaque one more time. *(It's truly astonishing to me how one can get so caught up in the pursuit of 'fools gold'.)* I then planned on taking at least six weeks off to follow my dharma. *(The compromise the Prince had worked out with his integrity.)*

The decision was made for me. To my utter bewilderment, as soon as I arrived at work that Monday morning, I was called into my supervisor's office. There sat the hatchet man and his sidekick, 'Billy'. I could tell he didn't understand what was going on, as he seemed as awkward as I that he had the unpleasant job of firing me.

At first, I couldn't believe it. I was stunned and baffled. My emotions ran the gamut from, sadness and guilt (what's my dad going to think?), to indignation mixed in with relief.

"Just doing my job," he offered weakly, after giving me the ludicrous official spin. I was well aware of the feathers I'd ruffled and the real reason for the dismissal, so after the initial shock and ensuing embarrassment (as I'd never been fired before), it took me all of about 30 minutes to realize,

"This was God doing for me what I couldn't do for myself."

The universe loves a made up mind, and the day the Prince marked the course in his calender, God had started orchestrating events to happen that would fullfill his deepest desire. Though the Prince likes to think he would have made that move on his own, deep down, he knew it took an earthquake to get him there, and it would have taken an earthquake to get him out. To see his dismissal, that quickly, as the 'blessing in disguise' it really was, felt like phenomenal growth to the Prince, and he quickly embraced the unlimited possibilities it offered.

ADD/ The Pilgrimage

"Opportunity is often missed because we are busy broadcasting, when we should be tuning in."

Author Unknown

*T*he synchronicity of leaving the corporate world and starting his creative U-turn on the same day, wasn't lost on the Prince. Since he believes that nothing happens by coincidence, accident, or chance, and that there is nothing random or haphazard about the universe he lives in, he took it as a sign he was definitely being guided on the right path.

A few months earlier, a friend, that knew me well, had dropped by my apartment quite unexpectedly. He told me, in the course of conversation, that he had recently been diagnosed with Attention Deficit Disorder (a neurological syndrome whose classic symptoms are impulsiveness, distractibility, and hyperactivity). Later, after having gazed around my apartment at all the piles of unfinished projects, he surprised me when he asked, "Have you ever been checked out for Attention Deficit Disorder? We seem to have many of the same symptoms."

I bought the book my friend recommended on the subject, 'Driven to Distraction', and wasn't twenty pages into it, before I was sobbing. I couldn't stop the flood, for well over an hour, and it seemed apropos that every page, telling my story, now had my tears all over it. They were describing my life and all the years feeling like I was somehow different from my fellows.

"You mean there's a name for this? I'm physiologically wired differently than other people?" I asked my mutually afflicted friend.

The book talked about ways to help the disorder, including support groups, organizational tools, and even medications that had brought startling results to some people. I could hardly wait to get an appointment with a doctor. He not only verified my diagnosis, but said, "You're a prime candidate to be a poster child."

It was like a brilliant spotlight had been turned on to reveal a place in my head that had acted like a black hole all my life; a place where things had disappeared, never to be heard from again.

Some of the tears were of sadness, wondering what my life might have been like had I found out sooner, but most were for relief that at least I finally knew about it, and it had a name. It would be a good year, before the tears of anger and frustration started bubbling to the surface. Ironically, that happened while standing in a 'Covey' store. (Created by the man who wrote 'The 7 Habits Of Highly Effective People'.) I was there trying to find what I needed to set up a day planner (a suggestion for all people with ADD), but I had gotten overwhelmed. Thank goodness, my sister was with me. Bless her heart, she patted me on the back, when she saw I was getting choked up, "Don't worry, I'll help you."

What a shame, it had taken three decades to discover there was a name for the Prince's greater than average tendencies to say or do whatever came to mind, his low tolerance for frustration and boredom, and his predilection for situations of high intensity. There was a reason, beyond his control, for many of the behaviors that seemed to plague him all his life.

The good news was, once I was diagnosed and began treatment, there were distinct advantages to having ADD as well; high energy, intuitiveness, creativity and enthusiasm, to name but a few. Once they were harnessed, they actually became a blessing and my life began to change dramatically. Just knowing I had the disorder made a huge difference for me, and even doing simple things, like making lists and keeping a day planner, brought discernible results.

Now that I had joined the ranks of the unemployed, I elected to take literally what a good friend had reminded me,

"God is your employer. Your job is to do whatever is put in front of you, to the best of your ability, and not to worry about the results. That's God's job."

That admonition was a big help and I was off and running. First,

I resolved to take some of that military discipline and structure, I had been so inundated with as a child, and put it to good use. I decided to break my life, and then my work day, down into four areas: physical, mental, spiritual and emotional. Then, I would create a schedule that reflected a balance of the four.

For the physical, I started working out every day, as I had long since recognized the importance of a healthy body. For years I had been admonishing the guys I worked with in 12 step programs. "In my opinion, if they had written the big book of Alcoholics Anonymous now, with all the new information available on health, they would have included a chapter on the importance of exercise and nutrition."

For nutrition, I chose to follow the teachings of Dr. Barry Sears, in his book, 'Enter the Zone'. It was a best seller that went against the grain of mainstream thinking on how, and what, to combine in the way of food, for optimal health and vitality. The idea was to eat the proper amount of carbohydrates, protein and fat at every meal, to get peak performance from one's body. Based on a formula that varied for each person, I quickly found it worked remarkably well for me.

Lastly, I settled on a simple, but daily, Hatha yoga routine to keep my body supple. *(Not to be confused with a daily Tantric yoga routine, though he hoped that might be forthcoming as well.)*

Since the expression was 'a healthy body, a healthy mind,' mental well-being was next on my list. I was already going to a number of 12 step meetings of different varieties, and I knew that would be the foundation, but I added weekly therapy to the mix, and went back to a wonderful therapist I had seen in the past. She was a surrogate grandmother for me, and was the voice that would always remind me,

"He was wrong, he was dead wrong," referring to some of the harsher lessons I had received from my father as a child.

I also diligently used a tool I got from the class I started the day I left the corporate world. First thing, when I woke up each day, I'd write three pages of free flow. Nicknamed 'the brain drain', it would clear my mind of all extemporaneous thoughts.

Spiritually, I had been practicing Jim Goure's 'seven step effective prayer', as well as the techniques I had learned from Deepak Chopra, on a regular basis. Now, I would do them more frequently, and for longer periods of time.

Last, was my plan for emotional well being. All of the above certainly contributed to that goal, but I found it imperative that I play music and write daily to maintain my serenity. Since I'd finally accepted my talents as a gift, not using them felt almost sacrilegious. I was taken aback, once I was reminded of how rewarding it felt to just pick up the guitar and play for a while, or write some new verse or prose.

Next, believing wholeheartedly in the verse "unless ye be like little children", I volunteered at my church to play for the children's choir. Recognizing one of their own, the kids were soon climbing all over me as I taught them how to yodel and make rhythms, using their mouths as their instrument. I don't know who had more fun, but it was just what the doctor had ordered. For whatever reason, I could connect with kids and animals on their own level. (I just wish adults were that effortless.) Countless people, over the years, had voiced their amazement when their cat or dog, that didn't like anybody, would be sitting in my lap after half an hour. I realized having kids and animals around me was definitely an important piece of the puzzle that had been missing. *

Also, around this same time, a good friend gave me a book by 'Sark', which proved to be an utter delight and reminded me once again, to not take it all so seriously. Reminding me to go fly a kite, hug a tree, take a walk, give a smile to someone, get a massage, take a bubble bath, laugh at myself, laugh at myself some more, eat more ice cream and fewer beans, which reminds me . . . I posted a poem up on my wall, which had appeared in my life, and I made a point to read it every morning upon arising. It was written by eighty-five year old Nadine Stair, who was dying and accepting her death. Here it is......

* Children's Song...Awakening Imaginations CD #1

"If I had my life to live over,
I'd try to make more mistakes next time.
I would relax. I would limber up.
I would be crazier than I've been on this trip.
I know very few things I'd take seriously any more.
I would take more chances, I would take more trips,
I would scale more mountains, I would swim more
rivers and I would watch more sunsets.
I would eat more ice cream and fewer beans.
I would have more actual troubles and fewer imaginary ones.
You see... I was one of those people who lived
prophylactically and sensibly and sanely,
hour after hour, day after day.
Oh, I've had my moments
And if I had it to do all over again,
I'd have many more of them.
In fact, I'd try not to have anything else,
just moments, one after another instead of living so
many years ahead of my day.
I've been one of those people who never went anywhere
without a thermometer, a hot water bottle, a gargle, a raincoat
and a parachute.
If I had it to do all over again, I'd travel lighter,
much lighter than I have.
I would start barefoot earlier in the spring,
and I'd stay that way later in the fall.
And I would ride more merry-go-rounds,
and catch more gold rings, and greet more people,
and pick more flowers, and dance more often. If I had to
do it all over again.
But you see, I don't."

It wasn't long, before I began to feel like myself again. The joy of playing and writing, brought back, not only the laughter, but the feeling of authenticity. Daily meditations and walks along the ocean, replaced the stifling air of the corporate environment I had just been freed from.

Eating right, working out, and yoga, brought back the dancer's body I hadn't seen in so many years. Therapy and twelve step meetings brought back that 'comfortable-in-my-own-skin' glow, that had seemed so elusive. The sparkle in my eyes, and my mischievous demeanor, returned. One day, I took myself to a train store and watched the model trains for hours. I thought to myself,

"I am today the best man I have ever been. I am becoming the man I always wanted to be."

Since the earthquake, I had felt the call of the wild; the urge for movement, for change, but my adult mind had been successfully talking me out of it. Thoughts like "grow up...be responsible...settle down", had been coming through, loud and clear, practically drowning out everything else. Now, I could feel that intangible quickening in the air; something stirring inside of me. Not sure what it was or where it was pointing, I started getting the overwhelming urge to start preparing for something.

One day, it dawned on the Prince, it had been quite a while since he'd been on a good old-fashioned adventure. (The type that feels more like a pilgrimage to Mecca than simply going on a vacation.) So, he chose to rectify the situation.

The Eagle, The Rabbit and The Snake

"A good traveler is one who has no fixed plans and is not intent on arriving."
Chinese Proverb

*K*nowing I was a bit rusty and out of practice, for being on the road, I resolved to take a couple of trial runs, to get my reflexes back up to speed.

For openers, going to the high desert for a twelve step/Zen Buddhist men's silent retreat sounded ideal. I had been invited before, but the idea of that much silence (especially when you like to talk as much as I do and you're with friends you haven't seen in awhile), hadn't tempted me before now. There would be some instruction on various Zen practices, such as open-eyed meditation and work meditation, but mostly, it would be hours and hours of quietude.

The day I was to leave, I awoke early to meditate and do my morning writing and work-out. I was eager to be off. By the time I had put a hundred miles between myself and the ocean, I could sense something special was in the air, and flashed on a memory of riding with Princess Claire, when she'd been visited by angels. That's when the old cliche came to mind, "This is the first day of the rest of your life."

In all my years, I'd never had that thought before, in fact, had always found it rather hokie, but for some reason, this day, I found the idea not only inspiring, but perfectly fitting. With the convertible top down, the balmy wind blowing in my face, and the comforting sound of a summer baseball game as background music, I wasn't sure where this was all leading, but I knew I was heading in the right direction.

Once I found myself in the rolling foothills of the mountains, the directions guided me onto a little-used, country road. Before long, the occasional gnarly tree, surrounded by boulders and waves of grain, was flying by as I was intently taking the curves, having somehow found myself in a sports car rally for one. *(Nothing quite like a vivid imagination.)*

Suddenly, as I flew around a sharp curve, there in the middle of the road, was the largest rattlesnake I'd ever seen. I swerved to miss it, though I assumed it was already dead. I had a fascination with snakes, having been born under the sign of scorpionic transformation.

Slowing immediately, I found a turnabout, where I could reverse direction and go have another look. (Remembering I was in no real hurry, I smiled at myself, once I realized what I had been doing when I had spotted the creature.)

After retracing my path, I was mystified to find the serpent was nowhere to be found. I even alighted from the car, to see if there was any blood on the asphalt. Then it dawned on me, "I must have blown right over the dragon, while it was napping on the warm pavement, disturbed it's rest, and it slithered off."

Next, I cogitated that the rattler was probably observing me from the brush, even now, thinking, "What a curious human, to speed by, veering impressively to miss me, and then going to all the trouble to come back and make sure I'm O.K. You know, some humans are all right."

With that train of thought, I knew I was back 'on purpose' and determined it was a good omen, having passed by the proverbial dragon unharmed. Then, my next thought brought even more clarity.

"I need to slow down. I wonder how many other auspicious omens I've passed by in this life and haven't even noticed?"

It wasn't long, before I arrived at my destination, or so I surmised, as the road had led me to a dead end. Sure enough, when I glanced at the written directions my friend had given me, they read, "When you get to the cul-de-sac, you've arrived. Wait and you will be greeted."

I climbed out of the car, to stretch my legs, after the long drive. Not seeing anyone, but distinguishing five distinct paths, all at odds with each other, I opted to just lean back on the trunk of my car and soak in the rays for a spell. The directions did say I would be greeted.

After half an hour of basking in the sun (being rather fair skinned), my face told me it had had enough, so I sat up. Ready to hear other voices besides my stomach, which was chatting quite a bit by now, I began to wonder which of the trails would lead to the monastery. I closed my eyes and did a little centering technique I'd learned from Jim, then upon opening them, went with my first instinct.

They all appeared similar, at first appraisal, but I headed toward the path left of center. *(That's different!)* No sooner had I taken a dozen steps in that direction, when a large jack rabbit came out of nowhere and hopped over to the beginning of that trail. I paused and introduced myself.

"Hello Bigwig, where's Hazel and Fiver?" (Names all taken from 'Watership Down', one of my all-time favorite books.)

Scrutinizing me curiously, for a few moments, 'Bigwig' then hopped down the path, a dozen feet or so, stopped, and turned back toward me, as if waiting for me to follow. I delightedly picked up my cue and ambled that direction, this time getting within three feet of my new friend, before kneeling down and picking up the conversation where we had left off. I moved my mouth a lot, showing my non-carnivorous teeth, while making what I thought were friendly reverberations. He wiggled his ears and whiskers in acknowledgment that I was attempting to communicate in his native language, since, after all, I was the tourist there.

While I chatted on, Bigwig busied himself, having found a cowslip by the side of the path (a sought after delicacy in every warren). After he had polished it off and scratched his ear for a while, he once again hopped a ways down the bunny trail and then stopped, turned around, and waited for me to join him again.

This went on for quite some time, until we came to a small wooden bridge where the sparkling of the water beneath was visible between the slats that forded the moss-banked, gurgling brook. Once there, I could make out a house up on the hillside, tucked in amongst a grove of gnarly old manzanita trees. Well, sure enough, Bigwig led me literally to the front door, and then found himself a luscious patch of cloverleaf and went on about his business.

Just then, Frank (the old and dear friend who had invited me to the retreat), came traipsing out of the woods with a bunch of flowers in his hand, his face displaying surprise I had found the house. I regaled the tale of my arrival, and even introduced him to Bigwig, whereupon Frank grinning, ear to ear, chuckled,

"I told you you'd be greeted, I just didn't tell you by whom."

I put an end to the one way conversation I'd been having with my midriff, using several pieces of fruit as silencers. Then, seeing as it was still early afternoon, I thought to strip down and let the rest of my body soak up some of the delicious golden rays of sun. Looking about for a spot to lie out, I came across a six foot raised platform, on the grassy knoll behind the house. Primarily, used by monks who wanted to sleep out under the stars at night, it was perfect.

Using my discarded tee shirt to cover my face, as it had already soaked in enough of the ultra violet, I must have fallen asleep, because I was abruptly awakened. Not knowing what had startled me back to consciousness, I lay there for a few moments, with my eyes open. Just as I reached up to pull the cloth away, a shadow momentarily blocked out the sun and a huge white-faced eagle, with a wing span of at least seven feet, passed no more than an arm's length over my head. Now I knew what had awakened me.

I hypnotically watched, as the powerful messenger circled overhead, one remaining loop, and then dipped his wing in farewell, before soaring back towards the mountaintop. I had actually felt the wind stirred up by the movement of those wings, and I knew I'd been blessed by an angel. That energy was mine for the asking; both the eagles vision and its ability to soar to new heights.

I couldn't ignore the omens and thought to myself,

"A snake, a rabbit, and now an eagle. All on the first day of the rest of my life? Thank you God...I'm paying attention, but what does it mean?"

The Prince spent the next four days in refreshingly contented silence, so

he had plenty of time to contemplate the signs. With no experience interpreting omens, he found he was in a bit of a quandary, but finally allowed the expressions 'more will be revealed' and 'all in God's time' to be perfect for the time being.

Then recalling Deepak's teachings about detachment, and how freedom is found in the wisdom of uncertainty, the Prince laughed at himself thinking, "I must be getting pretty wise then."

Farewell To The City of Angels

"When your work speaks for itself, don't interrupt."

Henry J. Kaiser

*S*oon, *the Prince was back in the city putting his old world in boxes. (Funny, how the 20th century has seemed to compartmentalize everything.) He now knew what he had to do. He was going on a pilgrimage, his journey to Mecca. Back to rediscover his roots and the roots of his forefathers. Instinctively, he knew there would be one big difference between this sojourn and those of the past, and had the thought,*

"This adventure is for life. I don't know when, or even if, I'll be back this way again."

Ever since that first day he felt his life was anew, the Prince had been paying close attention to any synchronicities that occurred, especially after it was assigned as homework in one of his classes. He had even grown to expect a certain amount, but what occured next, made even the Prince pause and wonder.

One day, as I was cleaning out my beach-front gilded cage, preparing for the upcoming pilgrimage, I came across some suitcases of lyrics and poetry I'd been carrying around for years. One valise went back almost two decades. Inside were limericks, sonnets, jingles, lyrics, dreams, notions, silly expressions and sentiments. I'd even made up my own language. They were jotted down on every type of paper imaginable, from menus, to napkins, to matchbook covers I had grabbed at random to capture the thought before it went back into the akashic records. I went through and sorted it all, putting in a couple hours to organize each day. One pile was for finished ideas, one labeled 'has potential...current project', another said 'needs work...future', and then did away with the remains in ritual fashion.

On this particular day, I came across a schedule of events that was over a year old. It was for a teacher whose work was based on the Neville material. Normally, any flyer, that out of date, would have hit the trash can immediately, but for some reason, I started browsing through it.

I came across a photograph with the name Tom Kenyon under it. The picture looked vaguely like an old dear friend of mine, but just barely. The guy I knew had been an excellent guitarist and songwriter, and he and I had wiled away many hours pickin' and grinning back in Greensboro, when I was there for music school. Besides our obvious bond of music, we had both been into metaphysics and curious about how to develop the unused portion of the brain. We had even been to psychics together, and Tom was one of those few lucky people that I had taken to Black Mountain and introduced to Jim Goure and Veneta. He carried many of my memories for me, but unfortunately, after I moved to Nashville, our nomadic lifestyles had sent us in separate directions, and we had regrettably lost touch. Over the years, I had often wondered what had happened to him.

With his upbringing as a military brat, the chameleon Prince had learned well the lesson of walking away and not looking back, though every now and then, he'd formed a friendship that felt like it was supposed to be for life. That had happened over two decades earlier with Tom, so finding this picture had brought back a flood of memories.

I figured what did I have to lose, and called the number on the brochure, leaving a message, "If by chance you used to live in North Carolina and play a mean guitar, this is a voice from your past."

As soon as he hung up the phone, the Prince remembered that, less than twelve hours earlier, he had been writing about his adventures in Greensboro and had thought about Tom then. As soon as he remembered that, he knew the number, where he'd just left the message, was that of his old friend. Sure enough, that very night, Tom called the Prince back, and they were reunited after almost twenty years.

During our conversation, Tom reminded me of a story about Jim that I had long since forgotten. It had happened the day I introduced them. Tom had not experienced much in the metaphysical realm, as yet, and this meeting was to alter the entire direction of his life.

It seems that shortly after I had introduced them to each other, Jim had told Tom to walk down the driveway, and when he got to a designated spot, he was to stop, focus his attention in a particular direction, and then return and tell Jim what he had seen. Tom did exactly as he was told, and was astonished to have a vision of a beautiful geodesic dome built on the mountain side. When Tom came back and related to Jim what he had seen, Jim just smiled and said, "I thought you might have the gift."

Three years later, the dome Tom had seen (The Light Center), was built right where he had envisioned it. Once that gift became apparent, Tom changed course and has devoted his life to learning how, and teaching others how to open up the unused portions of their brains. He has even written a critically acclaimed book on the subject called Brain States.

The synchronicity of connecting with Tom, the day after having written about him, reconfirmed for the Prince that higher forces were at work and that his pilgrimage was definitely being guided.

As I continued preparing for my journey, Salvation Army and Goodwill wound up on my daily list of places to go. For the first time in my life, I started giving away, rather than collecting belongings. Huge sacks of clothes, boxes of kitchen accessories, furniture I no longer wanted; it felt fabulous to let it go. Huge art pieces and furniture I'd been lugging around for years, were put on consignment. I ordered new custom cases for The Gordamer and The Dulsitar, as I was taking them on the road as well. I set a goal for myself to not only complete the reediting and re-mastering of both the Edgar Cayce and Rainbow CD's, but to finish the multimedia concept project I'd been working on the past two years, before hitting the road.

I spent hours and hours digitally editing the new CD, trying several different lineups and segue between the tunes. (Thank God, for my dear friend, Charlie Springer, who after twenty years at Warner Bros. Records, was one of the few people left in the business with both integrity and good ears.)

I also had visits with old friends whose feelings might be bruised if

I didn't say good-bye in person. The second of my trial runs was rapidly approaching, and I'd agreed to perform at a benefit concert for Native Americans the day before lift off. That seemed like a fitting way to say farewell to LA. Then, I was off to see the wizard . . .

For my second trial run, I decided to go camping again with some old friends up in the mountains around Idyllwild, California. It was with a group called 'Try God' (as in, "you've tried everything else, why not try God?")

According to Dennis Praegger (author and radio talk show host I admired), one of the essential ingredients to creating happiness was having things to look forward to. I had been on a dozen campouts with this group over the past few years, and it was easily one of the things I most looked forward to all year, and knew that I would sorely miss.

I had become the camp troubadour, and the bi-yearly event had somewhat satisfied my wandering minstrel urges. Both Frank, from the Zen retreat, and my buddy Charlie would be there, and I was taking my dear old friend (I can't watch you die) Ernie. We had lost touch, but magically reconnected seven years after he had expressed those sentiments. It came about through a mutual ex-girlfriend I rediscovered when answering a personal ad in the LA Times. It was quite a reunion, as he was sure I had long since crossed over to the other side.

My plan, was to test my state of readiness for the pilgrimage by seeing if I could totally relax on the camp out, knowing I'd left no stone unturned back in the city. For starters, I decided not to drive.

This might not seem like any great shakes to the ordinary citizen, but for a control freak, like myself, this was humongous. I always drove, reasoning I never knew when I might have to make a quick escape. But this time, believing it was healthy to sometimes take contrary actions, I made the conscious decision to be a passenger and let Ernie do the driving.

The whole weekend, was pure, unadulterated pleasure. I soon forgot about the city down below. There was a lot of pickin' and grinnin' round the campfire, that could literally float a spirit off on its sweetness;

quiet walks with dear friends through the forest, not needing to fill the air with words, but finding contentment in the silence; afternoon naps and meditations in the hammock, and best of all, just being... Being with God, being with myself, and being with people I loved and, who I knew, loved me. Not once, did I think about the journey coming up.

By the time we got back from the campout, my questions had been answered and I knew the timing was right. I felt complete with my adventure in 'The City of Angels', and was ready for whatever God had in store for me. I knew, because there was no fear or trepidation about what lay ahead; only soaring anticipation. My plan was simple; to stay out of my own way, as much as possible, and trust that I would be led where I could best be of service.

Besides the 'Try God' campouts, probably the thing I would miss the most, was one twelve step meeting, in particular. One of the tenets I had learned early on, when starting to 'trudge the road to happy destiny', was the importance of getting a home group. Still in my first year, I had been invited to a men's stag meeting which met every Sunday night in a different man's home. It wasn't listed in the AA directory, so you had to keep up with it to know where it would be. There were at least fifty men that attended regularly, and half of them had twenty years or more of sobriety. I used to love going to that meeting and wouldn't miss it, if I could help it. Often, I didn't even have to share. Just sitting on the floor, surrounded by my elders (many of them older than my father), had a profound effect on me. Looking back, I can see how healing and nurturing that meeting had been. To feel like I belonged and was 'a part of', for perhaps the first time in my life, was wonderful. And it wasn't just me; every new man that came in the door got the same welcome.

The Prince planned on taking all this with him. He knew he could start up his own men's stag meeting, and find other campouts like 'Try God', wherever he ended up. His chameleon brain also knew that friends were only a phone call away, and if he really just had to get a hug, the City of Angels was only a few hours journey.

Reunion

"Say 'I love you' to those you love. The eternal silence is long enough to be silent in, and that awaits us all."

George Elliot

*T*he Prince timed his departure so that he'd arrive back in North Carolina for the fourth of July family reunion. That felt like the perfect place to begin his pilgrimage; back to the farm where five generations of his family had been before him. There, he would do a 'reality check' on himself, and then 'the law of uncertainty' would hopefully open up the endless possibilities Deepak Chopra referred to in the sixth spiritual law of detachment.

Since the class where this had all begun fell on Monday nights, my plan was to leave on Tuesday, right after the course ended. Just to be safe, I allowed myself a week to make the drive from Los Angeles to Carolina. At long last, the day came to finally hit the road.

I hadn't driven across the country in nearly twenty years. In fact, the last time I'd made the trek, I'd been in the blue van with 'Follow Your Dreams' painted across the back, and Grendel the monster hanging out panting beside me.

As the miles receded, and then dissolved, in my rear view mirror that first day, I couldn't help but reflect on those times and how far my journey had taken me in the intervening years. It was a journey where even the despair and hopelessness could now be seen in a positive light; as both the struggles and the victories were a necessary part of the adventure, neither good nor bad, but just what I needed at the time.

Being a military brat, growing up as a chameleon, I was always saddened when we had moved in the past. I expected, at some point, that first day, to have the same feeling of loss come over me. It never did. Though I was leaving a number of dear friends behind, I realized, in the past, I had been powerless over the moves, while this time the choice was my own.

Then, I remembered this mecca had actually begun that day I'd encountered God's three messengers while at the Zen retreat. I felt such joy and exhilaration, from just being on the road again, I must have sung for the first two hours. (*The Prince had found, over the years, that many military brats like himself were quite comfortable when leading a nomadic life; much like a modern day Bedouin tribe.*)

As the scenery changed, names such as Painted Desert, Meteor Crater, Petrified Forest, Bucksnort, Black Hole, Bottomless Pit, caught my imagination and I would write down the images so they could be saved for later when I could break out my guitar. I had bought a lap-top computer, for saving thoughts, a digital tapedeck, for recording sounds, and a camera, for capturing sights, along the way. *You can be sure there will still be lots of scraps of paper, with the Prince's indecipherable hen scratching, collected as well.*

Not needing much sleep, since adhering to the regimen I'd put together back in LA, I found myself waking up each morning around four a.m., meditating, writing, doing either yoga or a physical workout, and still able to be on the road by six. I'd usually drive, pretty much, straight through till dark. I had always loved being on the road, and found it was a great place to think and organize my thoughts, as well as listen to music and other sources of inspiration, such as the Neville tapes. Averaging six hundred miles a day, I arrived in North Carolina at dusk on the fifth day. I watched the sun go down, over the oldest mountains on the planet, knowing I was right where I was supposed to be.

My plan had been to arrive at the farm a couple days before the reunion, as I had my usual job of organizing the damming up of the creek. It was a tradition in the family that had been passed down for over 150 years, and the job had finally been handed over to me. (*As much because of the Prince's eclectic ADD energy as anything else, since it was one sure way to keep him busy.*)

Over the years, that job was something I had become increasingly grateful for. The area alongside the creek had to be cleaned up and the brush along the waters edge needed to be cut back for each reunion. This allowed parents to feel comfortable letting their kids swim in the spring-fed waters. The pond itself could have been taken straight out of a Norman Rockwell painting. The creek came winding down through a pine forest, with huge boulders strewn about at random (as if God had been in a rock fight). It then gently flowed by what was known as the big rock, where people would sit alongside the six-foot waterfall and watch as the water dropped over the slippery falls into the pool area.

Thirty feet upstream from the pond, was a spring that had been the only source of drinking water for many of my ancestors. One of my favorite jobs was to clean it out, so the waters would once again run pure. For that extra touch, I would hang the ceremonial tin dipper on the tree next to it. Every new cousin or clan member had to go down at some point and take a token sip, straight from the underground pool, before they were officially family members. It was just that kind of ritual that I had become enchanted with over time.

Since I had built at least two dozen dams there over the years, I considered myself the authority. It had actually grown to feel like one of my responsibilities was to pass the knowledge and strategies of sandbagging the creek onto the teenage boys coming along in the family. Filling all those sandbags was a lot of hard work, so the last couple of reunions, I had been using reverse psychology on the teens, much like Tom Sawyer's ploy... *Now that he's just revealed his strategy here, I doubt the Prince will get away with it next year.*

The reunion was exceptional. All my aunts, uncles, and cousins from Mississippi showed up with each of their prospective broods. I believe the final tally was close to a hundred relatives. There have been as many as four hundred in attendance before, but this time was just my grandpa's descendents. Personally, I liked the smaller reunions better, since you got a chance to spend some quality time with each person. Since my dad keeps a half dozen acres of yard mowed, we had no shortage of room and set up a volley ball game, out by the fruit orchard, for those that were so inclined.

My sister (the organizer), had come prepared with a number of interactive games that were great icebreakers for the newer family members (second and third spouses etc.). Of course, there were the ever-present screams of delight coming from the creek, as well as the occasional, not-quite-so-delighted, screeches when one of the more rambunctious boys would find some critter and choose to share it with the girls. In times past, I was usually that boy.

Succulent aromas, wafting through the house, were usually a mainstay at these gatherings and this year was no different. There was one fifteen second flare-up of male canines, posturing for position, but that was to be expected.

Over the years I had grown to appreciate these get-togethers more and more, and especially so this time (probably because I made a concerted effort to be of service.) I found myself wearing three different hats; directing traffic for the younger generation, parking the cars for the older set; so they wouldn't have so far to walk, and video taping all the arrivals, as well as doing interviews for posterity's sake (as well as my mother's). Between my running comedic commentary, and my ability to get people to smooch on camera (not that our clan has ever been accused of being shy), I think I've been appointed to that position permanently.

My sleek foreign convertible proved to be quite a hit with the under-twenty crowd, and a conversation piece for others, so I found myself organizing quite a few trips with young traveling companions to pick up ice, watermelons, etc. My dad had been asking lots of questions about its engine size, how it handled, amount of torque, etc. (the kind of thing I generally don't have a clue about), so I shouldn't have been surprised when, one morning after the reunion, he asked if he could take it for a spin. We ended up traversing blue highways for half that day, with him at the wheel. *(In times past, most country roads were designated in blue on maps as opposed to highways which were red.)*

For years, I'd dreamed of hiring a back hoe to come dig out the pond area. Though I'd thought about it for a long time, you don't mess with tradition lightly around the farm, and I wanted all my ducks lined up in a row (my fathers blessing), before I tackled it. Knowing it was a delicate issue, I diplomatically got my dad involved in the decision making process by asking him, "Dad, do you know any good local backhoe drivers with their own equipment?"

The day after the reunion ended, my dream became reality. To everyone's surprise (except mine), it went off without a hitch. One of my uncles, who knew of the potential land mines involved in taking on such a project, made a point to come over and compliment me on using great tact and discretion in getting my dad's input on all the decisions. His comment was,

"You did that well. I was shocked it went as smoothly as it did, knowing of your history together." I smiled back,

"I knew I had it in the bag the whole time, but I've got to admit, I was a little nervous when the back hoe looked like it might tip over."

I found the longer I stayed sober, the more connection and healing was able to occur between me and my dad. The previous December, I was more than a little surprised when the annual Christmas card arrived with a check, which in itself wasn't unusual, except that this time, not only was the check in my dads handwriting (which was a first), but there was a letter from him as well. Until that day, I had never so much as received a single phone call, let alone a letter from him. When I called to thank him, I got an even bigger surprise.

I had given up hope of ever hearing him express any love for me, verbally, after an incident five years earlier. At that time, we had a conversation in which I had expressed regret for any pain I might have caused over the years. I then made the mistake of saying,

"I just wanted to tell you that I love you, while I still have the chance." His reaction was one of anger and left me dumbfounded with a line I'll never forget.

"The only people that use that word are mothers with their babies and prostitutes."

At that point, I realized I was probably going to an empty well (*probably?*), but recovered quickly and said, "Oh, just a matter of semantics dad. I've got a lot of respect for you." He had no problem with that one and responded "Thank you, son."

Only later, in reflection, did it dawn on the Prince how that one statement spoke volumes about the lack of nurturing and emotional nourishment he had received from his original role models, and why it had been such a constant theme in his recovery process.

From that time, to the Christmas conversation when I thanked him for the check and his letter, a lot of healing had taken place. Just as I was hanging up the phone, I unthinkingly said, "Love ya dad," at which point, he paused, and then said the words I'd waited all my life to hear,

"I love you too, son."

I was stunned; I mean, literally overcome. * Once I hung up the phone, I sat and wept. I wish I could say I was so evolved and conscious that it didn't matter, either way, how he felt about me, but the fact is, it did matter to me, just as I know it does with a lot of other men. It was without a doubt, the finest Christmas gift I had ever been given.

Just a month prior to heading out on his pilgrimage, the Prince had sent his dad a father's day gift from 'Cigars Around the World'. Since they both enjoyed a good smoke, the Prince had found it to be a common denominator and something they could enjoy together.

The day after the creek project, I was puffing away contentedly, out on the front porch swing, when it dawned on me that most of the affection expressed by my dad was shown in code. I realized that was something members from his generation (especially those with military bearing), were wont to do. Once you understood the language, though, you could pick up the real meaning underneath.

One example, would be the conversation we had about having never gotten along with each other because of being so much alike. (That observation, by my dad, almost caused me to swallow my cigar.)

A couple of days later, I said, "Dad, didn't you used to have a sense

* Tears Of Joy

of humor?" To which he replied completely deadpan "Yes son, I used to."
We both roared.

Another day, we took a drive, and he pointed out where he thought
the ideal place to build a trout pond would be. (One project, that he had
always planned on doing, but had just never gotten around to.) We
stopped the car and wandered around a bit, while he explained why he
thought it was the best location, and warned me of some of the pitfalls I
should be aware of. We lit up a couple of stogies, and while standing in the
middle of my future fishpond, we shot the breeze like any old friends
might do. I knew that was his way of passing the mantle onto me, and it
felt like a real honor. For just a few moments he let his guard down, and I
got to see him as just a regular guy; not my dad, not 'The Captain', not the
disciplinarian or husband to my mother; just another guy dreaming about
a fishing hole.

A couple of years earlier, he had offered to let me drive his little
convertible MG Midget. (The same one I used to steal back in high
school.) Looking back, with this new perspective, I could see how that had
been a token peace offering, and it touched me to realize it.

The most poignant moment of all, though, came the day before I
was to depart. I could already tell he was gonna miss our cigar powwows,
on the front porch, and we'd been talking even more that day than usual,
when out of nowhere he said, "Son, when I pass on, would you make sure
I get buried in Arlington Memorial Cemetery? I only want one service and
I want it to be held there, with full military honors."

I couldn't believe what I was hearing. The man I used to hate was
entrusting me with an honor that would have been inconceivable, even a
few short years before. You just don't get there from where we'd been. I
managed to croak out, "Yes sir, it would be my honor."

I was literally speechless. The boy in me wanted to shout with ela-
tion, but the adult managed to suppress such an outburst, afraid he might
take the words back. Without showing too much emotion, I kept rocking
on the porch, puffing on my stogie, in silence. My head was spinning and

it would be a few moments before the feeling subsided enough where I felt able to speak again. I then continued, "Would you put that in writing for me when you get a chance?" knowing mom had planned for them both to be buried at the local cemetery.

His pilgrimage had just received another major confirmation; he was on the right path. Though the Prince knew inside, with every fiber of his being, that he was a good man with a good heart, getting that acceptance and having a connection with his dad brought him enormous satisfaction. It didn't matter how many seminars on healing he did, how many twelve step meetings he attended, how many other people told him they loved him, none of it compared with hearing it, and seeing it shown, by one of the people that had brought him into this world.

Bagpipes Calling Me Home

"Build me a son, O Lord, who will be strong enough to know when he is weak, and brave enough to face himself when he is afraid, one who will be proud and unbending in honest defeat, and humble and gentle in victory."

Douglas MacArthur

*A*fter the reunion, the Prince planned to go and meet Clyde, at Grandfather Mountain, where The Highland Games (the largest Scottish clan gathering in the country) were to take place. Clyde had been inviting him for years, but the Prince had never been able to make it before. Now, that he was on this journey in search of his roots, something told him 'The Games' should go to the top of his priority list. He'd written it on his calendar, months earlier, but had no idea what he was getting himself into.

Never particularly enamored with the idea of either bagpipe music or of men wearing skirts, I thought I was going mainly so I could spend time with my old friend, Clyde, but I got so much more.

The two hour drive up was breathtaking, as I had chosen to go the circuitous route along the Blue Ridge Parkway. I put the roof down, tuned in to what had become one of my favorite radio stations, and waved goodbye to the farm. I arrived, mid-afternoon, and found Clyde (which was easy as he'd camped in the same spot for seventeen years), pitched my tent and unhoisted my guitar. (I've found over the years, that's an easy way to meet your neighbors and let them know you're a friendly buzzing around their skys.) After a couple of yodels, I set out to explore my new surroundings. There's something special about the Blue Ridge Mountains anyway, but being on a mountain named after Grandpa magnified the possibilities for adventure, even more than usual, in my way of thinking.

As I meandered through campsites, I noticed many different clan flags and crests proudly displayed, making it easy to find your own people. The lively mood was contagious, and there was lots of laughter floating through the woods. Many men brought their swords, for display, and each year Clyde had noticed that they became bigger and bigger. One year, Clyde had made a twenty foot wooden sword and stuck it in the ground near his camp as a humorous challenge. (You know, he with the biggest sword; that sort of thing.) Of course, someone came and stole it in the middle of the night, which was cause for much playful jousting the next day.

I wasn't there two hours, before I found out I was actually of Scottish descent, on my mothers side, and that our clan was probably represented there on the grounds. I researched the name, thoroughly, and couldn't wait to call mom and tell her about it. She replied, "Of course we're of Scottish descent. One of your distant cousins has already done all the research. Our family came over from Glasgow in 1784. I've even got copies of their birth certificates, and letters they wrote as well."

I was floored. I had no idea I came from such a rich heritage. That night, I went out to the parade grounds where a hot Scottish rock and roll band was using traditional Celtic instruments such as bagpipes and harp, together with electric guitar, bass, and drums. It was a joyous modern sound, yet you could hear strains of ancient overtones and harmonics blended throughout. I loved it. I found myself enamored with the music in a way I'd never known before. This piqued my interest.

The next day, I was witnessing the clans file into the arena (often, three and four generations from the same family), with their appropriate banners, tartans, and kilts, when I heard my first full pipe band. There must have been forty bagpipe players, with an accompanying drum corp, all marching together in full regalia, playing a haunting melody. All of a sudden, I became overwhelmed, as scalding tears started flowing down my cheeks, and my legs got shakey. I staggered to the ground, before I collapsed, and then closed my eyes. It felt like I was in a flying dream, being transported back in time by the music. I knew where I was, but it could have been at any point in Celtic history. After a few moments, the intensity of the experience subsided and I knew I was back in present day reality.

I sat there with the tears unabashedly streaming down my face, not caring who noticed. It had come over me like a wave and I couldn't help myself, as if the sound was affecting me on a cellular level. *

I call it an aural deja vu', knowing you've heard something before from another lifetime. From then on, the Prince was a man with a mission. He started finding out all he could about his clan, their castle back in Scotland, and the history that went with it. Then he found out his father's name had its origin in Scotland, as well, and found out their entire history.

Later that night, as I was telling Clyde of my experience with the bagpipes and the feeling of deja vu', he reminded me of a story that I had long since forgotten; how a number of our mutual friends saw me as having come back from the dead already.

During the twenty-five years he and I had been friends, my normal chameleon self just dropped by unannounced when I happened to be in the area. I never called anybody or stayed in touch, so there were periods when no one would hear from me for one or two years at a time.

Years earlier, back in the days of my 'Follow Your Dream' bread truck, it seems there had been a fiery crash between a semi and a van, that looked just like mine, on interstate 40 down around Morganton, North Carolina. The bodies had been burnt beyond recognition, but somehow word spread to all my friends it had been me. So the next time I came bopping nonchalantly in from my latest adventure, everyone was backing up like they were seeing some kind of apparition. At least I found out I was beloved by a few people, as they were genuinely glad to see me back from the dead. Clyde reminded me of that earlier phantom-like appearance.

The next day, I was still feeling awestruck by the depth of emotion from the bagpipe experience. As if that wasn't enough impetus to inspire me, a stunning redheaded lassie, I'd noticed earlier, dropped by my campsite. She had a beguiling sensuality that forced me to do a double take, the first moment I spotted her, and her figure was like a sharp unexpected jab to the solar plexus. She'd noticed my California plates, and struck up a conversation to be friendly. Seems she'd spent a few formative years in Santa

* Days of Old…Awakening Imaginations CD #8

Barbara, and wondered if I'd perhaps been there. We flirted a bit, and at some point in the conversation, she made the remark, "There's nothing sexier than a man in a kilt."

(Of course, it goes without saying, the Prince started shopping immediately for his.)

Just experiencing entire families together in one place, all with the same intention, was inviting enough, but 'The Games' with their dancing, music, camaraderie and tradition was something the Prince decided he was never going to miss again. These were his people, his clan, his tribe, and for a military brat, whose single greatest quest was to feel he belonged somewhere, this was a big deal. Once more, he realized how important this pilgrimage was becoming and he hadn't even been gone yet a month.

The Cemetery
and My Dream

"I do the very best I know how; the very best I can; and I mean to keep doing so until the end. If the end brings me out all right, what is said against me won't amount to anything. If the end brings me out wrong, ten angels swearing I was right would make no difference."

Abraham Lincoln

*A*ll his life, the Prince had heard the old expression, "You can't love someone else until you learn to love yourself." He had read hundreds of books that all basically said the same thing. In theory, it sounded like a great idea, but how to do it in real life was another thing? It certainly wasn't anything the Prince knew from his own experience. He had always looked outside himself for the answer, either in money, sex, power, fame, or material possessions, but they were all just substitutes for his true hearts desire. Once he'd realized that, the Prince tried meditation, fasting, psychoanalysis, martial arts, metaphysics, and religion, but none of these could take him to what he so passionately desired until he could truly love himself. He knew once he could love himself for the person he was, and could give that love away, then he would find real freedom.

Not too long after the Highland Games, the Prince figured he was being signaled by the universe when three different people, in three days, all told him about the same teaching that had profoundly changed their lives. It was a seminar called The Hoffman Quadrinity Process. He was surprised he'd not heard about it before, as it had been around since the mid-sixties. Though he believed the miracle stories he'd been told from his three messengers, his analytical mind was still observing, and his skeptical nature was still questioning. He had, however, requested some written information on the process. Three days later, it arrived, and he was reading how both John Bradshaw and Joan Boryshenyko (two teachers he held in high regard), had called it the most pro-

found experience of their entire lives. That was enough for the Prince.

"Where is it? And how soon can I go?"

It turned out to be in Harper's Ferry, West Virginia. There, one of the most startling and profound experiences of the Prince's life was to unfold. Due to the confidential nature of the process, the Prince can't tell you all the details of what happened, once he arrived, but I will share this much with you. By the time the process was over, he realized how everything, and I do mean everything, that didn't work in his life was a pattern that he had learned. He further realized that if it was learned, it could be unlearned. A big part of that unlearning or letting go, took place in a quiet cemetery there in Harper's Ferry.

I had gone there to bury the old negative love patterns I'd learned from my parents, once and for all. I was told to find a gravesite for each of them, and then visualize a ceremony where I buried everything that I'd learned from them that didn't work and hadn't served me. (My fears of intimacy, my need to look good at all costs, my belief that love was something that had to be earned, etc.)

I had been told by my instructors that I would know exactly which site to choose, once I got there, and it would be perfect. Well, sure enough, as I got about 75 yards from the cemetery, I saw a large foreboding gravestone that looked very autocratic and militaristic and thought immediately it looked perfect for my dad. Was I ever in for a surprise; written on the gravestone, were the names Myers and John. During the week, I'd realized a lot of my dad's negative patterns were from being a middle child, brought up during the depression, and always having to fight for everything he got. His two older brothers were named, Myers and John. *"OK, just a coincidence. We'll let the Prince sit there and smoke his cigar and leave it at that."*

After I finished the ritual and felt complete, I left a flower propped up against the headstone. Then, I went searching for the final resting spot for my mom's negative traits. Finally, from way across the field, I saw the one that looked perfect. It was tall and statuesque, with flowers and musical notes carved into the stone. I knew, immediately, that was the place. When I finally got close enough to see what was written on the marble, I almost lost it... my mother's name, my last name, was deeply engraved there. She was born in 1846 and died in 1933. *OK don't freak out, there's got to be a reasonable explanation...right?*

I finished the ritual I had prepared for my mom, and after symbolically burying her negative love patterns in my visualization, I told her how much I loved her and how grateful I was that she had brought me into this world. I then started to slowly get up, but found I was still a bit shakey. *I wonder why?* Determined to follow the directions I'd been given, I still had one more ritual to do. Last on my list of assignments, was to find a gravesite where I would witness my own funeral. (The one that would take place in twenty years, if I didn't change the patterns I'd identified weren't working in my life.) Now that I realized I was at a crossroads, and did have a choice, I was to visualize how it would look if I continued on the old road.

I tried not to think about the strangeness of what had already transpired and started heading down the hill towards the river and a tree that looked like a good final resting spot. I was thinking about how my biggest fear in life was to end up all alone, because I'd pushed everyone and all the love away, due to my fear of intimacy. I was lost in those thoughts when, all of a sudden, I tripped over a rock the size of a shoe box sticking out of the ground. There was nothing else around, no gravestone, no flowery words of wisdom, nothing. I looked down and almost had a heart attack. Carved in the top of the rock, were my initials GWC.

After my initial shock wore off, I lay down on the grass to have a talk with my maker. We talked for a long time, and then I witnessed my funeral. In brief, here's how our discussion ended.

"OK God, I surrender. I have no doubt who's running this show."

Not too long after that wake-up call in the cemetery, I had a telling dream. In the dream, I was in the entourage of one of the worlds richest men. One day, he sent an emissary for me who brought me to where he was sitting in his wheelchair. He signaled for us to both get aboard, and we stepped up onto the running boards that were on either side. We went rolling off and after awhile, he stopped the chair and told his emissary he could leave us, as he wanted to be alone with me. Then he told me he wanted me to take him dancing. So I took him to a place that had a wooden dance floor with beams that ran from the floor to the ceiling. The dance hall was almost deserted, except for a couple people who were getting ready for the evening rush. They didn't pay us any attention, and we started to dance. Since he was an invalid, and his legs didn't work, I picked him up and held him close, while I started spinning and dancing all over the floor. Pretty soon, we were twirling all over the place and then I started to teach him the tango. After a while, we were both laughing so hard, I tripped and we both went sprawling. We lay on the floor and laughed, uproariously for a long time.

The next scene, we've rejoined his entourage and we're out dancing again. This time, we're in public where everyone can see us. Once again, we started laughing so hard, from all the twirling and the fact that we're feeling so alive, it caused us to land one more time on the wooden surface. This time, everyone from his entourage came rushing out to give him a hand, only he waves them all off. We lay there on the floor trying to catch our breath from all the laughter.

The richest man in the world who's an invalid is me. That's how I've felt most of my life. Finally, after doing the Hoffman process, I've been able to embrace myself and reunite all the parts of my being. My intellect and my emotions no longer have to fight between themselves, like some sort of sibling rivalry, and they've both agreed to let my spiritual nature run the show. It seems I'm finally starting to love myself, just the way I am.

What's the 'moral of the story'? Beats me. My only job is to tell it.

Epilogue

The Prince had lived in a magical kingdom of his own making. His father, a King of great power and authority, was known to dispense justice fairly to all the warriors of the kingdom. Unfortunately, when it came to his own son, the Prince, he had been much more withering and was unable to dispense it with either love or compassion.

After many battles, in which they had both been bloodied, the King had enlightened the Prince that once he attained the age of maturity, he was to be banished to the hinterlands. The Prince, glad to be out from under his father's tyrannical roof, had chosen to seek his fortune in the world, rather than follow in his father's formidable footsteps.

Being a gifted, ambitious and single-minded youth, he had cultivated the musical talents of his time and became a troubadour amongst the highest ranks. He had found himself with other eminent musicians of his time, playing for prominent people and vast crowds, not to mention performing and frolicking with royalty from both far-reaching material and spiritual kingdoms.

Though he was a Prince in disguise, he had fallen into the life of the men whose company he shared, reveling in wine, women, and song (an ancient version of drugs, sex, and rock and roll).

After many years spent in such revelry, the Prince had become dissatisfied with the life of a commoner. He knew he was really a Prince, and would one day be a king. But princes do not become kings, unless they prove themselves deserving of such an exalted position. So, the Prince had set his mind to becoming kingly material.

He had gone into the wilderness and engaged in rituals to become a man. He had fought in many battles and slain many dragons, including those with names such as Alcohol the Beast, Drugs the Dreadful Dragon, and Money the Madness Maker. Though his opponents were cunning, baffling and powerful, the Prince, with the help of his good friend and ally 'Sir Endertowyn' (pronounced surrender to win), had emerged victorious.

Eventually, after many years away from home, he had returned to his father's kingdom and was welcomed, with great joy and open arms, by both the King and Queen.

The Prince was very happy to have made his way home again, no longer the rebellious youth he was when he had left, but now a man who deserved to be called 'Sire', and unquestionably destined for the revered position to which he aspired.

But the Prince felt he still had one more dragon to slay, in order to take his rightful place in the world as a king. That dragon, was called Big-Time Fame and Fortune, and was one of the hardest of all to slay, because it was so elusive. Many men had endeavored to slay this dragon, and many men had been eaten in the process. The Prince had already slayed a smaller dragon, called fame and fortune, but he had a huge appetite for life and had dreams and desires beyond those of ordinary men.

One day, while the Prince was embarking on his latest quest, he came upon a personal ad that caught his attention. 'A sparkling diamond seeking a gem of a man'. Having witnessed his best friend, Prince Ebeneezer, meet his true love in this manner, he felt no qualms about responding. So, he sent up his favorite carrier pigeon and their first dialogue lasted a surprising three hours. I say surprising, because the Prince had been spoiled by the many maidens who had thrown themselves at his feet and into his bed over the years. Having won the hearts and bodies of many women, handily, he was more than a bit skeptical that she would be that much different.

He was mightily intrigued after their first exchange, though, as he had tested her with a dare which no woman before her had ever accepted. This was to let him take the lead, no matter what, intimating he might choose to deflower her much quicker than the current romance novels and women's magazines prescribed. She was to trust him totally to set the pace on their courtship. She not only agreed, but had a dare of her own. That, if he found her comely, he was to passionately embrace her within moments of their first meeting.

The Prince applauded her mettle. He even fancied the thought, "if this woman looks as good as she sounds, and is truly a Princess, I might have final-

ly met my match."

The day came they were finally to meet, and the Prince was waiting at the pre-appointed place, when in walks a woman with a beatific smile and an hourglass figure, and he beseeched the Gods that she be the one. His prayer was answered, and the Prince began to woo her heart, in earnest.

Her name was Princess Marigold and, because she was a Princess from another kingdom, he didn't realize she was unlike the fair maidens with whom he had heretofore warmed himself on cold wintry nights. Maidens did not expect much from the men that bedded them, nor offer much in return, but Princesses were another story, altogether. They were not to be taken lightly, for they had the singular power to intoxicate men and inspire them to great exploits.

Thus, Princesses expected those who courted them to prove they were Princes among men by recounting their many exploits; especially all the dragons they had slain, and demonstrating their chivalrous intentions through serenades in poetry and song and tokens of love and affection.

The Prince wasn't at all sure he was ready for all this. He was afraid all this time, spent wooing and courting, would be time away from his task of slaying the dragon of Big Time Fame and Fortune; time he could ill afford to waste. But, there was another voice that kept telling him the only reason he wanted to slay that dragon was to get the approval of his father, the King, and win the love and admiration of a Princess, like his mother, when both were already within his grasp.

*Could it be that 'True Love' was the dragon he was really afraid of and needed more than anything else to conquer? * Was it true that a real Princess would only enrich his life and enhance his creative powers, not distract from his life's purpose? How was he to know she wouldn't love him and leave him? Better to love and leave her first, like all the rest, so his heart would stay intact. After all, he had spent much of his life moving from place to place and avoiding any real intimacy. She says she will intoxicate and inspire me, and I know she will warm my bed nicely, but is that enough to take such a risk? ***

The Prince brooded and pondered, and it finally dawned on him that

---

* What You Gonna Do When Love Comes Calling…Awakening Imaginations #5
* I Don't Know How To Do This

he and Princess Marigold were like yin and yang, as described in the mysterious Chinese texts from across the sea. The Prince had built almost insurmountable barriers around his heart, while Princess Marigold had none around hers and showed no respect for the barriers he had erected. And the Princess had built almost insurmountable barriers around her body, while the Prince had none around his and showed no respect for the barriers she had erected. Thus, he figured they were perfectly suited to dismantling each other's old and rusty armor.

Princess Marigold must have figured all this out, as well, because it wasn't long before they had hurdled the first set of walls and were heading to the largest gathering of cave dwellers in the kingdom to celebrate the Prince's birthday. The Prince had been there before, but it had been many years, and at the time, he had seen little more than the insides of a recording studio belonging to one of the kingdoms' most illustrious minstrels of the time.

Knowing this, Princess Marigold decided to show the Prince the Big Apple, as she knew it, as part of his birthday present.

The Prince resolved to be adventurous from the get-go and try alternative transportation. Rather than ride his trusty steed, he would go by way of special caravan. Not only did this caravan have a carriage entirely devoted to serving delicacies for the palate, it also had its own flock of carrier pigeons, so you could communicate with other realms of the kingdom while you traveled.

Since it was his birthday, after all, the Prince decided to treat himself and send a greeting to the King, who he thought might be feeling a bit lonely, as the Queen was off visiting her relatives. He had surmised correctly, and the Prince and his father had a most enjoyable exchange about the King's own first visit to the Big Apple.

Upon arriving, the Prince had a bit of a rude awakening. Mostly, due to rumors he'd overheard during his exploits, he had created an expectation that many people in this land of caverns and cave dwellers were dishonest and not to be trusted. Sure enough, as soon as he alighted from the station, he was hoodwinked by a couple local rogues, offering to carry his luggage, and he had his wish fulfilled. "Not the best way to start off an adventure" he thought, but was reminded by Princess Marigold, back at the inn, that he was lucky to get the lesson out of the way early and so cheaply, as it could have been a lot worse.

Truly, the only real damage done was to the Prince's pride, and as he was nursing his wounded ego, he sat reflecting to himself, "They must have seen me coming. I wonder if I still have hayseed in my hair?"

To ease his mind off the subject, Princess Marigold decided to take the Prince to be fitted for his birthday present. She had made arrangements, with one of the finest tailors in the land, to create for the Prince a swagger coat with matching breeches made out of the queen's purple.

That evening, the Prince marveled to find crowds of people, in very elegant dress, being kept waiting at entrances to all the establishments they visited. However, when he and the Princess were seen approaching in the queen's purple, each and every door was held wide open for them as they strolled arm in arm through the parted crowd. For the first time, the Prince was able to experience what it felt like to walk through that invisible wall that holds most people at bay. It was intoxicating, and they danced till the wee hours of the morn.

The next day, the magic really began. Princess Marigold had made reservations at The Tavern on the Green (a very elegant eatery in a huge wooded area that reminded the Prince of Sherwood Forest).

The two lovers were holding hands, while the Prince had been recounting tales of his early exploits and how he had come to join an exclusive group of the most serious party people in the land. He had just quoted the twelve basic tenants, that held it all together, and was recounting the tale of the two men who started it all, saying "one just doesn't get there from here, I'm grateful just to be alive," when he got so choked up he had to stop.

Just then, the Prince looked over, through misty eyes, and discovered that an old fashioned, very wide, 24-carat gold wedding band had miraculously appeared right next to their table. It was as if it had been dropped from the heavens, as the Prince knew it hadn't been there before, and he reached over to pick it up. Princess Marigold had a look of astonishment on her face, as she had witnessed the whole thing. Then the Prince reached for her hand and placed the ring on her finger. It fit perfectly, and they were both speechless, for a change. *

Desirous to keep it, but equally sure it would be sorely missed by the owner, they commissioned an artist to capture the two of them sitting there with the ring under glass. On the way out, the Prince went to the maitre d' to leave his carrier pigeon number in case someone reported the ring missing. The Prince figured he would then, at least, have a chance at offering a great sum, in case they were willing to barter. Princess Marigold gaily laughed at his idea saying,

"Who in the world would sell you their wedding band?"

The Prince just smiled and said, "You never know."

As soon as the Prince got to the front desk and reported it, the maitre'd said, "Oh sire, a countess reported losing a ring a little while ago, I'll send someone to see if she is still here."

The Prince couldn't hide his disappointment, but it still made for a good tale, and at least they had the picture. A minute later, a grateful countess appeared and, lo and behold, after the Prince and Marigold told her the story of how they had met and came upon the ring, she insisted they keep it, saying, "It has brought me and my husband nineteen years of the most wonderful marriage and he recently bought me another ring anyway. Please, you keep it, with our blessings."

Wanting to know all the details behind the miracle, Marigold asked the countess to show them where she had been sitting when she lost it. It turned out to be a good twenty-five yards away from their table and all they could figure, was that a waiter must have kicked it somehow so that it had just suddenly appeared beside them.

After taking down the countess' address, in a far-flung region of the kingdom, they promised to let her know how it all turned out. Besides, the Princess wanted to send her a thank-you gift, as well. After saying good-bye, the Prince took Marigold's hand and they walked back out in the park, both lost in their own thoughts.

On the way back to their inn, they stopped by the Playhouse that was

* Destiny

across the street, in which a very sought-after show was playing that evening. Since they hadn't made advance reservations, and the performance began in two hours, the odds of getting seats, at all, would have to be considered slim, at best . . . but they were feeling lucky.

Just as they approached the ticket window, a carrier pigeon landed, bringing news that not only was there a cancellation, but it was for two of the best seats in the house. The Prince and Princess looked at each other and burst out laughing, "I wonder which angels have decided to take such an interest in us?" said the Prince, when he could finally catch his breath.

The next day, they made plans to go see the Rockettes (a line up of 36 of the kingdoms finest fillies high stepping together), performing in the annual Christmas show at a great venue called 'Radio City Music Hall'. The Prince was overwhelmed, and it brought tears to his eyes, as he had never seen such a production before; dozens of dancers and children in colorful garb, a veritable zoo of animals from cows to sheep to camels, and an orchestra that sat on a disappearing stage and would appear at appropriate times for effect. As they were leaving, the Prince touched Princess Marigold's heart when he described the performance as, "Delightful, mesmerizing, enchanting, wondrous beyond belief. I wish every child in the kingdom could see this."

By this point, the Prince was becoming enamored with Princess Marigold, and was imagining "could she truly be my life partner?", though he hadn't said anything to Marigold as yet. * The Princess, though, was a bit more verbal (some things never change), and that same night, as they were embracing each other while standing beneath a drizzling rain in Times Square, she gazed up at the Prince and whispered, "Is this for real?"

The Prince didn't say a word, just turned her around and pointed to a 100 foot neon sign that could only be seen from the angle they happened to be standing. Princess Marigold burst out laughing when she read, emblazoned across the night in huge letters, "As serious as it gets." *

I'm sure you're finding this hard to believe, cause I know I did and I was there, but it gets even better.

Two days after the Prince and Princess had returned from the Big

* You're Everything To Me

Apple, back to the land of the Celtics, the Prince was recounting his weekend saga to another fair maiden whom he had been courting, and since he had made up his mind to not see anyone else but Marigold, he thought it only honorable to be out with it. As they strolled across the crimson campus (on the way to meet his best friend for a banquet), the Prince had just come to the part about finding the wedding band, when he noticed a burgundy pouch lying at the edge of the curb. He walked over, picked it up, and after untying the draw strings, was astonished to discover...a diamond engagement ring.

I swear it's true.

The Prince, needless to say, is dumbfounded and thinks to himself, "OK, Princess Marigold's ring size is unusually tiny, If this ring fits as well . . . "

His friend at the banquet had already been regaled on the legend of the Big Apple, and had even seen the old-fashioned wedding band, so when the Prince arrives, breathless, and unveils the new ring, he almost fell out of his seat. The Prince could hardly wait for the feast to end, and raced all the way home to put the two rings side by side. Sure enough, it was the exact same size, and the Prince burst out laughing,

"OK, God, I get the message." *

* Merlin's Theme...Chameleon CD #1

Songs & Poems

A U Yah

It came without warning
But the message was clear
Each man had his own reason
As to why he was there

We were men of ever color
We were men of every creed
Our world was crying out
we all had felt the need

We knew when we arrived
We were all taking a chance
You don't give a man a weapon
'Til you've taught him how to dance

      Be you black man red or white
      You're still precious in His sight
      A U Yah

One man came there to kill
But instead learned how to pray
I'm sure that doesn't happen
Lord, just every day

One kissed the earth with passion
And then he told us with pride
He said, "Excuse me
while I kiss the sky"

Something else was said
That I'd never heard before
If you're gonna tell the truth
Better have a horse right by the door

At one point we didn't know
If we'd get out alive
But thank the spirits up above
The entire tribe survived

A man with rhythm in his hands
Summoned the gods to play
Another brother led the dance
And we held hands to pray

Be you black man red or white
You're still precious in His sight
A U Yah

I used to think that once upon
A time was just for kids
I changed my mind cause grown men
Just don't cry for kicks

This time will be remembered
Long after we are gone
January '92
When we few lived this song

Be you black man red or white
You're still precious in His sight
A U Yah

ANGEL OF PURE LOVE

I must be
The luckiest guy in the world
You should see
The heavenly angel I call my girl
Words cannot describe
The feelings from deep down inside
She's the one to guide you to pure love
She inspires pure love

Love like this
Is, oh, so rare
Joy turns to bliss
For all to share
Maybe once in a lifetime
When the stars are right up above
You will meet an angel of pure love
She inspires pure love

(ANGELS) SHINE ON

I've got a message, I've been carrying for years
A story so incredible, it's always brought out tears
Of gladness, of gladness

I'm sure it sounds quite crazy, but I know inside it's true
And if you'll just be still and look within, you'll know it too
That there's angels, heavenly angels

> Shine on people, let your love shine on
> Sing it to the world let your life be your song
> Fill it 'til it overflows, and joy it abounds, live in
> Perfect harmony and then hear how it sounds to be
> Happy and carry on...

I awakened to the sound of music all around my head
And then I saw the angels hovering gently near my bed
So gently, so gently

And then I heard them singing, oh, the sound was true and free
Way down inside I couldn't hide, these words were said to me
So sweetly, so sweetly

Everyone a king upon his own domain
Know your wealth is in yourself
That way you'll have a reign of peace, of peace

> Shine on people, let your love shine (repeat)...

CHAKRA SONG (WHAT'S COME OVER ME)

One job I've been given was to fill you in
About the powers of the rainbow
Now, where to begin my story of what's come over me?

Don't you know man's plight
Has been to find the white light
That's the way it's been on earth since it's conception
If you want to find bliss
You better listen to this
'cause I don't believe you'll find an exception

First you start at the red, orange, yellow and green
Move up to blue and indigo, you know what I mean
Then there's violet, yeah and there's violet

It was half past eight I was feelin' great
Don't know why but I was feeling in love
I'd been downtown just cruisin' around
Imagining the one from above

When suddenly appeared the girl of my dreams
She had angels all around her
At least that's what I seen
I said, "Oh my! What's come over me?"

Well, I rubbed my eyes but it was no disguise
There she was just looking at me
I started to howl, but all I got was a growl
As the rest of me went in a deep freeze

I thought "Oh my god! Don't you know I love you?"
I was changed, rearranged from a red to a purple-blue
I thought "Oh my! What's come over me?"

When I came to the same purple-blue hue
Was deep within me but my angel was gone
I started to cry but then I got awfully high
When I realized that she left me this song

Don't you know we're all channels trying to tune to the flow
What a lovely state of being just to be in the know
To tell you people what's come over me

Well, it happened to me and it could happen to you
Like a beacon shining bright in the night
Once you learn you're divine, then you'll get along fine
From the indigo into the white light

CHAMELEON

Wild man, predator
He sometimes calls the beast
She wants to take to bed with her
So together they can feast

Hypnotized deep in the trance
Black garter on the floor
He finally cries, "cut me, cut me"
And still she's wanting more

Elusive as a shooting star
From the bed he does emerge
Tries not to leave visible scars
Though often that occurs

    Hope it's not somebody, somebody I know
    You're gonna reap just what you sow
    What goes around soon be coming back at you

Thunder clappin' its mighty hands
Everyone heard the crash
Silhouetted up against the blackest night
She saw the jagged flash

Close to home, she knew at once
No way it could miss
Like a cobra or a rattlesnake
He gave himself away with a hiss

    Hope it's not somebody, somebody I know
    You're gonna reap just what you sow
    What goes around soon be coming back at you

CHILDREN'S SONG

Let there be peace
All over this world
Let the wars all cease
All over this world

It's time we stop killing our brother
It's time to start loving each other

> Love is the answer
> Love is the key
>
> Love is the answer
> Love is the key to open the
> Door to the answer
> Love is the key to open the
> Door to peace

Listen to the sound
Of the children crying
Out for all to hear:

"Find a way to end
All the strife and hatred
Especially all the fear."

> Love is the answer
> Love is the key to open the
> Door to the answer
> Love is the key to open the
> Door to peace

COWBOYS AND INDIANS

When I was a boy and I'd come home from school
What I most enjoyed, what I longed to do
Was put on my cowboy hat, strap on my gun
Tie on my chaps, then my boots one by one

Then I'd go next door, I can still hear me say
Can Johnny come out? Can he come out and play?
Since I had the outfit and he was my friend
We'd always play cowboys and indians

> I can still here me say
> Can you come out and play?
> Cowboys and indians

Then I grew a bit older and put away my toys
I still wore my boots, went out with the boys
First longnecks, then ladies had become my best friend
Now the game was for real, there was no more pretend

> Still sometimes to this day
> I still want to play
> Cowboys and indians

Those simple days have passed us by
Longing for them is making me sigh
Ain't no use in asking why
Only makes me want to cry

Now I'm all grown up, I still act like John Wayne
I still fancy the ladies I don't show no pain
I'm teaching my son to fight the good fight
And wherever you can try to stand for what's right

> Still sometimes to this day
> I still want to play
> Cowboys and indians
> I can still hear me say
> Can you come out and play?
> Cowboys and indians
> It's such a nice day
> Come on over let's play...cowboys and indians

DANCING GIRL

I want to take you in the moonlight
Out dancing 'til the dawn
Feel your sweet caresses
And sing to you this song

All the love that's inside
I just can't hide how I feel
It'd be a shame to deny
It's making me fly
It's so real

> Don't you know by now
> That I love you
> Yes I love you

Dancing girl the perfect pearl
All I want is the chance
To show you how we can dance
I said, "Dancing girl
Give me a whirl
Won't you open your shell
And come dancing with me...with me?"

I want to take you in the moonlight
Out dancing till the dawn
Feel your sweet caresses
And sing to you this song

All the love that's inside
I just can't hide how I feel
It'd be a shame to deny
It's making me fly
It's so real

> Don't you know by now
> That I love you
> Yes I love you

DAYS OF OLD

Seems like yesterday I woke to the sound of your laughter
Seems like yesterday I thought we would be forever after
I thought you said a love like ours could never die, then why
Have you left me?

Days of old running through my mind
Days of old reliving the time
I was with you

Now it's time to put my feet on the ground
Pick up the pieces before that I drown
I don't regret, the day we met, now it's time to forget
Those days of old

Seems like yesterday I was watching the lovelight in your eyes
Seems like yesterday there was certainly no thought of sad good-byes
You were the moon, I was the sun so happy together we were as one
But now you've gone and left me

The love we had it set me free
Now all I have's the memory
Since you left me

Now it's time to put my feet on the ground
Pick up the pieces before that I drown
I don't regret, the day we met, now it's time to forget
Those days of old

DESTINY

First time I saw her standing there
Smile in her eyes flower in her hair
I knew right away
There was nothing to say
She was mine
She came over, took my hand
The look in her eyes let me understand
She knew it too
There was nothing to do
I was hers

> Something's come over me
> Seems like destiny
> Something's come over me
> Call it destiny

All of my life I've been looking to find
That girl of my dreams that would make my life shine
The harder I tried the more that I cried out in vain
'Til finally I felt that there never would be
That one in the world who was just there for me
Then it happened, you and me, it was ecstasy

> Something's come over me
> Seems like destiny
> Something's come over me
> Call it destiny

DIRTY TALK

Many a girl, I told to stop
It brought me down, 'stead of lifting me up
I used to think, it was just perverse
But now I learned the art
Of how to converse

> In dirty talk
> Sure is fun
> Dirty talk
> I'm glad I've finally begun
> Don't you know it really turns me on

Never thought I had it in me
Never knew that I could
Even if I did
I didn't think that I would
By day I'm as straight
As a person can be
But at night behind closed doors
I turn 180 degrees

> With my dirty talk
> Sure is fun
> Dirty talk
> I'm glad it's finally begun
> And you should hear the way
> It makes my girlfriend moan
> Listen to her moan (harmonica solo)

Anything suggestive
That's what she wants to hear
Always wants me
To whisper in her ear

> Some dirty talk
> Sure is fun
> Dirty talk
> I'm glad we've finally begun
> But you should hear the way
> It makes my girlfriend moan
> Listen to her moan (harmonica solo)

DISCOVER YOURSELF

Well, it seems to me
If you want to be
Happy all the days of your life
First eliminate
Don't hesitate
All the things been causing the strife
Some are without
But most are within
Take a good look now, don't be shy
Get down to the source
There's your answer of course
Don't waste your time asking why

       Discover yourself
       There's a whole world inside you
       Discover yourself
       It's just waiting to be found
       Discover yourself
       It's time for you to be true
       To yourself....to yourself

Inside of you
There's a gold mine too
Just laying there waiting to be found
Now and then be still
And you'll begin to feel
The presence of your creative sound
Once you let it flow
Then you'll start to know
What it's like and that you got it to
Then just give thanks
And join the ranks
I swear it's all you've got to do

       To discover yourself
       Know that your God's creation
       Feel His exhilaration
       Dance to His motivation
       You are His greatest sensation

FALLING IN LOVE AGAIN

I sure do love you but you're cold as ice
If you'd let me warm you, it'd be oh so nice
I don't believe I've fallen in love again
No sense denying, no need to pretend
It's oh so sweet
If we could just keep
This love together
Forever and ever

Last time it happened she knocked me off my feet
The pain of getting up was more than I could meet
I don't believe I've fallen in love again
No sense denying, no need to pretend
It's gonna get better
Yeah better and better
We'll stay together
Forever and ever

Your love reminds me of the rising sun
Your warming rays making me wanna come
A little closer, yeah closer to you
With all this love inside, it's all that I can do
To keep myself from falling in love again
'Cause if I do, I'd know it'd be the end

FEVER

After the love we knew, after the warmth of you
Disappeared in the morning light
Like a thief in the night, now you're clean out of sight
And I'm left sitting here in the dawn

Why is it always the same? I'm just no good at the games
Seems the rules are changing all the time
Now I'm alone again, just like it's always been
An empty room inside that's just for crying

> When you got the fever, when you got it bad
> When there's no one there to hold you
> And the silence drives you mad
> When you got the fever, when you got it bad
> The days are long and lonely
> But the night you start to dread

When all those strangers' lies, and all their empty eyes
Reflect the pain of being all alone
When all you had they took, and everywhere you look
All you see are hearts without any homes

That's when you start to cry, that's when you realize
The ache of being left here in the dark
Still you keep reaching out, you keep dreaming about
The flame somebody will spark

      When you got the fever, when you got it bad
      When there's no one there to hold you
      And the silence drives you mad
      When you got the fever, when you got it bad
      The days are long and lonely
      But the night you start to dread

FIRST TIME LOVERS

When you're a first time lover
It's so great to discover
All the love two people can share
Just hold them to you tight
Rock them gently through the night
Speak of dreams and fantasies without a care

      First time lovers
      And all time mothers
      That's the strongest kind of love known to man
      You know life is worth the living
      And the joy is in the giving
      Just try it don't deny if you can

Treat that magic like it's gold
'Cause it's something you can hold
When all the temporary things are gone
Give freely and completely
Don't try and box it neatly
As you know there's different beats for every song

If you're one who's been passed by
Never known that first love's high
Or it came and went before you saw the light
Don't worry, don't despair
Treat the next love with more care
And gently rock that new love through the night

FIVE SENSES

I feel, finally the time is right to tell you how much I love you
Even the stars at night fail to shine as bright as you do

I see, nothing but you when I fall asleep and dream at night
Being close to you, my love makes everything all right

Your smell, reminds me of honey-suckle blossoms in the springtime
I can't help but wonder if you were sent just to be mine

The taste, of your lips on mine is far beyond imagination
Never knew before that love's the ultimate creation

I hear, angels singing when you whisper soft and sweet I love you
Always bringing me to where pure ecstasy is in view

FOR YOU

Baby did you see the sunrise today?
I long to be that sunlight shining your way
I'll shine on you the purest love
Like the sun upon the moon
I'll sing to you my precious one
Won't you let me hear your tune

>You always make me sigh
>With your sweet lullaby
>If you'll just play for me
>I'll sing the harmony for you
>Darling just for you
>I'll sing the harmony just for you

Darling did you see the sunrise today?
Rainbow colors all around showing the way
Like a lily at winter's end
About to burst in bloom
All I need's to see your face
And here you sing your tune

>You always make me sigh
>With your sweet lullaby
>If you'll just play for me
>I'll sing the harmony for you
>Darling just for you
>I'll sing the harmony just for you

FREEDOM

Freedom is all in getting clear of your mind
Like clouds hiding rays of a brilliant sunshine
Let the winds of change blow them by and be

> Free as the wind
> Spirits blend
> In harmony
> Free as the light
> Shining bright
> On you and me

Freedom is just in learning to be
And giving pure love is surely the key
It's there for you, it's there for me, so let's be

> Free as a dove
> Up above
> In heavenly flight
> Free as a flower
> Such a power
> Made such a beautiful sight

Unlock the chains, unharness the reins and be

GO BEYOND YOUR DREAMS (FOR HEAVEN'S SAKE)

Have you ever gone beyond your dreams
Beyond all space and time
To a place so far from earthly schemes
That peace is all you'll find?

Have you ever really noticed a bird in flight
Or a rose garden in spring?
You too can know of such delight
Close your eyes and see what I mean

> Find what it means, beyond your dreams
> Find what it means to create
> Find what it means, beyond your dreams
> Do it now for heaven's sake

Have you ever set sail your mind to sea
And given your soul free rein?
What you'll find is a divine
Walk down lover's lane

Find what it means, beyond your dreams
Find what it means to create
Find what it means, beyond your dreams
Do it now for heaven's sake

GOOD-BYE (SUICIDE) BLUES

Don't know what to do
To get over these blues over you girl
Better do something, do it fast
'Cause I don't know how much longer I can last
I got them suicide blues

    You should have shot me in the head
    Without your love I'd rather be dead
    Hope I got enough pills to do the trick
    Last thing I need is just to get sick

Don't know what to do
To get over these blues over you girl
Now all my tears, have run dry
Guess it's time for my last good-bye
I got them suicide blues

Don't know what to do
To get over these blues over you girl
Wish you'd said something, anything at all
Prepare me for this terrible fall
I got them suicide blues

    You should have shot, me shot me in the head
    Without your love girl I'd rather be dead
    Hope I've got enough pills to do the trick
    Last thing I need is just to get sick
    I got those suicide blues

GROOVIN' ON LOVE

Stars in her eyes
No way she could ever disguise her love
Surprise, surprise
To find she's the woman I've been dreaming of
Since I've found you no other woman will do
They all seem to be just shadows of you

First time I met her we both knew right away
We both smiled when our eyes met
There was nothing more we had to say
She walked over to me said "Hey there,
What's your name?"
I don't know why, but I think I'm in love
And I hope you're feeling the same

> Groovin' on love movin' to the rhythm of love
> Groovin' on love movin' to the rhythm of your heart beat

I can't believe I'm the lucky one
Those baby blues are for
'Cause every little thing about you
Don't you know girl I adore
I remember the first time
Pillow talking in your arms
I'm willing to bet there doesn't exist
A girl with more hidden charms
Since I've found you no other woman will do
They all seem to be just shadows of you

> Groovin' on love movin' to the rhythm of love
> Groovin' on love movin' to the rhythm of your heart beat

GYPSY DANCE

Gypsy, gypsy dance
Rhythm, of romance
Take a chance, take a chance with me

Moon flower in your hair
Think now, do you dare
Take a chance, take a chance with me

> It's your heart that I'm out to steal
> I know the way, if you got the will
> Let's put it all, put it all on the line
> Take the chance, take the chance of a lifetime

Passion, that's your name
Never, never been tamed
Take a chance, take a chance with me

Mister mystery
Only way to be
Take a chance, take a chance with me

> It's your heart that I'm out to steal
> I know the way, if you got the will
> Let's put it all, put, put, put, put it on the line
> Take the chance, take the chance of a lifetime

HABIT FORMING

Creatures of habit...this one's for you

I have always tried to keep an eye out for the early warnings
Keeping me away from anything that might be habit forming
But I have come to the conclusion, even when there's ample warning
Everything that I enjoy potentially is habit forming.

> Habit you had enough?
> Habit your own way
> Habit forming

Overeating, over sleeping, being late for work each morning
These are just a few examples how we keep those habits forming
Just when you think you have licked the habit you can bet it's scorning
Knowing that the odds are definitely with the habits forming

> Habit you had enough?
> Habit your own way
> Habit forming

Even nuns have habits
You either habit or you don't
Well odds are if you habit, I habit too

> Habit you had enough
> Habit you own way
> Habits forming

I habit in the palm of my hand
Do you habit? I don't habit
Habit you had enough?
Habit you had enough yet?

HILLS OF BEVERLY

Hills of Appalachia
How I love them so
The Rockies and the Ozarks
Now them 'der hills I know
But the hills that make me crazy
The hills that can't be seen
Are the hills down there in Beverly
Where everything's a dream

I went to see the cowboys on Rodeo Drive
I think I saw a Stetson as a limousine drove by
I did not see no horses, didn't see no show
'Less you count that pig on the leather leash
With the rhinestone hat and bow

      Hills of Beverly, hills of Beverly
      Ain't no sign of wildlife
      'Cept all them furs I see
      Did not see no river
      Nothing running free
      Ain't no sign of country in them hills of Beverly

They got Giorgio and Gucci
And Liz Taylor perfume
They got fancy cars and movie stars
And plastic plants in bloom
I went to get some coffee
As I walked around
But they gave me some espresso
And I'm still trying to come down

If you ever go to the hills of Beverly
Don't you be surprised by the things you will not see
You will not see no horses
Nothing running free
'Cause there ain't no sign of country in the hills of Beverly

(I COULD BE) THE BOY NEXT DOOR

She's met her match
But she doesn't want to get attached
She thinks there's a catch somewhere

Oh boy I just woke up
I guess that was just a dream
Wonder why you're always on mind?
I wonder what that means?
Can't get you out from under my skin
I wish that now we had never been introduced
But what's the use now it happened?

> I love you with a passion
> Though I know that's not the latest fashion
> Everybody's trying to play it so cool
> But me I'm just the kind of boy who always wants
> To break all of the rules
> I can be the boy next door
> You're the one for me
> I can be the boy next door
> I'm the one for you (repeat)

Oh boy...I just woke up
I guess that was just a dream
I wonder why you're always on mind
I wonder what that means
You're crying tears of joy
'Cause you met your boy
And it's me

> I love you with a passion
> Though I know that's not the latest fashion
> Everybody's trying to play it so cool
> But me, I'm just the kind of boy who always wants
> To break all of the rules
> I can be the boy next door
> You're the one for me
> I can be the boy next door
> I'm the one for you (repeat)

I DON'T KNOW HOW TO DO THIS

I'm both a monk and yes a lover, through the ashes I must sift
To find a clue that answers, both this burden and this gift
I see with stunning clarity my love of solitude
But just as clearly I can see, that love is my heart's food

Ambrosia, God's sweet nectar, the fruit of life divine
Must be shared one with another, of this I am not blind
But I have no real experience in taking the next step
I must leap into the chasm and trust God there is a net

> I don't know how to do this
> It overwhelms me so
> Completely lost, over my....
> Head says I should stop; heart says I should to go

Both startled and yet mesmerized, like a doe out in the road
If love is blind I guess that I'm destined to what unfolds
Been yearning for the learning, think I've finally got the tools
But just like everything they're only good if they are used

> I don't know how to do this
> It overwhelms me so
> Completely lost, over my....
> Head says I should stop; heart says I should to go

Afraid of being swallowed up, consumed within her fire
Afraid I'd lose my solitude, she'll quench my great desire
I must think of what I'm gaining, instead of what I'll lose
Because freedom becomes bondage when I'm too afraid to choose

> I don't know how to do this
> It overwhelms me so
> Completely lost, over my....
> Head says I should stop; heart says I should to go

God, I don't know how to do this

I LOVE YOU

Thinking about you again
Wishing I, I could spend
One more night just one more night with you
I'd give anything in this world for the chance to

Saw an old friend yesterday
Didn't have a chance to say
All the things all, those things that were overdue
I'd give anything in this world for the chance to

      I'd give anything in this whole wide world
      For the chance, for the chance just to say
      I love you

Saw your photograph today
Even though you're far away
There's so much, so much I want to say to you
I'd give anything in this world for the chance to

      I'd give anything in this whole wide world
      For the chance, for the chance just to say
      I love you, I love you, I love you

I WANT TO LIVE

Ancient ritual is planned
Initiation as a man
Led by elders of the tribe
Feelings that you can't describe
A hundred silhouetted men drumming 'round the fire

    I want to live
    I want to live like that

Like a knight who's iron clad
Slaying dragons in his head
Knows the wild man deep within
Some call the beast, he calls my friend
Excaliber the mighty sword glinting in the fire

    I want to live
    I want to live like that

Stalking tiger on the prowl
Hear the wolf, his midnight howl
High above where spirits fly
Sighting with his eagle eye
Phoenix-like the soul of man rising from the fire

    I want to live
    I want to live like that
    I want to live, I want to live
    I want to live like that
    I want to live, I want to live
    I want to live like that

I'D DO ANYTHING

(feminine)
I've been searching for that special one
Who understands my love
Will accept it, not reject it
Fly with me high up above

(masculine)
One who understands my purpose
And will help to see it through
And when the time is just right
Is there to say I do
(together)
   I'd do anything just to see you smile
   I'd do anything to stay with you awhile
   I'd do anything you know that ain't a lie
   Anything for you, I know will make me high

(feminine)
When he puts his arms around you
Like the circle round the sun

(masculine)
With her magic eyes a dancing
And she tells you, you're the one

(feminine)
Then he comes and lays beside you
And puts his hand in yours

(masculine)
Says, I'll be yours forever
And then she starts to purrrrr....She says

(together)
   I'd do anything just to see you smile
   I'd do anything to stay with you awhile
   I'd do anything you know that ain't a lie
   Anything for you, I know would make me high

(together)
   I'd do anything and more that's for sure
   I'd do anything just keep your motive pure
   I'd do anything just hold it to the light
   The darkest night is over now it's time to shine so bright

IN THE BEGINNING

People fighting over just how it all began
Is it evolution or God's image that created man?
What's the difference? More importantly we need to understand
How to change what's going on before it gets too out of hand

Brother fighting brother, everybody's leaving home
Even though the family could be the most precious thing you own
Got to be your brother's keeper, you can help him on his way
But you can't live in the past or future, only in today

If you'd do unto your fellows as you'd have them do to you
It doesn't take another prophet to see just what it would do
If this all seems overwhelming, yet you want to do your part
Know the longest journey takes you from your head into your heart

IT'S ONLY A MATTER OF TIME

It's only a matter of time 'til we break up darling
We got to get out from under this spell 'fore it's too late
I got so much to give, that's my reason to live, so do you darling
But together any farther, we'll be making our first mistake

Now, don't get me wrong, I don't want to come on as complaining
You sure were good for me with your love so free of explaining
But we both know it's time, you can't miss the signs in our love making
Once the thrill is gone, it's never too long 'fore you're aching

> I still think you're divine
> You got me praying to the Lord
> I'd say that's a good sign
> But it's simply come the time of my leaving

Before I go I just want you to know that I love you
But please don't ask me to stay 'cause there ain't no way
Though I'd like to

> I still think you're divine
> You got me praying to the Lord
> I'd say that's a good sign
> But it's simply come the time of my leaving

LIFE AS WE KNOW IT

Baseball, hot dogs, mom's apple pie
Hollywood stars, politicians that lie
Drugs and sex and Rock and Roll
We are the ones for whom the bell tolls
Monday night football, Kentucky moon
Wheel Of Fortune, Name That Tune.

Life, life, life as we know it

Wall Street Journal, Rodeo Drive
Asphalt jungle where the fit survive
Harlem shuffle right up to your door
Consumer index gimme, More! More! More!
Rose Bowl, prom and even U2
Too much time, with nothing to do

Life, life, life as we know it

S & L bailouts, national debt
Homeless bourgeois to the new jet set
Toxic cleanup, acid rain
Everything's different, but it stays the same
20th century's legacy, America the beautiful
Wait and see

Life, life, life, life as we know it

Carson, Oprah, Abdul Jabbar, Magic Johnson, Eisenhower
Fonda, Star Wars, I.B.M., Eagles, Elvis, Letterman
General Motors, Loony Tunes, Rocky, Jaws, and Daniel Boone
I Love Lucy, Burger King, Richard Nixon, Wild Thing
Z.Z. Top and Wells Fargo, Star Trek, E.T., Way To Go
Leave It To Beaver, make my day, New York, Boston to L.A.
Thirtysomething, Liberty Bell, M.T.V., Gee, that's swell
Eat your Wheaties, James Brown, Arsenio Hall get down

LIVING A LIFE OF LOVE

Blue moon, summer night, aha
Crystal sea in the starry light, aha
Shooting stars going out of sight, aha
The pounding of the ocean like the meeting of hearts
Is only tryin' to tell us that it's time for us to start

      Living a life, living a life of love

Cool rain on the silver sands, aha
It's been the same since time began, aha
Learning to live in love again, aha
It's the rhythm of the ocean, jasmine on the wind
Mountains in the morning it's there for you my friend

      When you're living a life, livin' a life of love

A new dawn another day, aha
Sunshine shows the way, aha
Getting back to what is real, to what we got to do
Following the way you feel will lead you to the truth

      When you're living a life, livin' a life of love
      Living life, livin' a life of love

LOVE WAS JUST A WORD ('TIL SHE SAID IT TO ME)

I've seen eyes that filled with starlight
I've touched a golden woman's hand
I've laid my weary body down with angels in the sand

The word was often mentioned
But it fell like dew upon the sea
'Cause love was just a word 'til she said it to me

      'Til she said it to me love was something slipping by
      'Til she said it to me love was something I'd been denied
      But now I have found what the feeling can be
      Yes, love was just a word 'til she said it to me

Of all the miles I've traveled
And the women I have known
I've laid me down beside them
But I've always been alone

My heart was standing open and
Still they tried to find the key
Yes love was just a word
'Til she said it to me

 'Til she said it to me love was something slipping by
 'Til she said it to me love was something I'd been denied
 But now I have found what the feelings can be
 I know love was just a word 'til she said it to me
 Yes, love was just a word, 'til she said it to me

MARIA

Maria, I need ya,
I need you like the sea needs the shore
But I need you a whole lot more

Maria, I need ya,
I need you like a flower needs the sun
I need to know I'm the only one

 A woman of the world
 Is what I'm looking for
 With the innocence of a child
 When we close the door

Maria, I need ya,
I need you like a bird needs the air
I need to know you'll always be there

Maria, I need ya,
I need you like the stars need the night
'Cause only you can make me feel so right

 A woman of the world
 Is what I'm looking for
 With the innocence of a child
 When we close the door

Maria, I need ya,
I need you like the forest needs the rain
I need to hear you whisper my name
Maria, I need ya,
I need your touch if you only knew
How much I really do need you

A woman of the world
Is what I'm looking for
With the innocence of a child
When we close the door

MERRY GO ROUND

Merry go round, dance to the sound of the angels
Merry go round, feet leave the ground as we fly
Starts as a dream, soon turns real
Those who've learned express what they feel

　　　Radiate your creativity
　　　Try it once if you've ever wanted to be free

Merry go round, dance to the sound of creation
Merry go round, love must be found inside
The more you give, the more returns
The light inside it brighter burns

　　　Try it a while and see just what I mean
　　　What meets the eye is not always what it seems

Merry go round, dance to the sound of the angels
Merry go round, feet leave the ground as we fly
I am you as you are me
Talkin' about the divinity

　　　Haven't you noticed that we're all in this together?
　　　This life may end but we will live on forever

This life may end but we will live on forever
This life may end but we will live on forever

Merry go round go round go round go round go round

MY OLD LADY

Some men call her darling
Some say she's my girl
I'm sure you've heard "Meet my cheri"
In some parts of the world

Of course there's always honey
Or even sugar bear
You might have known a concubine
Though that's a bit more rare

      She might just be your mistress
      You might call her your doll
      But to me she'll always be
      My old lady

      Old-a-la-dy, old-a-la-dy, old-a-la-dy
      Old-a-la-dy, old-a-la-dy, oooooo
      To me she'll always be
      My old lady

Some say she's my fiancee
Or maybe my soul mate
Some say that she's my better half
Though I just don't relate

She certainly is my equal
Or maybe my partner in crime
She might have been a gangster's moll
In another place and time

      She might just be your mistress
      You might call her your doll
      But to me she'll always be
      My old lady

      Old-a-la-dy, old-a-la-dy, old-a-la-dy
      Old-a-la-dy, old-a-la-dy, oooooo
      To me she'll always be
      My old lady

NATURE OF OUR CALLING

Everyone I see is a reflection back of me
Mirrored in my soul from way back when
Everyone I know, running here, to and fro
Needs to hold his peace and take a look within

Rainbow man that I am beginning now to understand
The hues and tints and colors of the spectrum
The colors they don't fade away
It's just your mind that turns to gray
So radiate the light of your perfection

      That is the nature of our calling
      That is the nature of our calling

Radiate the light on through the night
Shine on everybody that you meet
Let a little love out and you'll love a whole lot more
It's felt in places you can't even see
Yes, it's felt in places you can't even see

      That is the nature of our calling
      That is the nature of our calling

Bathing in the light, frees your soul and gives you sight
To see and know the all there is to give
The love you have inside, let it flow don't let it hide
For love and light is really all there is
Yes, love and light is really all there is

      That is the nature of our calling
      That is the nature of our calling

The perfect love from up above's upon us now
On winged dove, open up your soul unto this rhyme
Let it flow down deep inside before the light
Nothing can hide and know throughout your being
You are divine! You are divine! You are divine!

Get your education, share with all you can
When you find your work it's time you should begin
To make this world a better place especially for the children
On earth as it is heaven
Yes, on earth just as it is heaven

NEW AGE SHUFFLE

I been rockin' and a rolling since the break of day
You bet your sweet Urantia I was feeling okay
I'd found me a friend and a new guitar too
And they were talking to me just like I'm talking to you

>'Bout a new age dawning where we'll all see the light
>There's a new age dawning it's gonna be dynamite
>Here's the new age song let's get down
>And do the new age tonight

I'd been honky tonkin' Nashville 'bout three years ago
Met a sweet petite young lady who tuned in to my flow
I said, "Sweet petunia, won't you come on home with me?"
She said, "You're still in the old age mister. Don't you see?"

>There's a new age dawning where we'll all see the light
>There's a new age dawning it's gonna be dynamite
>Try a new age song, then get down
>And do the new age tonight

Well I pondered on her words about a minute or two
I thought the old ain't nothing special, hell I'll try something new
The loving I've been getting never seems to last long
I'll stop taking, start giving, maybe write a new song

>Called the new age shuffle where we'll all see the light
>There's a new age shuffle, don't it feel dynamite?
>Here's the new age shuffle get down
>And do the new age tonight

Well this all happened back in '75
My head changed, rearranged what a joy to be alive
And just today I heard a DJ on the radio
And he was talking 'bout a tune that seemed to be in the know

>Called the new age shuffle where they dance to the light
>It's the new age shuffle and it's sure dynamite
>It's the new age shuffle get down
>And do the new age tonight

OCEAN SONG

The ocean is a subtle sorceress
Weaving dreams of loving
In all who comes to know her beauty
All who feel her wave's caresses

     I feel the gentle peace of the ocean
     Lying in your arms

The rhythm of the ocean's lullaby
Softly rocks the lonely seeker
Washing clean the pains of living
Making clear the road before him

     I hear the haunting call of the ocean
     In the love you sing to me

The wonder of the ocean's magic is
Written in the moonlight's glimmer
The beauty of her blue-green canvas is
Painted with a starlit shimmer

     I see the loving peace of the ocean
     Deep within your eyes

     Together we can be like the ocean
     Reflecting heaven's sighs

ODE TO THE BLANK PAGE

Good morning, dear friend
It's truly a joy to see you again
I don't notice until you are gone
It's for you most of all my heart does long

I need your openness, the choices you bring
Which voice is next? Whose turn to sing?
The dancer, the writer, the singer, the muse
Ballet shoes, ink pen, which one shall I choose?

Potter or painter, sculptures of clay
Are all on the path, they all show the way
Photographs, etchings, first drafts of prose
It's all in the process, I think I'll do those
It's here you remind me, it's all getting clear
It's you, mister blank page, you've become oh so dear

OFF THE HOOK (HANG UP THE PHONE)

Please baby, please baby, please baby hang up the phone
You been off the hook, out of touch girl for far too long
I'm not one to think the worst
But since I've known you girl
This is a first
I'm going crazy going out of my head
I keep remembering something that you said

> Nothing lasts forever, all things must pass
> Never say never 'cause nothing lasts
> Slow down, you're moving too fast
> You can't change it once the dye has been cast

Please baby, please baby, please put it back on the line
The longer it's off, the more that I feel like dying
Maybe I'm mistaken and then maybe I'm not
I'd do anything to keep you girl
You're all that I've got
I didn't comprehend, she was talking so fast
I can't believe our love is a thing of the past

> Nothing lasts forever, all things must pass
> Never say never 'cause nothing lasts
> Slow down you're moving too fast
> You can't change it once the dye has been cast

Please baby I'm beggin' you, put it back on the track
My world's closing in, everything's looking so black
Nothing to live for, girl except you
I don't even want to think of
What I might do
I'm going crazy, going out of my head
I keep remembering the last words that you said

> Nothing lasts forever, all things must pass
> Never say never 'cause nothing lasts
> Slow down you're moving too fast
> You can't change it once the dye has been cast

OPPOSITES ATTRACT

Good, bad to the bone
Tell me who's to say
What's good for you might be the death of me
Then who will pay?

In or out of touch
With reality
It's an in house attraction
Won't you please come in and see?

Up down, way down yonder
It's up to me you say
Then don't get up in arms
Just because you're down today

      Opposites attract, that's a fact

Beautiful or ugly, there's two sides to everything
If no one's right and no one's wrong
Then there's no one to blame

High, low, there you go, what's wrong with in between?
Living on the edge
Isn't always what it seems

      Opposites attract, that's a fact

Left right on the money
Right between the eyes
Left to my devices you might just be surprised

Here, there, can't be everywhere
At the same time
I swear it's neither here nor there when it comes your time

      Opposites attract, that's a fact

PEACE OF MIND

Well I found most every sound
In Nashville town
From jazz to funk, even country
But if you're still listening to find
Some peace of mind
I got some now will start you wondering

Take a deep breath
And close your eyes
Look for the light
Lord don't be surprised

If the feeling you get
Has always been denied
'Cause the sound that you hear
Comes from down deep inside

PLAY ALONG

Play along at the rhythm of life
Not thinking of, but from your desire
Expect to see
What you want it to be
And it will
Yes, it will

Play along at the rhythm of love
Not thinking of, but from your desire
Expect it to be
What you wanted to see
And it will
Yes, it will

Play along at the rhythm of devotion
Not thinking of, but from your desire
Expect to see
How you want it to be
And it will
Yes, it will

Play along at the rhythm of forgiveness
Not thinking of, but from your desire
Expect to see
Where you want it to be
And it will

Play along at the rhythm of peace
Not thinking of, but from your desire
Expect to see
When you want it to be
And it will
Yes, it will

PRACTICE MAKES PERFECT LOVE

Flowers to start her day
Afternoons our time to play
I'm her doctor, she's my nurse
We take turns on who goes first

We believe like they say
Pardon me, but to coin a phrase
Who am I to contradict?
Practice makes perfect love...practice makes perfect love

When we close the door at night
And shadows dance by candlelight
Her every wish is my command
Just the way true love was planned

I give her everything she needs
I don't stop until she pleads
Even Casanova knew
There's always room to improve...practice makes perfect love

Alligators round the bed
So much safer here instead
Don't you know, I'm sure you knew
I'm here to slay your dragons, too?

Sometimes we pillow fight
Then pillow talk throughout the night
Couple children having fun
It's the secret to keeping young...practice makes perfect love

When the feeling comes on her
No matter where it might occur
I tell her give me the eye
At first she was oh, so shy

But now she doesn't hesitate
You know there's some things just can't wait
Love has a mind all its own
It's not for sale or even loan...practice makes perfect love

PRIMA BALLERINA

Her momma was a prima ballerina
They knew it from the day she was born
By the time she turned sweet sixteen
She'd taken the world by storm

Soon after that she had her own little girl
She was pretty as a picture could be
Lo and behold like a fairy tale told
That baby fell in love with me

    Momma had to take a second look
    What has this guy got?
    He's hypnotized baby
    I wonder just maybe
    If he's the one I've always sought

It wasn't long he had her singing songs
And he put a big smile on her face
What she'd been after was love with laughter
That was woven like the finest of lace

    Momma had to take a second look
    Only way to find out
    I got to give it a chance
    I think he might enhance
    But there can not be any doubt

PUT YOUR MONEY WHERE YOUR MOUTH IS

Step right up, folks, put your money where you mouth is

Step right up, folks, and come on in
The greatest show on earth is about to begin
I know you got a ticket or you wouldn't be here
So gather 'round people, let's all come near
Spinning the wheel now, watch as she goes
Round and round to where nobody knows
Life's roller coaster, up and then down
Or you can play it safe like on the merry go round
   You want the merry go round
   Then put your money where your mouth is
   At this carnival called life

Rockin' and rollin', winning and a spinning
Lucky winner coming up nine
Put your money on a color, first one then another
October won and done it this time
You get what you pay for, there's no free rides
Look at the fat man, there's no disguise
Bearded lady, her ducks in a row
Shoot 'em, or shave her, it's a part of the show
   It's a part of the show so
   Put your money where your mouth is
   At this carnival called life

House of horrors, can you relate?
Remember what happened when you came home late?
Double or nothing, increase your wealth
House of mirrors, can you see yourself?
Make it or break it, you pay to play
I don't care just what they say
Life's a risk, it's all a big chance
It's up to you, but if you want to dance
   But if you want to dance then
   Put your money where your mouth is
   At this carnival called life

We've got hogs, frogs, all kinds of dogs, Winnie the Poohs and kangaroos
It's one thin dime, one tenth of a dollar, you can't win unless you play
There goes another one, look at the size of that one
Ain't nothing to it, but to do it
A shot in the pot, A roll in the hole
A load in the commode
They're all the same
No shit that's the name of the game
No poop, just the straight scoop, when you play over here

QUANTUM LEAP

Many moons before this song was wrote
The planets managed to stay afloat
Through trials and traumas tough enough indeed
But on occasion, now and again
We're truly inspired by a cosmic wind
And we're led to make the mighty quantum leap

> Quantum leaps go round full circle
> Quantum leaps are universal
> Quantum leaps can be in harmony
> Be you black man, red or white
> You're still precious in His sight
> Be prepared to make the mighty quantum leap

Heights you can reach will have no end
Just be sure and don't pretend
As motive is the sole priority
If you stay in love it stays in you
Just the way God meant it to
And know throughout your being you'll soon be free

RAINBOW BLUES

I was cruising down the open road
Gonna see a long lost brother
Head in the sky, thoughts twice as high
Had the blessings of our mother
Now him and me had been tight you see
Together we'd slayed demons
But I surmised through his disguise
He'd lost that rhyme and reason

> Just radiate the light, let your love flow all around
> I'm singing about the rainbow sound
> Erect your bubble upon the ground
> Every little thing is gonna be alright
> When you're bathing in the light of the rainbow blues

Release and replace all the darkness with the light
Keep in the flow learn to rock and roll
To the rhythm of his might
You got plenty of help if you'll just tune in
Let go your inhibitions
Go beyond your mind, listen to the rhyme
To what the women call intuition

> Just radiate the light, let your love flow all around
> Singing about the rainbow sound
> Erect your bubble upon the ground
> Every little thing is gonna be alright
> When you're bathing in the light of them rainbow blues

Let the light shine down upon us, omnipotent healing power
Out of the haze, into the rays, bathe in that rainbow shower
It'll feel so fine when it touches your mind
And penetrates your soul
You can't deny it will make you sigh
Lord you know it feels so fine

> Just radiate the light let your love flow all around
> I'm singing about the rainbow sound
> Erect your bubble upon the ground
> Every little thing is gonna be alright
> When you're bathing in the light of the rainbow blues

RAINBOW LIGHTS

Rainbow lights day or night shine on me
Begin to show how to flow like the sea
Take me there I'll be the air in the wind
We'll take it slow teach the flow to my friends

As I was floating through the blue green world
My mind was truly kissed
Until the rainbow floated by
And my joy it turned to bliss
I saw myself a magic man
Down deep beneath the sea
My wand of light the rainbow hues
It spread the bliss in front of me

Rainbow lights day or night shine on me
Begin to show just how to flow like the sea
Take me there I'll be the air in the wind
Take it slow teach the flow to my friends

And as the sun gave way to moon
And the stars began to shine
The love I know began to flow
Far beyond my naked mind
You'll flow below the surface realm
Leave your body far behind
And know your life is so much more
Than the body's finite mind

Rainbow lights day or night shine on me
Begin to show how to flow like the sea
Take me there I'll be the air in the wind
Take it slow teach the flow to my friends

SINGING FOR HEAVEN NOW (I'M SINGING)

Please, please, somebody please
Won't you lend me a hand
I've been down so down
Yeah, the third times coming round
(it's) three strikes you're out I understand

If this ain't the time
Then better let me know
'Cause I'm getting close to the
Proverbial end of the rope

Don't believe his knocking
He's standing at my door
Unless this S.O.S. is heard
My number's up for sure, and I'll be

      Singing for heaven, yes I'm singing

Can't take much more of this
I'm down here on my knees
Praying for you Lord
Please show me, won't you please?

It doesn't really scare me
Just didn't think He'd be here this soon
I see my angels coming now
I hope they like this tune

So I turned to my left
Sang "How do you do?"
I hope soon to be an angel, too
Then I turned to my right
She liked to hear me sing
I asked her then and there
"How did she earn her wings?"

      She said, "By singing
      Just by singing"
      So I'm singing for heaven now
      Yeah, singing

STOP PICKING ON ME

You got the pick of the crop
Like it or not, you got the pick hit of the week
You can pick your friends
You can pick and grin
You're always free to pick your seat
You can pick the plot where they'll lay you down
And the grass will grow over you
You can pick your teeth, even pick your brains
Pick anything you want to

> You can pick to win, place or show
> Pick the pocket of who's in the know
> But stop picking on me

You got the pick of the litter
If you don't get the jitters, you're free to go pick a fight
You got your pick up spot
Like it or not sometimes you got to pick a diet
You got your picket line, pick your favorite sign
Sometimes you gotta pick up the phone
You might pick apart someone you love
Just because you need to be alone

> You can pick to win, place or show
> Pick the pocket of who's in the know
> But stop picking on me

You got your picket fence
It don't make sense unless you pick the color white
Pick up your clothes, you can pick your nose
In public it still ain't right
You can pick your turf
And when you go to surf
You're always free to pick your wave
You can pick a peck of pickled peppers
Even buy them at the Pick and Save

> You can pick to win, place or show
> Pick the pocket of who's in the know
> But stop picking on me

SWEET, SWEET DARLING, ANGEL DIVINE

I gotta tell you baby, that I love you
That you'll always be on my mind
I just wanna let you know that I adore you
You're the one that makes me feel so fine

  Sweet, sweet darling, angel divine
  Take me by the hand, let your love light shine

And I just wanna tell you honey, when I see you
Tryin' so hard to make it divine
That your gift of love shines all around you
No matter where I am I feel it all the time

  Sweet, sweet darling, angel divine
  Take me by the hand, let your love light shine

I just wanna thank you girl, for your sweet loving
You taught me how to love, oh you showed me so fine
Now it's come full circle and I know for certain
That your hand in mine can make the sun shine

  Honey how I love you, wanna set you free
  Put no one above you, you're the one for me

TEARS OF JOY

A.A. it's not a new drug, it's a place I go when I need a hug
When I found my life had gotten out of control
From too much drugs, sex and rock and roll
Well I swallowed my pride, that was hard to do
But I'd bitten off more than I could possibly chew
But lo and behold you know what I found
After choking on my ego it finally came down

> At A.A. they take it day at a time
> It's brought me to tears of joy
> That's what I've been crying
> Tears of joy running down my face
> Tears of joy, boy that ain't no disgrace
> Welcome back to the human race

Step one, powerless
Over alcohol and everything else
Step two, came to believe
Need another power to keep my sanity
Step three, made a decision
To turn my life over to God's great vision
Steps four and five, I told myself
I told it all to God, I told someone else
Step six, became entirely ready
You can't marry God but you can sure go steady
Step seven, got on my knees
Humbly asked Him, relieve my shortcomings
Steps eight and nine, list of people I've harmed
Making my amends they said, "I'll be darned"
Step ten, continued on
Admitted right away when I was wrong
Step eleven, sought God in prayer
And His will for me I want to always be there
Step twelve, I gave it all away
That's the way to keep it or so they say

Having had a spiritual awakening

TENNESSEE HOSPITALITY

I was cruising along, just singing my song
'Bout the Asheville, Nashville run
One side of me was looking to see
The other side was looking for fun
I was into the Smokies down Knoxville way
My truck blew up, Lord I started to pray
I said, Lord, grant me a bit of hospitality

    I said, Tennessee hospitality
    Yeah, I said, Tennessee hospitality
    Well, I've been around some of the most renowned
    Folks on the planet today
    But I don't know where they begin to compare
    With the folks down Tennessee way

Vancouver was nice, Jamaica was fine
I almost stayed in Brazil
Amsterdam once was the plan
Hawaii was quite a thrill
But all through my travels
I've yet to find a place quite as nice
'Cept maybe ol' Carolina
So I reckon I'll be from sweet Tennessee
Where the people still treat you so fine

    I said, Tennessee hospitality
    Yeah, I said, Tennessee hospitality
    Well I've been around some of the most renowned
    Folks on the planet today
    But I don't know where they begin to compare
    With the folks down Tennessee way

THAT'S HOW IT IS

(my first poem, December 1975)

Listening to the fire glow
Deep within my very soul
Watching my lives unfold before me

So good to know just where I am
Along this path called God's great plan
Heralding Thy works before Thee

Releasing all unto the light
Frees my soul and gives me sight
To see and know the all I have to give

Erect your bubble all around
From earth to sky and underground
And know throughout your being that's how it is

THAT'S HOW LOVE SHOULD BE

Moon shining down on your face
I can see by the smile in your eyes
That you feel comfortable here with me

      That's how I want it to be
      That's how the love should be

I can tell by the look on your face
That you feel what I feel and it's real
And you know that it comes from deep inside

      That's how the love should be
      That's how the love should be
      That's how the love should be

Wind in the sky like the sound of your sigh
Singing soft and so free
Like the birds and the bees in perfect harmony

      That's how the love should be

As the sun kissed your skin
I could feel it again coming up from inside

It's the love that is guiding me
Oh! And it set me free

    That's how the love should be
    That's how the love should be
    That's how the love should be

(THAT'S THE WAY TO) CREATE PURE LOVE

Girl you're fine, so glad your mine
If only for a little while
I'm here to stay forever and a day
Only a fool would leave that smile

Don't you know we've got a love
People think is just in fantasy?
But when we come, together we go
Far beyond reality

Sometimes I feel, when we make love
What better way to end
Than going out, spirits together
Souls that then transcend

    That's the way to create pure love
    Can you say, that's what yours is made of?

Quality, not quantity
Seems to be the rule of thumb
Take care, always be there
When your baby's wanting some

The best relations are built on foundations
Strong as they can be
If you don't, they'll surely crumble
Like sand castles close to the sea

It's not as hard as it might seem
Once you've made up your mind
Open up your heart, that's when it starts
You can not miss the signs

    That's the way to create pure love
    Can you say, that's what yours is made of?

THERE OUGHT TO BE A LAW

There ought to be a law to help the lover
Like when the humming bird in flight decides to hover
Over the rose that it has chosen for its nectar
'Twere I a king I'd right this thing with my scepter

I cried down deep inside, didn't want to bring you down
But the pain you left behind's about to turn my head around
You left me standing here with my back against the wall
Two years of time like bitter wine, there ought to be a law

I'm coming to you sweet mama, got to see you once again
The song we sang was sweet love, but that was way back when
We got to start all over to find the place that rhymes
The sounds that blend know how to send us off in perfect time

> We're talking about harmony
> Gotta have harmony
> Looking for the harmony
> Sweet, sweet harmony

It's the past and the future keeps you in your earthly ways
Release it all and feel it thaw your soul with lovin' rays
The present is the only time, gotta learn to be here now
Don't ever cop no attitude of holier than thou

> When you want harmony
> Gotta have harmony
> Looking for the harmony
> Sweet, sweet harmony

There's a spiral from your inner being that leaves from your third eye
It goes up and joins the spiral coming from the sky
Don't you know when these two meet it'll energize your soul?
You can do it too, go on it's as easy as rock and roll

> When you want harmony
> Gotta have harmony
> Looking for the harmony
> Sweet, sweet harmony
> We all need harmony

TIME

Time, more precious all the time
Especially now that I
Soon must go

Time, together for all time
And forever you'll be mine
First I want you to know

I was meant for you
You were meant for me
It was fate we met
It was destiny

One last time the gypsy must roam
One last time this eagle has flown
One last time must be on my own

But I'll be back for you
Yes, I'll be back for you

UPRISING

Now for the first time in many years, the path of peace may be open.
No one can be certain what the future will bring, but history and our own conscience will
judge us harshly if we do not now make every effort to test our hopes by actions, and this
is the place to begin.

Bring down the walls in China, we did the same in Berlin
There's still so much oppression but it's a place to begin

    Uprising

Times are changing, we made Mikhail man of the year
Secession from the union, now, that the peace talk's in gear

    Uprising, uprising, uprising, uprising

Let's feed the hungry people, shelter the poor and the weak
Broken and homeless children, we'll get them off the street
Environmental issues, the information confused
But if you don't believe me, just watch the 6 o'clock news

    Uprising, uprising, uprising, uprising

Drugs are taking over, you know we're losing that war
A generation dying, addiction par for the course
It's time we got together, it's time we all took a stand
Instead of nasty lyrics, ignorance should be banned

Uprising, uprising, uprising, uprising

THE VISION THAT I SAW

Rainbow a rising
That ain't surprising
'Bout time to start wising
Up to the truth
There's work to be done
By each and every one
You don't have to be young
Just remember your youth

Letting your mind drift lazy
On a sunny afternoon
Feeling the strength of the earth
As you go back to the womb

Feeling your back against the tree root
Knowing it's all a part of you
Dancing with joy for the love's inside
What else is there to do?

Knowing we're all in this together
Yeah, there's one within us all
It's been like this forever
Went the vision that I saw

Rainbow a rising
That ain't surprising
'Bout time to start wising
Up to the truth
There's work to be done
By each and every one
You don't have to be young
Just remember your youth

WE'RE ALL IN THIS TOGETHER

I've been flying, flying, flyin' all across this land
Sowing reaping, mostly seeking players for the band
Players who like me just want to shine a bit of light
On all the darkness giving hope we'll make it through the night

     'Cause we're all in this together!
     'Cause we are all in this together!

I know it seems quite crazy after all the times you've tried
Might even seem a bit insane after all the tears you've cried
Just dedicate your life to helping all you can
Just help yourself and learn to love, then help your fellow man

     'Cause we're all in this together!
     'Cause we are all in this together!

There is one responsibility we all have while we're here
To teach the ways of love to our brother who's in fear
Just shine that precious love light that comes from deep within
It doesn't matter who you are or where that you have been

     'Cause we're all in this together!
     'Cause we are all in this together!

Be you black man, red or white
You're still precious in His sight
Love is what we've come here for
If we're to make things right
Rich man, poor man, beggar man, thief
We're basically the same
Some like to dance in sunshine
Some like to dance in the rain

     Still we are all in this together!
     Yes, we're all in this together!
     'Cause we are all in this together!
     'Cause we're all in this together!

WHAT YOU GONNA DO? (WHEN LOVE COMES CALLING)

What you gonna do when love comes calling?
Whispers in your ear, "won't you come fly away?"
What you gonna do when love comes calling?
Will you open up your heart and let it have it's say?

Or will you listen inside your head?
Begin to question why?
Does it really make the world go round?
Should I even try?
Then by the time you got it figured out
It's gone and passed you by

What you gonna do when love comes calling?
Whispers in your ear, "won't you come fly away?"
What you gonna do when love comes calling?
Will you open up your heart and let it have it's say?

Telling you of all the joy it brings
But you've seen the other side
Your heart says "Go", your head says "Whoa!"
Think of all the times you've cried
You can pretend it's the same in the end
I've never known love to be denied

WITH OR WITHOUT YOU

I ain't been sleeping so good like I used to
Since the first time I got into you

     I can't live...with or without you

This tossing and turning throughout the night
Passing the hours 'til the dawn of light

     I can't live...with or without you
     I can't live...with or without you

Yes, no, maybe, won't you make up your mind?
You've been driving me crazy for such a long time

     I can't live...with or without you

It's almost as if a spell had been placed
Woven together with the finest of lace

     I can't live...with or without you
     I can't live...with or without you
     I can't live...with or without you

I need some peace in my body and soul
Guess I gotta stick to my rock and roll

     I can't live...with or without you

I wish I'd known then what this was coming to
Now it's too late cause I'm in love with you

     I can't live...with or without you
     I can't live...with or without you
     I can't live...with or without you
     I can't live...with or without you

WITH YOUR LOVE

You're the piece of the puzzle
That makes me whole
The link to complete the chain
The spark that ignited the light in my soul
When I was lost in the rain

You're the sun in the morning, the joy in my life
My reason for being alive
You're my strength and my weakness
My rod and my staff
With you love I get high
With your love I get high

You're the peak of the mountains
As vast as the sea
In you I have found all I need
You're the wind in the willow
So wild and so free
I will follow wherever you lead

The last ray of twilight as it fades out of sight
The beckoning stars in the sky
The first golden moonbeam that shines through the night
With you love I get high
With your love I get high

WIZARD'S RAY

Near the castle courtyard in Black Mountain
There lived a maid so fair
Her eyes of blue oh such a hue
Of golden was her hair

But in the castle courtyard
The fountain had gone dry
The dove above was cold, no love
It made me want to cry

Dragon's breath had singed the mood
Fire had seen its day
Seven years now the cloud did pass
When the wizard used his ray

A wizard's ray I've heard it said
Is made up of all the light
So that any soul that gazes there
Can see it through the night

I've also heard it said before
That if the ray hits you
Your sight is changed and rearranged
And all you feel is new

WOMEN

It don't matter how long I live to be
One thing for sure will stay a mystery
All you guys out there, know what I'm talking about
Even Adam watching Eve pick the apple
Had to have his doubts

> About women, w-o-m-e-n
> They may drive me crazy
> But I wouldn't want to live without 'em

I could live without anything else, but having my girl
Nothing else I've found will do in this whole wide world
I've just been stood up, standing here, wonderin' what for
But the rewards so enchanting, I'm going back for more

> Talkin' 'bout women, w-o-m-e-n
> They may drive you crazy
> But I wouldn't want to live without 'em

I used to try and figure them out, had to give it up
Nothing seems to work, except lady luck
One thing though, I know for sure, they're my inspiration
I reckon this song's my way of a dedication

> To women, w-o-m-e-n
> They may drive us crazy
> But I wouldn't want to live without 'em

YODEL AWAY

As I was walking upon the planet earth
Down in Black Mountain
I heard my angel calling
She said "Boy get yourself together
before it's too late."

Today I found that angel again
I was torn and battered from a harsh life's wind
My energies low and needing a friend
She kissed away my pain

I told her to come away with me
On my journey to flow to know the sea
The wind, the birds how I want to be free
To find the light again

Then we walked away, oh
Then we walked away, oh
Gonna yodel away
Gonna yodel away
Yodel eda lay ee o

       Have you not heard the divine rhyme of things?
       It permeates all has effect on all beings
       Makes you to laugh, and cry and sigh and sing
       Just open up your hearts and you'll hear the truth ring

Gentle, so gentle I'll caress your soul
And teach you the ways of becoming whole
Leaving the games and playing the roles
And becoming all that you can

First you must release the fears
The past, the negatives, the tears
Replace them with the light of the spheres
And know you are divine

A child of God, a heavenly being
Build your castle, become the king
Rest assured you'll hear the ring
And rhapsody of the rhyme, of the rhyme

       Have you not heard the divine rhymes of things?
       It permeates all, has effect on all beings
       Makes you to laugh and cry and sigh and sing
       Just open up your hearts and you'll hear the truth ring

THE CHAMELEON

Open the door, let the love flow through
        Become a channel for the old and the new
        Sing soft your harmony, no need to feel blue
        As we're all together in the hereafter, too

We got words to make you laugh
We got words to make you smile
Words to make you cry, but only for a while

As there is so much bliss about
Just open up your eyes
And see the wind song softly sail its ship
Upon your sighs, upon your sighs

Speaking of a new age on the planet earth
We've joined in love, have conceived a new birth
A new day is dawning, I think it's getting near
A new ray is dawning, God, I do believe it's here

        Look beyond your mind, hear the rhyme divinity
        Look beyond your mind, hear the rhyme divinity
        Gonna yodelee-le-lo

YOU ARE MY FIRST LOVE

Since I met you I don't think I'll ever be the same
From the depths to heights of ecstasy and back again

> You are my first love
> My only girl
> You are my first love
> You are my world

Never knew what love was really all about before
You appeared and gently guided me right through the door

> You are my first love
> My only girl
> You are my first love
> You are my world

All my life I'd heard how wonderful love could be
Love was just a word 'til you said it to me

I'm so thankful you're the first to steal my heart
You have showed me ways of love, with which I'll never part

> You are my first love
> My only girl
> You are my first love
> You are my world

Even all my fantasies cannot compare with this
You and me in ecstasy and beyond into bliss

> You are my first love
> My only girl
> You are my first love
> You are my world

All my life I'd heard how wonderful love could be
Love was just a word 'til you said it to me

YOU BETTER BE SURE

Planets in a new age
Lord knows it's going round
The further out the planet gets
The higher grows the sound
New frequency vibrations
To open the third eye
Time to be aware that there's a
Rainbow ray of light

Don't be afraid, the rainbow ray
Is only here to heal
To ease the pain and stop the reign
Of beings who aren't for real
Knowingly they'll drag you down
And drain you of the force
Unless you use your gift from God
The rainbow ray, of course

But let me warn you here
And make it clear
Your motive must be pure
To use that light
With all its might
God knows you better be sure

YOU CAN'T GO BACK

You can't go back
Once you've seen the light
No you can't go back
Try as hard as you might

You've heard it time and time again
Now you're gonna hear it some more
Ignorance is bliss?
Who needs this?
Go on and unlock the door
But you can't go back
No you can't go back

You can't go back
But you can fly so high
You can't go back
No sense in denying

When the love of God is deep within you
The harmonics of your soul will radiate through
Just release and replace all the darkness with the light
And your life can begin to shine so bright

But you can't go back
No, you can't go back
Please, you mustn't go back

YOU GOT TO BE THE STAR OF YOUR DREAMS

You got to be the star of your dreams
At least that's the way that it seems
You can part the water
If you need to then you oughta
You just got to be the star of your dreams

Wherever you go, try and tune to the flow
Try and leave a little love where you been
If we all tried this, don't you know there'd be bliss?
And you know it's what we'd call a Godsend
Keep yourself high, don't you know by and by
You'll be helping those that only pretend
So make that music sweet, sweet music with your friends

You got to be the star of your dreams
At least that's the way that it seems
You can part the water
If you need to then you oughta
You just got to be the star of your dreams

YOU'RE DRIVING ME CRAZY

I ain't been sleeping so good like I used to
Ever since I got introduced to you
This tossing and turning throughout the night
And passing the hours 'til the dawning of light

     Is driving me crazy
     Making me hazy
     And all because of you
     Driving me crazy, making me hazy
     Lord have mercy, what should I do?

I wish I'd known then what this was coming to
Now it's too late 'cause I'm in love with you
It's almost as if a spell had been placed
And woven together with the finest of lace

Can't you see girl, what I'm going through?
Keep myself from fallin' about all I can do
You grabbed my head girl, and twisted it around
Don't even know if whether I'm up or I'm down

There's just one more thing that I've got to say
If this is love I don't believe that's the way
To find some peace in my body and soul
Guess I'll just stick with my good old rock and roll

YOU'RE EVERYTHING TO ME

Waited for so long
To sing you this love song
First had to belong... To you
Of all creation
You're my inspiration
This dedication's... Past due

      Girl can't you see?
      You're the sun, the moon
      You're everything to me

When you're beside me
I want you so badly
I've fallen madly... For you
Want you so much
Got to have your touch
Don't you know you're such... A jewel

      Girl, can't you see?
      You're the sun, the moon
      You're everything to me

Angel come down
To you I am bound
It's heaven that I've found... In you
Love you forever
Always together
There's nothing that I'd rather... Do

      Girl, can't you see?
      You're the moon, the stars
      You're everything to me

Remember the first time
Your eyes they met mine
Something divine... Began
Such a surprise
Contented soft sighs
It's only now I... Understand